Berkeley College

From the Library

of

Praise for
The Momentum Effect

The Momentum Effect offers hundreds of ideas to help managers and their firms deliver higher and better growth. These ideas are ingeniously organized in a roadmap for systematic and compelling value creation. JC Larreche's latest book is an extremely valuable tool for every business executive.

—Henri de Castries, Chairman of the Management Board, AXA

Professor Larreche's long experience and deep insights, not only as a business academic but also as a corporate director, are powerfully evident in his latest book, *The Momentum Effect*. His rigor of analysis, incisiveness of deduction, and clarity of expression make for a highly stimulating read to which the ambitious manager will refer time and time again. The challenge of migrating the vision and drive of inspirational leaders into a systematic sustainable management ethos has eluded all too many once great companies. Professor Larreche may well have identified a route to shortening the odds.

—Sir David G. Scholey, Senior Advisor UBS Investment Bank, formerly Executive Chairman of S.G. Warburg Group plc.

A masterclass from one of the greatest of business thinkers. *The Momentum Effect* clearly describes the fusion of forces that can propel exceptional and sustainable performance in organizations. A must-read!

—Lord Birt, Director-General of the BBC, 1992-2000; Strategy Adviser to the UK Prime Minister, 2000-2005

The Momentum Effect paves the way to sustainable profitable growth by combining innovation, customer, and marketing excellence into a coherent momentum strategy. And the art is to create that momentum!

—Jean-François van Boxmeer, Chairman Executive Board, CEO, Heineken NV

At last, a pragmatic perspective on how CEOs can place the customer at the center of their firm's strategy with the objective of delivering sustainable profitable growth. *The Momentum Effect* clearly shows that exceptional organic growth is based on the mobilization of brains to obtain more for less, more value to the customer at a lower cost, more value to the firm for less spending.

—Pierre Bellon, Founder and Chairman, Sodexo

This book shows you how to build momentum and leave your competitors trailing in your wake!

—Sir Richard Branson

J.C. Larreche's book, *The Momentum Effect*, is a must-read. It highlights why more marketing spend and further value extraction are not the key determinants for future growth. To create powerful momentum for exceptional growth, it is essential to offer innovative value to the marketplace. *The Momentum Effect* outlines just how to achieve this. The results are illuminating.

—W. Chan Kim & Renée Mauborgne, Authors of *Blue Ocean Strategy*

How can companies achieve exceptional and sustained growth? *The Momentum Effect* explores this challenge and reveals successful strategies for originating new sources of growth and value from customers with the power to unlock great potential.

—Dr. Daniel Vasella, Chairman & CEO, Novartis AG, Basel/Switzerland

This book has immense insight, the world would be a better place if all CEOs put this into practice. Constant customer-driven innovation always creates more value for shareholders, for customers, and for society. Larreche not only proves it, but also shows how it generates its own inevitable momentum. He has codified the holy-grail of self-sustaining growth.

—Alan Hughes, CEO First Direct Bank 1999-2004

THE
MOMENTUM
EFFECT

THE
MOMENTUM
EFFECT

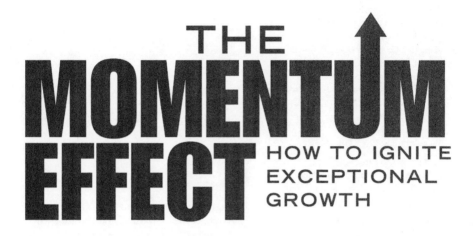

HOW TO IGNITE
EXCEPTIONAL
GROWTH

J.C. LARRECHE

Vice President, Publisher: Tim Moore
Associate Publisher and Director of Marketing: Amy Neidlinger
Wharton Editor: Yoram (Jerry) Wind
Acquisitions Editor: Martha Cooley
Editorial Assistant: Pamela Boland
Development Editor: Russ Hall
Digital Marketing Manager: Julie Phifer
Marketing Coordinator: Megan Colvin
Cover Designer: Alan Clements
Managing Editor: Gina Kanouse
Project Editor and Proofreader: Chelsey Marti
Copy Editor: Keith Cline
Indexer: Lisa Stumpf
Compositor: Nonie Ratcliff
Manufacturing Buyer: Dan Uhrig

Wharton School Publishing offers excellent discounts on this book when ordered in quantity for bulk
purchases or special sales. For more information, please contact U.S. Corporate and Government Sales,
1-800-382-3419, corpsales@pearsontechgroup.com. For sales outside the U.S., please contact
International Sales at international@pearsoned.com.

Printed in the United States of America

Second Printing May 2008

ISBN-10 0-13-236342-9
ISBN-13 978-0-13-236342-6

Pearson Education LTD.
Pearson Education Australia PTY, Limited.
Pearson Education Singapore, Pte. Ltd.
Pearson Education North Asia, Ltd.
Pearson Education Canada, Ltd.
Pearson Educatión de Mexico, S.A. de C.V.
Pearson Education—Japan
Pearson Education Malaysia, Pte. Ltd.

Library of Congress Cataloging-in-Publication Data

Larreche, Jean-Claude.
    The momentum effect : how to ignite exceptional growth / Jean-Claude Larreche.
        p. cm.
    ISBN 0-13-236342-9 (hardback : alk. paper) 1. Industrial management—Handbooks, manuals, etc.
I. Title.
    HD38.15.L37 2008
    658.4'01—dc22
                                                    2007047718

Contents

Acknowledgments

Over the many years of discovery, research, teaching, consulting, and practice during which this book has developed and matured, I have benefited immensely from the contributions of my colleagues, friends, clients, and students. My most sincere thanks go to all of them. Unfortunately, I cannot name every person who has influenced my work, but I would like to recognize a few people in particular.

My first thanks go to those who have shared my passion for the momentum effect and have contributed the most to the current expression of ideas, concepts, and models presented in this book: Alan Hughes, Zohra Jan Mamod, Prashant Malaviya, and Stephen Partridge.

The many projects that laid the foundations for this work benefited from the devoted efforts of dozens of people in my research teams, and I would like to acknowledge the valuable contributions of Cole Aliel, Marc Alzieu, Anne-Marie Cagna, Heather Chopra, Priti Jain, Ruth Lewis, Estelle Mense, Gueram Sargsyan, Nishi Shah, and Julia Yaziji.

Many thanks must also go to those who took the time out of busy schedules to review the book in various stages and make detailed comments: Marc Beauvois-Colladon, Mike Brimm, Pierre Chandon, Victor Cook, Hubert Gatignon, Christoph Loch, Christian Pinson, Subi Rangan, and Petra Saf.

Several colleagues at INSEAD have helped shape my ideas over various discussions around meetings, in lunches, along corridors, and in offices, including Reinhard Angelmar, Ben Bensaou, Miguel Brendl, Ziv Carmon, Amitava Chattopadhyay, Markus Christen, Morten Hansen, Jill Klein, David Midgley, Paddy Padmanabhan, Philip Parker, Werner Reinartz, Miklos Sarvary, David Soberman, Charles Waldman, David Weinstein, and Klaus Wertenbroch. Sadly, our friend and esteemed colleague Erin Anderson left us as this book was in production and her constructive optimism is deeply missed.

INSEAD provided support for my activities through the Alfred H. Heineken Chair, and I would like to thank Dean Frank Brown and Dean Anil Gaba for their encouragements. The Heineken company created this Chair in honor of its late chairman and main shareholder, "Freddy," who transformed the company, established the brand as the leading global beer, and created exceptional growth. I am extremely grateful to the firm for its generous funding of the Chair and for the valuable interactions we have had over the years.

My personal understanding of market phenomena was helped by many academics whom I had the pleasure of working with as co-authors, or whose work found some resonance with my own quest. First, my advisors and colleagues on many projects, Dave Montgomery and the late Harper Boyd. And then George Day, Leslie de Chernatony, Dominique Hanssens, Dipak Jain, Johny Johansson, Kamran Kashani, Kevin Keller, Philip Kotler, Christopher Lovelock, Sandra van der Merwe, Reza Moinpour, John Quelch, Seenu Srinivasan, Donald Sexton, Ed Strong, Terry Vavra, Jerry Wind, and Gerry Zaltman.

In the field of strategy, many authors have shaped our response to the challenge of creating value. Those whose inspiring work has most influenced my thinking are undeniably Chan Kim and Renée Mauborgne, both of whom are my colleagues at INSEAD, and Jim Collins, Michael Porter, and C. K. Prahalad.

Some of the concepts in this book started to emerge when we were deploying the Markstrat simulation in many large global corporations. The firm I created, StratX, was based on the success of Markstrat, and many consultants and computer developers contributed to improving and extending it. I have spent many hours working with colleagues and associates from StratX offices in Paris, Boston, and Tokyo, helping clients deliver sustainable growth through customer focus, innovation, and marketing excellence. Interacting with them in different meetings and assignments has always been the source of personal learning. I would like to thank all of them, and in particular Laurent Bonnier, Philippe Latapie, Remi Triolet, Jeff Schnack, John Wills, Mario Castaneda, Dana Allen, Steven Flostrand, Sabine Fabbricatore, Laurent Schmierer, Jean-Michel Chopin, Thibaud Claudeville, Patricia Cormier, Marc Dimancescu, Sebastien Lamiaux, Alan Slavik, Gavin Strok, Etienne Auvillain, Paul Ritmo, Marie-Caroline Turmel, Bruce van Barthold,

Raymond Ouellet, Douglas Ross, Stephan Hasse, Donald White, and Niall McDonagh.

Over the years, I have been privileged to learn and debate with literally thousands of business executives and managers. Some were clients, others students, and others friends. Many others were interviewed by members of my team. They came from all levels, CEOs to product managers, from all functions, and from all types of industries. I have operated in an international environment all my life and have been fortunate to meet and exchange with business people in North America, South America, Europe, Asia, and Africa. I would like to thank all of them for what they brought me in additional wisdom, and recognize some of them more specifically: Laurent Beraza, Lord Birt, Peter Blackmore, Jean-François van Boxmeer, Jonathan Browning, Jan Carendi, Pierre Douaze, Pier Carlo Falotti, Roger Greenwood, Matt Hall, Han Hendricks, Heiner Hochreutener, Michel Jacques, Rick Johnson, Rod Jones, Michel Lambert, Jim Nyquist, Alan Pedder, Allan Polack, William Powell, Georg Reiff, Steve Ridgeway, Michael Rubenstein, Johannes Schmidt, Sir David Scholey, Geoff Skingsley, Philippe Vivien, and Emmanuel Wolff.

Many thanks to all those in Pearson and in Wharton School Publishing who organized the publication of this book with great expertise, and especially Keith Cline, Megan Colvin, Martha Cooley, Russ Hall, Chelsey Marti, Tim Moore, Julie Phifer, Laura Robbins, and Richard Stagg.

I am deeply indebted to Suzanne Sellier Di Sano and Joan Bryant, who went through the tedious details of the book, checked, corrected, and helped me in so many ways.

My gratitude goes to those whose journalistic skills greatly contributed in making this manuscript more accessible and pleasant to read: Rudy Chelminski, Elen Lewis, and Laura Mazur.

And finally, this book is dedicated to my children, Sylvie and Philippe, and all the young people of goodwill like them. May this work, even in a modest way, help them live in a better world where customers, employees, and other stakeholders of the business community can prosper in harmony.

About the Author

J.C. **Larreche** is Professor at INSEAD, the famous international business school, where he holds the Alfred H. Heineken Chair. It was as a student at Stanford that he was first nicknamed "J.C." by his friends. It was also there, in the midst of Silicon Valley, that he developed an interest in the way some firms achieve exceptional growth while others don't. Since then, his research, teaching, and consulting activities have focused on the discovery of systematic and practical ways to help businesses achieve quality growth that is not only exceptional but also sustainable.

J.C. has always combined his academic life with a business career, and is particularly sensitive to the practical day-to-day realities which executives have to deal with. He is a renowned consultant with leading global corporations, most of them listed in the global Fortune 500. Aged just 36, J.C. was appointed a nonexecutive director of the multinational firm that became ReckittBenckiser, and he kept that position for an exceptionally long tenure of 18 years. He is the Founding Chairman of StratX a strategic development consultancy with offices in Boston, Paris and Tokyo.

His academic work concentrates on fostering the fundamental capabilities that impact a firm's ability to deliver growth and especially marketing excellence, customer focus, and innovation. J.C. is the author and coauthor of many books and articles, including Markstrat, the leading strategic marketing simulation used by more than one million executives worldwide. He has won many awards, including Marketing Educator of the Year and BusinessWeek's European Case of the Year award. J.C. is also a respected executive educator whose programs are among the most highly rated in INSEAD's excellent portfolio.

Preface

Delivering profitable growth year after year is the number-one, non-negotiable imperative facing today's business leaders. Many firms struggle to meet it, others achieve it in fits and starts, but only a select few consistently exceed it—sometimes extravagantly. How do these world-beaters do it?

The answer lies in the *momentum effect*.[1]

The momentum effect is a tremendously potent phenomenon by which, under specific conditions, exceptional organic growth is created—growth that feeds on itself. Momentum accumulates energy from its own success and provides ever-increasing acceleration for firms smart enough to build and harness it. These firms go from success to success, buoyed by a self-sustaining growth which sweeps all before them with disconcerting ease.

Momentum allows you to deliver exceptional growth without the stupendous efforts most firms are forced to make every day. It is this self-fueling characteristic of the growth produced by the momentum effect that leads us to call it *momentum growth* and to use the word *exceptional*. Momentum growth is exceptional for two reasons. First, because it is characterized by an exceptional *rate* of growth—exceptional, that is, compared to normal expectations based on history, market trends, or competition. Second, it offers an exceptional *quality* of growth, one that both generates higher profits and consumes fewer resources.

This book reveals evidence for the momentum effect, demonstrates how it works, and then offers you a pathway to harnessing its power.

The first inkling that a force such as momentum might explain some firms' exceptional growth occurred during my business studies at Stanford University. There, in the heart of Silicon Valley, I became fascinated by the way some businesses suddenly took off, experiencing almost unimaginable growth, whereas others, with what appeared to be technologically superior offerings, sank without a trace. Since then, I have sought out the engines of growth that help companies to create superior value, aided in this endeavor by different teams over time. We began by investigating marketing excellence. We examined customer focus. We scrutinized innovation. Each of these is a useful tool with an undeniable impact on growth, but painful experience over the years has taught us that marketing excellence by itself does not create sustained growth any more than does customer focus or innovation in isolation. We discovered that momentum growth requires a delicate combination of a number of specific elements, working cooperatively and simultaneously. This combination can occur by chance or by design. But even with the best-laid plans, it can work its full magic only if it is executed within a special culture and under a certain type of leadership.[2]

The momentum that builds as a result is what drove the extraordinary performance of Microsoft, Wal-Mart, and Dell, momentum that then deserted them, and momentum they are struggling to recover. The same near-irresistible energy is powering Apple, Toyota, Virgin, First Direct, and Nintendo today. But if those companies fail to maintain it intelligently, they too could wake to find the momentum behind their growth deserting them. That's the tricky thing about momentum: It is transitory. Without constant care, its power will prove fleeting.

Momentum is dynamic. In business, success can vanish in a flash unless it is constantly renewed. Several of the firms we studied lost their momentum because their leaders failed to understand or nurture the drivers of this force. Many of the stories we tell are of firms that are no longer excellent. And, almost certainly, some of the companies whose praises we sing will lose their momentum all too soon. But all these firms have built momentum and ridden it for all it was worth, some of them for decades. The ability not only to build momentum but, more importantly, to retain your grip on it is one of this book's key takeaways.

After sketching out the first rough outlines of the momentum effect, we embarked on a systematic investigation to expand and refine our comprehension of how it worked. We confirmed its existence as a long-term phenomenon through an empirical study of the world's largest firms, examining their growth in revenues, profits, and shareholder value over 20 years. We conducted in-depth studies of a vast number of small and large firms that enjoyed periods of exceptional growth over the past 50 years. We have generally considered that if a company has sustained this growth for at least ten years, the forces behind that growth were worth investigating—even if that growth has subsequently slumped. We often learned as much from the slump as we did from studying the initial growth. We have made exceptions to this ten-year rule only for recent ventures such as Skype, Nintendo's Wii, and Facebook. We used computerized simulations to replicate the phenomenon and to test different drivers of momentum. We advised client companies on specific aspects of momentum strategy, and tested their implementation.

What we learned was so wide-ranging that it would not sit comfortably within a single book, and we must leave many of our findings to subsequent publications. In these pages, we focus on a single purpose: to present a systematic approach for the design and execution of momentum strategy. This involves an eight-step process creating the specific conditions required to set the momentum effect in motion and to maintain it. This process integrates in a single framework a number of contributions that have emerged in the past decade, in academia and in business, mainly in the areas of customer focus, innovation, and marketing excellence.

Taken individually, each element of momentum strategy is very simple. It is part creativity, part business acumen, part psychology, and part simple common sense. You have to have smarts, not a Ph.D. Many entrepreneurs who created momentum for their firms and held it over several decades never completed university studies, either because of necessity or because they were impatient to go into business—Thomas Edison, Henry Ford, Steve Jobs, Luciano Benetton, Richard Branson, Michael Dell, and Bill Gates, to name a few.

But if the concepts are simple, successfully implementing a momentum strategy is challenging. "In strategy," wrote Clausewitz, "Everything is very simple, but not on that account very easy." This is keenly pertinent to momentum strategy, where the challenge is to first build and then maintain the balance that creates momentum and sustains it over time. For this, we offer a framework that assembles the pieces of the momentum-strategy puzzle into a coherent whole.

This book is divided into four parts. The first, *Discovering Momentum,* provides the evidence for the momentum effect and explains the phenomenon. It then presents the concepts of momentum strategy and demonstrates its role in value creation before describing a framework for momentum. Each of the eight steps of this momentum process is then examined over the two central parts of the book: *Designing Momentum* and *Executing Momentum.* The final part, *Total Momentum,* closes the loop. It concentrates on the creation of internal momentum and on the leadership competences required to successfully implement momentum strategy and create exceptional growth.

Like sports, the business environment of today's globalized, hypercompetitive world will increasingly become divided into leagues. The top league will consist of momentum-powered businesses enjoying exceptional growth. All the others will be trying to play catch-up. Given the choice, wouldn't you prefer to spend your future in the excitement and accomplishments of the Momentum League? Our most sincere wish is that this book helps you to create and experience to the fullest the stimulation and rewards of momentum.

PART **I**

Discovering Momentum

1

The Power of Momentum

Where's the Impetus?

Momentum. Most businesses get it at some point: the impression that everything they undertake succeeds effortlessly, as if they're being carried along by a tailwind that increases their efficiency and propels them on to exceptional growth.[1]

Some hold on to it. Most don't. Slowly, imperceptibly, the tailwind turns around and the momentum disappears, without anyone quite realizing what has happened. The company is still growing, but not as strongly as before, not as efficiently. Everyone's maxing out, but it seems like there's molasses in the works. Sound familiar?

Sooner or later, it hits you in the face. Imagine you are meeting up with a senior analyst whose opinion counts with some of your company's biggest investors. You think you're on safe ground—after all, your company is doing better than the competition. But the analyst is in full gimlet-eyed, illusion-killing mode. "That's nothing to crow about," she says. "Yeah, you've got reasonable growth, but it's nothing exceptional. You're a safe bet, nothing more. Okay, I might tell my mom to buy, but

3

then she's happy with inflation plus one. The way we see it, you're really grinding it out. We reckon the strain's getting harder, too. There's no impetus—no momentum."

Words like that can really take the gloss off a day. The next time you gather your team, you don't congratulate them on beating their targets—you want more. Sure, our results are up, you say, but that's not enough—where's the impetus? When are we going to do something exceptional? With all the resources at your disposal, when are you going to start building some momentum?

The team members look at their papers. Then Paul, an anxious member of your team, looks up and says: "Okay. Got any ideas about how?" What are you going to say?

What's Holding Us Back?

This book sets out to answer one question: How can I find a way to deliver continuous, exceptional growth, year after year?

By *exceptional,* we mean exceptional relative to expectations: growth that sets you apart. In some high-technology markets, this might mean 60 percent. In others, 6 percent might really stand out from the crowd if the market average is just 3 or 4. What we are talking about is growth that puts serious distance between you and your competitors. That is what this book is offering. It shows you how to get the traction you need to make sure that none of your effort is being wasted—to make sure that it all goes toward delivering tangible results. It will help you break free from the grind.

After all, grind is what most businesses endure. Most firms that manage to deliver growth do it the hard way. Measures that improve profitability often hold back top-line growth, while measures that drive revenue growth require investments that can drag down profitability. As one foot starts to run, the other starts sinking in the mire. It's devilishly hard to get the balance right and break free: It seems that all you can do is keep pushing. Companies have to push sales forward with big marketing investments while at the same time harrying their employees to become more productive and nagging their suppliers and partners for better deals. Pushing is hard work—it's exhausting and it churns through resources.

We thought: "There just *has* to be a better way than this." Some of our earlier work[2] showed that firms with certain shared characteristics were delivering substantially better results than others. The performance of these firms suggested that, under certain conditions, there existed a phenomenon whereby growth could be achieved more efficiently. The disproportionately higher growth these firms delivered hinted at some hidden energy driving their growth—an energy that seemed to feed on itself without the need for excessive resources. Their progress has been natural, highly efficient, and realized with almost frictionless ease. Because they were not held back by the sheer weight of resources others were employing, they were able to get some speed up. They had momentum. We went looking to find out exactly what this momentum was and how these momentum-powered firms acquired it.

The insight came when we realized that if momentum was powering a firm's success, then its *relative* marketing spend should be decreasing. Contrary to conventional "spend money to make money" wisdom, our hunch was that firms with momentum achieved superior growth while spending a relatively smaller percentage of their revenue on marketing than those pursuing the traditional "push hard" methods.

To test our hypothesis, we investigated the effect of marketing investments on the long-term growth of large, established firms. We looked at the conduct and performance of well-known corporations among the world's 1,000 largest, covering a 20-year period from 1985 to 2004. We looked at these firms' marketing behavior and tracked the effect that changes in this behavior had on sales revenue, net earnings, and stock price.[3]

The results were astounding.

Pushers, Plodders, and Pioneers

We divided the firms into three groups according to how their marketing behavior could be described: Pushers, Plodders, and Pioneers. Because we were interested in the effect of extremes in marketing behavior, our three groups were divided in a 25:50:25 split. For simplicity, let us illustrate the results of our research with an example from one sector, the largest: consumer goods and services.[4]

The Pushers were those companies that pushed their businesses hard in the traditional way, seeking to drive sales through aggressive increases in relative marketing spend. In our rankings, these were the firms in the quartile showing the highest increases in their marketing-to-sales ratio over the 20-year period. This group, on average, increased its marketing-to-sales ratio by 3 percent over this time.

Then there were the Plodders. These were the firms grouped around the middle of our sample—fully half of those in the study. Their marketing-to-sales ratio remained more or less constant for 20 years. These middling firms stayed in the safety zone of past behavior and took no drastic action one way or the other.

Finally, there was the remaining quarter—those firms that were, either boldly or foolhardily, heading in the opposite direction from the Pushers, and decreasing their relative marketing spend. Taking these firms' average marketing-to-sales ratio, we see a 4 percent drop over the timeframe.

This 4 percent cut was made while competing against the Pushers who were plowing in a 3 percent rise. In other words, the Pioneers cut their relative marketing spend by seven points when compared to the competition. Given the preeminence that marketing spend has among the tools most firms use to drive growth, this is a big, big call. Would these unconventional firms, which we dubbed the Pioneers, discover other avenues to growth, or fall behind as a result of their foolhardiness?

We expected these three strategic behaviors to have an impact on the firms' performance in creating shareholder value. What was not expected was the size of that impact.[5]

When looking at the percentage change in shareholder value over the 20-year period of our three groups, as compared to the change in the Dow Jones Index,[6] shown in Figure 1.1, we immediately see that remaining in the safety zone of stable marketing spend is not a viable option: The Plodders underperformed the stock market by 28 percent, achieving only 72 percent of the Dow Jones Index average growth.

As most analysts would have predicted, the highest increases in advertising ratio did produce significantly more shareholder value than did the Plodders' relatively stable marketing spend. Pushers managed, on average, to create shareholder value exactly in line with the evolution of the Dow Jones Index, thus demonstrating the soundness of the conventional faith in the power of active marketing spend to contribute to increasing shareholder value.[7]

What conventional analysis probably would *not* have predicted was the performance of the Pioneers. Despite having *decreased* their advertising-to-sales ratio, these momentum-powered companies created shareholder value 80 percent *above* the Dow Jones Index over the 20-year period. Eighty percent!

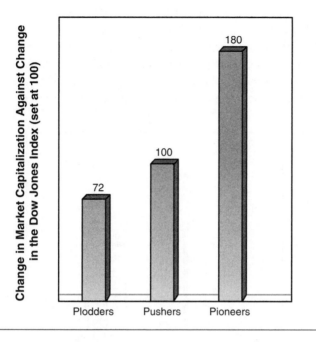

Figure 1.1 The three leagues, 1985–2004

As the limitations of the Plodders' inertia are obvious, let's leave them aside. Understanding the difference between the Pushers and the Pioneers—the "good" and the "great" in terms of growth in shareholder value—was both more challenging and more rewarding.

The first clue to the difference in the strategic behavior of these two groups appears in the top-line growth of the Pioneers, as shown in Figure 1.2. Over the 20-year period, using the Pushers' performance as a reference, the Pioneers' revenue growth was 93 percent better—almost twice as high. They achieved this massive revenue growth despite decreasing their advertising ratio. And remember: This is in comparison not to underperforming firms but to firms that actually matched the Dow Jones Index.

If we compare the *profitability* growth of these two groups, we can see that the Pioneers also did much better, with average earnings growth 58 percent superior to that of the Pushers.

A 58 percent advantage in earnings growth is very impressive, but it is noticeably smaller than the difference in revenue growth. Despite the Pushers' much poorer performance on revenue growth, *and* the fact that they were increasing their spending on marketing, they managed to claw back some lost ground: Their relative gap on earnings growth is less severe than one would expect. How did they manage that?

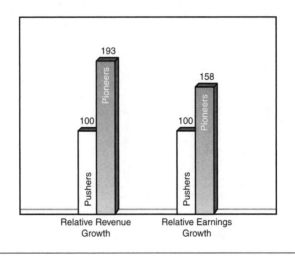

Figure 1.2   The two top leagues: Pushers vs. Pioneers, 1985–2004

They cut down on other costs, especially in manufacturing and R&D.[8] These combined cuts and efficiency economies more than compensated for the increase in advertising-to-sales ratio, and enabled the Pushers to peg back some of the Pioneers' huge top-line advantage when it came to earnings growth. Despite this partial catch-up, there is little doubt about where one would like to invest or work when one compares these two types of companies. The stock market recognizes this: The share-price premium of Pioneers over Pushers—80 percent— is significantly higher than the differential in their earnings growth.

The bottom line: Although the combination of pushing hard with marketing investments and slashing other costs can deliver growth, the Pioneers' achievements demonstrates that there is a more creative, exciting, and smarter alternative that delivers even better results.

Obviously, it is not as simple as cutting the advertising-to-sales ratio. A straight cut in advertising would almost certainly result in a drop in growth. In fact, our study shows that the momentum-powered Pioneers actually increased their total marketing expenditures in real terms. But while their marketing budgets were increasing, the proportion of their revenue that this expenditure represented was decreasing. In other words, because of the Pioneers' superior revenue growth, their advertising-to-sales ratio was coming down despite the fact that they were spending more.

In a world of increasing competition, marketing resources must also, inexorably, rise. But if they are to create sustainable, profitable growth, these expenditures must be invested in an effective manner. Compared to the Pushers, the Pioneers' increases in marketing investments were more effective: They got superior growth while reducing their marketing-to-sales ratio, thus improving profitability.

The question is: What was improving the efficiency of their marketing investments? This is not simply a case of great marketing, although marketing excellence is a key part of the mix. These firms achieved greater efficiency with their marketing because they found a different path to growth: They exploited the momentum effect. They created specific conditions that ignited an exceptional organic growth that feeds on itself: momentum growth.

We meet several firms that have managed to do this in the course of the following chapters. They come from domains as disparate as banking and ball bearings, but the central fact that unites them is this: It is their brains, not their muscle or money, that create the force to power them from success to success. They are momentum-powered firms.

Momentum-Powered Firms

The results of this research might seem counterintuitive at first sight, but they are perfectly logical. Too often, companies invest more in marketing to compensate for something: an inferior product, a poor pipeline of new products, deterioration of growth prospects, or a general lack of creativity.

Firms with such a limited vision compensate for their less-than-spectacular offers by pushing them on an unconvinced market using heavy-handed marketing resources. Even more compensation is required when, to fund this expensive marketing, they are forced to cut costs on the very activities that could improve the attractiveness of their offer: operations and R&D. This kind of behavior eats up resources and destroys firms from the inside out. These businesses will never build momentum. They are *momentum-deficient firms.*[9]

The Pioneers show there is an alternative. These momentum-powered firms don't have to push so hard because they have built up a momentum that improves their efficiency. Rather than just better-than-average growth, they deliver exceptional growth. Their growth is exceptional on two counts: It is both higher and more efficient.

Many of them manage to maintain their momentum for decades. Table 1.1 lists several, along with an estimate of the length of time during which they felt the momentum effect.[10]

Table 1.1 Momentum-powered firms

Firm	Years	Firm	Years
Apple	10	Nike	10
BMW	30	Rentokil	20
Dell	30	Sony	10
Enterprise Rent-A-Car	30	Starbucks	10
FedEx	30	SWA	10
First Direct	15	Swatch	10
IBM	50 plus 10	Tetra Pak	20
IKEA	20	Toyota	10
Johnson & Johnson	30	Virgin Atlantic	20
Microsoft	20	Wal-Mart	30

Of course, momentum can never be taken for granted. Even those firms that have managed to build their own wave and ride it to unimagined success can come crashing down through a moment's careless inattention. Fortunately, it can be regained, as the case of IBM shows—that is why we have noted that it enjoyed two separate periods of momentum: a prolonged spell in its early years under Tom Watson Sr. and Tom Watson Jr., and then the famous and oft-quoted recovery under Lou Gerstner.

We look at most of these firms throughout the book. Many of them are well known internationally. Others, such as Rentokil and First Direct, might not be. But all have enjoyed the power of the momentum effect. Indeed, we hope to convince you that momentum offers a more rounded explanation for their success—and, in some cases, subsequent fall from grace—than the usual explanations that you might have already encountered. If you think you've heard all there is to hear about oft-cited companies such as Microsoft, Apple, IBM Swatch, Wal-Mart, and Toyota, for example, read on—you might be surprised. And you might also discover some new momentum-powered firms from whom important lessons can be learned.

Over the next two chapters, we examine the source of momentum and how to exploit it through a momentum strategy and the momentum process, but for now, let's just see what it looks like in action.

The Power of Momentum in Action

Wal-Mart and Toyota are two apparently dissimilar firms. They operate in two different industries and come from different countries and cultures. But they are two of the world's 15 richest companies, and each is number one in its own industry. More importantly, both got there by creating the conditions needed for the momentum effect to emerge. Although one has lost its momentum, the other is still in full swing.

Wal-Mart

Sam Walton launched his company with a focus on customers. What is remarkable is the way that this customer focus created exceptional growth and continued to power Wal-Mart for many years after it had become a major industry force. Whatever its current challenges—and there are many—for the better part of a generation Wal-Mart was a momentum-powered firm.

Sam Walton knew about retail, but his main asset was the fact that he knew about customers. His strength was this: He liked to listen to them and observe them, and he understood their needs. When he started out, he related deeply to a very specific kind of customer—people like him, people from the United States' rural South.

Walton's customer orientation made him aware of the potential of this region's smaller towns. In 1962, when Wal-Mart was launched, the standard wisdom held that large retail operations could not survive in towns with fewer than 100,000 residents. But Walton decided that this was where opportunity lay, and he deliberately opened stores only in small towns where there was no large-scale competition.

Walton understood that these customers would value his offering, that they would appreciate being able to shop locally, rather than making long journeys to larger towns. He also realized that these shoppers were worth more than they seemed. Although their wallets weren't as full as those of people in large cities, Wal-Mart was able to command a higher share of their spending because there was no competition. The combination of cheaper premises, lower labor costs, no competition, and prices slightly higher than big-city competitors meant that Walton's customers were extremely profitable to service.[11]

This winning combination gave Wal-Mart the traction it needed to start building momentum. As the firm mushroomed, it continued to improve all aspects of its operation, from customer service to supply chain and supplier relationships. Eventually, Wal-Mart was able to glean economies of scale in purchasing to achieve its mantra of "Every Day Low Price" (EDLP) and gain further momentum.

EDLP runs counter to traditional retail promotions that lure customers into stores, hoping that they'll also end up buying more expensive products. The famous expression to describe retail strategy in the days before Wal-Mart was "an island of losses in an ocean of profits." It was really an island of bait in an ocean of arrogance and customer abuse. It was akin to duck hunting—attracting customers the same way hunters attracted wild ducks with decoys.

With EDLP, Wal-Mart turned the relationship with customers upside down. It moved from duck hunting to a vibrant partnership. Wal-Mart's competitors, to their discomfort, failed to understand that, although EDLP was jargon on the surface, it expressed a strong, hidden emotional value deeply appreciated by customers: trust. This customer trust powered the company's growth for decades.

Unfortunately, momentum doesn't look after itself. There is a perception that Wal-Mart slowly began to pay less attention to many of the key drivers of its success—respect for employees, local communities, and suppliers—and began to lose its momentum as a result. Momentum is dynamic: Unless it is constantly nurtured, it will ebb away. However, the reward for that unstinting attention can be immense—it can make you number one in the world.

Toyota

When asked in May 2007 about the prospect of Toyota becoming the world's number-one car manufacturer, company president Katsuaki Watanabe refused to take even a minute to gloat about beating his competitors. "Rather than think about other companies," he said, "I feel that we must do our utmost to satisfy customers around the world. There is plenty left for us to do."[12] This simple statement, reflecting an unswerving customer focus, demonstrates why companies like Toyota are able to develop a detailed and subtly nuanced understanding of customers—and why they are able to deliver better results.

It also shows that there is much more to Toyota's success than *Kaizen* and lean production. That is just the base: its excellence and efficiency at extracting value from its business. It is Toyota's ability to create new, original, and compelling value in the first place that drives its growth. Its secret is its ability to connect totally with customers' sense of self, to create products that are more than mere goods but complete, perfect, and compelling presentations of value. The Prius, for example, offers a package of utterly compelling value to environmentally aware city-dwellers: With its low carbon footprint, practicality for city driving, and celebrity association, it is more than just a car—it is a statement. The Lexus offers a totally different package of value to a totally different market, but the package is just as compelling, if you are part of its target market.

Consider the contrasting histories of the U.S. auto industry and Toyota. American car manufacturers are among the best illustrations of the limitations of the Pusher's strategy. They have given everything a try in terms of efficiency drives, but although they are now leaner, they are no fitter. They sought to drive top-line growth through expensive advertising as well as sales promotions to generate volume, along with deep discounts to move inventories of finished goods. These expensive tactics were needed to compensate for the failure of their products to really connect with customers.

Toyota, on the other hand, has become the world's largest and most profitable car manufacturer, riding a fantastic wave of momentum. Its success is based on a number of factors, but underlying its achievement is a deep understanding of its customers. First, Toyota proved that it could consistently deliver reliable, impeccably engineered automobiles. Once this crucial plateau had been achieved, it went on to innovate its range with cars that were somehow more than mere vehicles. Models like the Prius and the Lexus range appeared in their showrooms. Both of these cars connect on an emotional level with their drivers' self-image and aspirations—green and clean for the one, luxurious and status based for the other. This level of customer engagement did not happen by chance—it was the result of a focused, iterative process that created the conditions under which the momentum effect, and the efficient momentum growth it delivers, could flourish.

Join the Momentum League

We have spent many years focusing on the difference between the majority of ordinary firms and those few that deliver truly exceptional results.

Our research has shown that increases in marketing pressure can lead to significant profitable growth. The Pushers delivered good performance and matched the Dow Jones average over a 20-year period. But who wants average growth when there is a much better option?

The Pioneers—those momentum-powered firms that decreased their marketing-to-sales ratio—achieved revenue growth 93 percent greater than the Pushers. That is the sort of growth that gets companies noticed, that drives exceptional increases in value for all stakeholders.

How did they do it? By creating the conditions that are needed for the momentum effect to take place.

Ask yourself the question prompted by that meeting with a financial analyst at the beginning of this chapter: When are we going to start building some momentum? Momentum offers an easier, more efficient, and exceptional form of growth. But it requires the ambition to break free from the traditional reflex of using more resources to fuel it. The very things that seem to push you forward are holding you back. Momentum does not happen by chance. Nor can it simply be willed into existence. Achieving momentum requires an understanding of its source, and then the relentless application of a systematic process. It requires a momentum strategy.

Momentum leaders are not lucky—they are smart. They have discovered the source of momentum and, with it, the beginnings of a smarter way to exceptional growth. Managers often talk about "riding the wave." Momentum leaders aren't that passive. They live by this motto: First build your wave, *then* ride it.

2

The Source of Momentum

The Day Gary Kildall Went Flying

One fateful week in August 1980, two different leaders from similar companies in similar sectors faced the same singularly important opportunity. The decisions they made that week set the direction their companies took and, indeed, each man's entire future success. One company began to build a momentum that would see it become one of the world's largest corporations, while the other faltered, stumbled, and failed to fulfill its promise. It was the end of one era and the beginning of another.

The first leader was named Gary Kildall. On the day he was due to meet a delegation from another company about a possible new business deal, he decided to go flying in his plane instead. Insulted, the visitors took their business to the second leader. His name was Bill Gates, the customers were from a company called IBM, and the new business was a contract to develop the operating system for personal computers.

The rest is history—the software that Microsoft provided became the de facto operating system for PCs. Microsoft entered a period, lasting almost two decades, during which it generated exceptional, momentum-powered growth and established itself as the leader of a new and crucial industry.[1] Whatever its current challenges, during the 1980s and 1990s Microsoft was an exemplary momentum-powered firm: Its growth was phenomenal and created enormous value for its stakeholders. While Gates became one of the richest men on the planet, Kildall struggled along, a half-forgotten software pioneer. His company, Digital Research, had created the dominant operating system for the microcomputers of its day, which was why IBM approached him. He had enormous technical vision and talent, he had shaped his industry and was respected by his peers, but he failed to harness the momentum that was his for the taking: Digital Research became a momentum-deficient firm. It simply did not see the huge value-creation potential that lay behind IBM's plans.[2]

This failing is a stark illustration of how one company can kill potential in the bud while another grasps it. We do not pretend that if we had looked at Microsoft in 1980 we could have predicted its astonishing success. But we *can* say that Gates intuitively knew how to seize opportunities and had an accurate vision of customer needs. This understanding led his company to develop or acquire the capabilities to realize a virtually unlimited potential for growth. For at least two decades, it felt the full impact of the momentum effect.

The Source of Microsoft's Momentum

An analysis of Microsoft reveals that from the very start the source of the company's momentum has been its deep understanding of its customers. Bill Gates was always a customer-focused leader with a clear view of who his customers were. At the start, these were just normal people, amateur programmers who wanted independence and the ability to use small computers. He developed and offered them inexpensive compilers for easy-to-use programming languages such as Basic.

When Bill Gates was approached to help develop a program to power the new IBM PC, he immediately agreed. He didn't quite know how to do it, but IBM was IBM, and he wasn't about to miss out on the potential of a collaboration. He had no operating system on hand, but he managed to find where to buy one. It was called MS-DOS, and Gates offered it to IBM's customers for as little as $40, because he wanted it to reach a mass market.

The momentum was building. Microsoft's customers were satisfied, and Gates kept improving the offer to keep them satisfied. The more his customers worked on PCs powered by MS-DOS, the more likely they were to become loyal to Microsoft, because they grew accustomed to the system and because other programs would be designed as "MS-DOS compatible."

Microsoft refined and expanded its offer, confident that the corporate world would create more value for the company. Now Gates's engineers developed more applications: word processing, spreadsheet programs, and presentation software. Observing Apple's success with an icon-based and user-friendly operating system, Microsoft developed Windows. The Microsoft story has many other examples of this sort, but the point is this: The company never stopped developing packaged customer solutions with more features, more convenience, and at lower prices than previous offerings. Microsoft was not just technologically driven—it knew how to develop compelling offers that would have customer traction and create exceptional growth.

In retrospect, it all seems obvious, almost inevitable—but why Microsoft and not Digital Research? What set Gates apart from Kildall? *Momentum strategy:* a coherent set of actions focused on creating the conditions needed to produce momentum. To understand what momentum strategy is, and why it is so powerful, we must first understand the source of momentum. And that lies at the very heart of the process of value creation.

How Value Is Created

All businesses, whether they are the most aggressive private enterprises on the prowl for market share or purely altruistic nonprofit charities, exist solely to create value for their stakeholders.[3] *Value* and *stakeholders* can be defined in different ways, but no business—private, nonprofit, or public—deserves to exist if it is not creating and delivering value.

Value is not something that just exists, waiting for firms to come along and harvest it. Before value can be plucked, it must be created. However, the phrase *value creation* is confusing because it is a term used readily by different people in different sectors—fund managers, marketing directors, and salespeople all mean something different by it.

In our case, by *value creation* we mean the entire process by which a business creates the value that it was established to distribute.[4]

Value creation starts with customers who spend their money to have their needs satisfied. Customers are the original source of all the value that firms can distribute to their stakeholders. A firm's ability to move that value from its customers to its stakeholders depends on its capacity to execute three fundamental business competences, set out in Figure 2.1: *value extraction, value capture,* and *value origination.*

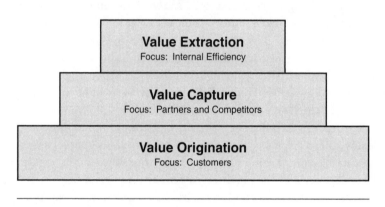

Figure 2.1   The value-creation process

Value extraction is about ensuring that the firm is efficient enough to not waste large amounts of the value it captures before passing it to its stakeholders. The first five years of Jack Welch at the top of General Electric were marked by his successful efforts in making the company leaner and extracting more value out of its activities. The dramatic changes—particularly the rows of empty desks—actually earned him the nickname Neutron Jack. Any number of corporate turnarounds and mergers have been based on so-called cost synergies improving a business's ability to extract value.

Value capture is the process through which value is gained by the firm, either from competitors or partners—that is, through gains in market share or by making sure that the firm is obtaining its fair share from alliances with third parties such as suppliers or resellers. A famous example is the competitive battles between Coke and Pepsi—the "cola wars"—and the occasional display of power between Coca-Cola and its bottlers.

Finally, value origination involves the creation of new products or services that customers esteem highly enough to pay for. Almost every successful, new, and innovative product results in value origination. It is called *origination* because it is the starting point of the value flow that the firm creates. The examples mentioned in Chapter 1, "The Power of Momentum," are in this category: The Wal-Mart stores in small communities and Toyota's Lexus and Prius models originated new sources of value.

A firm's capabilities in these three competences determine its performance. Each one is crucial, but their relative importance in generating long-term sustainable growth is totally different. Only one of these capabilities offers the potential for unlimited growth.

Where Is the Unlimited Potential?

Figure 2.1 illustrates the upward flow of value, welling up from its source to the firm's stakeholders. The pyramidal structure of the figure shows how these three competences are built on each other. But there is one striking feature of this process: No matter how well a firm performs at each of its stages, the maximum value that it can potentially pass on at any stage is limited by the value it acquired at the preceding stage. A firm cannot extract more value than it captured, and cannot capture more value than it has originated. It is immediately obvious that there is only one stage in the flow with unlimited potential to deliver growth: value origination.

To gain and maintain momentum, a firm must excel at all three of these strategies—otherwise, the value that is originated will not flow through the system. Obviously, value extraction is essential: An inefficient business can squander the value it creates. Indeed, in some particularly troubled situations, a firm will find it easier and faster to improve its results by focusing its efforts on extracting more value from current operations than on originating new sources of value. However, when a business has extracted every last cent through cost cutting, quality management, and other similar initiatives, there is no more to be found.

Likewise, value capture. For the past few decades, the field of business strategy has been dominated by a focus on value capture through competitive strategy, largely under the influence of Michael Porter.[5] A company must compete effectively and capture value from its competitors or it will disappear. Porter's work has been vital in helping firms improve their capabilities in this area. Ultimately, however, as with value extraction, growth through value capture can go only so far, because traditional competition is a zero-sum game. Even if a company were not hindered by antitrust barriers and could secure a dominant market share, its potential would be limited by the size of the markets it serves. The best illustration of the limits of competitive strategy is offered by Chan Kim and Renée Mauborgne with their brilliant and original work on Blue Ocean Strategy.[6] They show how successful organizations concentrate on their customers, deliver innovative solutions, and eventually, in the authors' memorable phrase, "make the competition irrelevant."

Capturing and extracting value are fundamental to the way we do business today, but organizations have been striving to become more efficient and competitive for years and many still find delivering consistent profitable growth a challenge. Why? Because the battles they are fighting blind them to the unlimited potential available at the very source of value creation.

To capture value, you must focus on your competitors and partners. To extract value, you must focus on your own internal processes. But these are not the source of the value-creation flow.

Where is that source? With the customers.

The waves of restructuring, downsizing, outsourcing, and total quality management—aimed at improving efficiency—have caused many leaders to become obsessed with value extraction. Michael Porter's work led others to fixate on the combative drive to succeed in the Red Ocean of competition. Kim and Mauborgne's exciting work opened the eyes of others to the unlimited potential of the Blue Ocean.

In the end, to deliver exceptional growth, firms must navigate effectively across all three levels of value creation: origination, capture, and extraction. This is what momentum strategy achieves. We expand and deepen the explanation of the way momentum strategy works throughout the book, but to start with, here is the broad picture in a nutshell. The source of momentum lies in value origination, but the momentum inherent in that source can be exploited only when certain conditions are aligned and reach a sufficient level of intensity. First, firms need to be able to develop offers that are perceived as compelling by customers. The customer traction that stems from these compelling offers gives an initial, rapid, and efficient burst of growth. This growth is maintained and accelerated by customer retention and engagement, and by systematic actions aimed at nurturing the momentum. Next, the momentum-powered firm is able to capture all the value that it has originated because the speed of its growth makes it difficult for competitors to react effectively. In a sense, it leaves its competitors trailing in its wake. In the last stage, the momentum-powered firm exploits the strengths of its compelling offers and high customer engagement to extract as much as possible of the value that it has captured. It is able to do this because its operations are targeted at supplying the high growth of successful products and its marketing simply has to reinforce the underlying customer traction, rather than compensate for market resistance.

In short, momentum-powered firms originate more value through compelling offers. They capture more value by being continuously ahead of their competitors. They extract more value with more focused operations and more efficient marketing. The coherent combination of actions at these three levels creates a momentum strategy.

Drivers of Momentum Strategy

Momentum strategy rests on some key competences, including customer focus, innovation, and marketing excellence, but it also requires an interactive involvement of multiple functions within the firm. The avenues for the successful design and execution of a momentum strategy are implicit in the brief exposition previously described. They are the key drivers of exceptional growth: exploring the customer's space, crafting power offers, and mobilizing for growth.

Exploring the Customer's Space

The traction that provides the initial grip needed for momentum to develop comes from novel insights into the customer's world. A large part of the success enjoyed by Nintendo's Wii, the TV-based home computer game system, comes from the simple insight that moving is more fun than sitting still, and that when people move their bodies they naturally interact more with those around them than they do when they're sitting down. From that insight, it becomes obvious that using your arms to control a virtual tennis racket, baseball bat, or boxing glove feels more real than using your thumb.[7] Also, that by standing side by side with your opponents rather than sitting next to them, you will look at them more, touch them more, talk to them more, and generally become more engaged and active—in short, that you will have more fun.

To acquire those insights, however, firms must explore their customers' space, their worldview, and the emotions that drive their behavior. Consider the example of an elderly woman who was a member of a focus group on anti-inflammatory drugs. Suffering from chronic back pain, this unfortunate woman regularly used an anti-inflammatory gel. In the focus group, she explained that she was unable to reach her back herself to apply the treatment and that she lived alone and had no one to help her. Her solution—ineffective, impractical, and humiliating—was to smear the gel on her shower door and then rub her back against it. Obviously, there had to be a better way. The company, Novartis, invented a special applicator to be included with the gel in a special package for back pain.[8]

Not all avenues for momentum strategy can be so directly pointed at by customers. As Henry Ford memorably said, "If I'd asked consumers what they wanted, I would have invented a faster horse." Exploration means being ahead of others, including customers: ahead down new paths that open up valuable avenues for them. It is the insights revealed by this exploration that uncover original sources of value and drive exceptional growth. To exploit these growth opportunities successfully, firms must craft offers that have a powerful appeal to customers, just like the Wii.

Crafting "Power" Offers

"Power" offers lie at the heart of momentum. They are offers that are so resonant, so compelling, so powerful that customers are drawn magnetically toward them. The crafting of power offers is not just another name for product development. It's not concerned with just the product, and it involves much more than development. Power offers have both breadth and depth. The complete offer includes the image, a relationship, the trust, the kudos that "membership" of the "club" of users brings, the reliability, and every other component of the value that a customer acquires. Crafting involves shaping all aspects of the complete offer to maximize both its perceived value to the targeted customers and the equity of these targeted customers to the firm.

The crafting of power offers also reflects an ambition to go beyond the norms to achieve something exceptional for the customer and for the firm. It expresses the collective care that an organization places in the realization of an offer, in the same way that true craftspeople put all their heart and ingenuity into creating a beautiful and unique piece of work.

Nowhere is Toyota's ability to craft a power offer that generates traction better illustrated than the Scion, a range of cars aimed at young drivers. For them, value is all about customization and individuality, with the Internet playing a pivotal role in their lives. So what has Toyota done? It has crafted a car that doesn't look like Mom's or Dad's car, that can be designed by the customer online, and that is packed with optional extras such as extreme sound systems and radical paint schemes.

And because Toyota is focusing on the drivers of tomorrow, it has entered a sponsorship deal with Whyville, a virtual-reality world aimed at 8 to 15-year-olds, which means that kids can buy, customize, and "drive" their own virtual Scion. The sponsorship supports Whyville's underlying educational purpose by teaching kids math—in the context of arranging their virtual-car financing.

The Wii and the Scion are examples of offers that could not have been designed by traditional product-development processes. They are the fruits of firms that had the ambition to craft offers that are so perfectly aligned with their customers' desires and sense of self that they feel as if the offers were designed personally for them.

Mobilizing for Growth

An effective momentum strategy requires a shared ambition across the firm, an objective that must trickle down to all levels of employees. Everyone in the firm must be focused on satisfying, retaining, and, most important, engaging customers. Inspirational leaders such as Richard Branson at Virgin, Steve Jobs at Apple, Lou Gerstner at IBM, and Sam Walton in Wal-Mart's first three decades are all excellent examples of this.

Effective mobilization also involves a sense of urgency. Michael Ruettgers, the former CEO of data-storage manufacturer EMC, once took a novel approach to making staff realize the importance of customers. The firm was way behind on its sales targets and had consequently accumulated a vast inventory. "So to make sure everybody understood how important this was," Ruettgers explained, "we took all that extra inventory and put it in people's offices. People had to climb around crates to get to their desks. Miraculously, by the end of the next quarter, we had met our sales targets. And all of the offices were empty."[9] His action was effective in this context because it was coherent with other measures aimed at mobilizing employees to create value for their customers.

Momentum Strategy at Work: The iPod

If you want an example of momentum strategy at work, just look for a pair of white earbuds. Whether you're on a plane or in a coffee shop, at a shopping mall or the beach, the little white buds of an Apple iPod are ubiquitous. The iPod has become the decade's defining consumer item, and iTunes, its related music store, sells millions of licensed music files every month. But think back to 2001: Napster was effectively threatening the future of the music industry by enabling users to download unlicensed digital copies of songs for free, Sony was taking its powerful Walkman brand into the digital age, and Apple's main product was the iMac, a beautiful-looking computer aimed at a relatively niche market that prized design and simplicity over compatibility.

What happened? How did Apple manage to create so much value so fast? It was all due to excellence in value origination. One of the key factors Apple has always understood is the importance of design and of the customer interface, but the iPod is much more than a user-friendly, good-looking gadget. It is *cool*. It captures its customers' imagination. Even today, with dozens of cheaper alternatives offering similar functionality, the iPod is still top of the tree.

But it is the iTunes website that stands out as the greatest achievement of Apple's momentum strategy. Remember that in 2001, illegal copies of songs were being shared across the Internet for free and with no digital rights-management restriction embedded in the files. Who would have predicted that a service offering the same files, with restrictions on excessive copying, could become a successful paid-for service?

It worked because Apple understood their customers' space. They knew that they were ripping CDs and illegally sharing files not because they were dishonest but because their sense of honesty and fairness was affronted by the music companies' business model: They felt that most CDs contained only one or two hit songs and a large number they didn't want but were forced to buy to get the ones they did. By offering users safe and legal access to the specific tracks they wanted, at a price they perceived as fair, iTunes originated new value for its customers. It created a market-leading service, selling a product that just a few months before was regularly being exchanged for free.[10]

The momentum effect Apple is enjoying is based in value origination, but the company has also improved its performance on the next two levels of value creation. Both the iPod and iTunes have captured significant value from Apple's competitors. iTunes in particular is also a great example of value extraction. An offering that not only sells you a music player, but then continues to sell you music to play on it, will obviously extract much more value than from one that consists of a player alone. Indeed, not doing so would be like Gillette selling razors but not selling blades. Obvious, sure, but Apple was the only company to do it successfully.

In mid-2007, Apple launched the iPhone. Early indications are that the company has done it again. Despite a hefty price tag, the one millionth iPhone was sold just 74 days after launch.[11] The new Apple momentum that started with the iMac and took off with the iPod and iTunes might be beginning a new phase. It's an impressive record.

How Momentum Growth Opens a New Efficiency Frontier

One of the defining themes of momentum is how it both ensures growth opportunities and exploits them more efficiently. You can say it in three words: more for less.

Efficiency, of course, represents one of capitalism's most ancient and never-ending quests. Ever since the Industrial Revolution, managers have devoted their waking hours to cutting production costs by improving organization, seeking cheaper or more productive labor, and installing better technology. Pushing the boundaries of cost-based efficiency enables firms to increase profits—but this alone cannot create sustainable growth.

The result is that while efficiency has progressed in operations and organization, marketing costs have been increasing as a percentage of revenues, so much so that in many companies marketing expenditure has become the value chain's number one component. This is typical of the Pushers. Winning the old-style efficiency battles can still provide growth, but that growth is limited. Pioneers, on the other hand, have discovered that there is a new efficiency frontier—one that focuses on providing customers the best *offer* in the most efficient way. This is the one that creates momentum.

Moving from Compensating to Momentum Strategy

Most businesses compensate for inadequate products and poor customer targeting by pushing their products on a skeptical marketplace. They attempt to batter their way to their customers' wallets through advertising, special promotions, hard selling, or discounting. To compensate for this expensive marketing, they are forced to cut costs on the very activities that could improve the attractiveness of their offer: operations and R&D. This is exactly how the Pushers we looked at in Chapter 1 behaved. We call it *compensating strategy*. It is the long-term cancer of business—eating resources and slowly weakening the firm from the inside out. It is not sustainable.

The return on the marketing investment might even be positive, increasing both growth and profits in the short term. But our research reveals that penalties appear in the longer term. Even a good return on a marketing investment supporting an inferior product does not necessarily mean that it should be made. Investing first instead in product improvements is a better option for profitable growth.[12]

Unfortunately, the first reflex of marketing managers facing a challenge is to ask for more resources. It's natural. Everybody knows that a large part of marketing resources is wasted, but this has become acceptable. In business meetings, managers laugh at the old adage, attributed to John Wanamaker, "Half the money I spend on advertising is wasted: The trouble is I don't know which half." They shouldn't laugh. They should cry. They should fall down on their knees and beg forgiveness for such profligate inefficiency.

Indeed, top management should give marketing and sales investments much closer scrutiny. This is where the new efficiency frontier lies, rich with opportunities for improvement!

We do not intend to bash marketing people. Marketers are often among the most able, innovative, and dynamic people in an organization, much closer to the customer than others in the business. Marketers and salespeople are skilled communicators, capable of connecting with customers and presenting images and ideas that resonate with their desires. And this holds for both sides of their crucial function: upstream in guiding the creation of offers to fulfill unsatisfied needs, and downstream in diffusing them to customers in the most effective and efficient way. Unfortunately, most spend a disproportionate amount of their time downstream, outspending the competition on existing product categories. It is upstream toward which they should turn their eyes—to outsmarting the competition through innovation and discovery.

Consider the Apple iPod again. The iconic advertising campaign—a silhouetted figure with white headphones and an iPod against a bright, solid color—was totally integral to the value being offered to the customer. The ads didn't just try to sell the value: They were a fundamental part of the value being offered. The design strength of these ads—and their successors, incorporating musicians as diverse as U2, Eminem, and Wynton Marsalis—contributed to the iPod's appeal. They were cool and looked great, just like an iPod. They were clear and simple, just like an iPod. They expressed enjoyment and variety, just like an iPod. This is true marketing excellence—not just spending money to try to force-feed the public with a product but actually adding to the value of the offer itself. It is the whole process of understanding the customer and thereby inspiring the insights that makes such ads effective. This is marketing's role in momentum strategy.

Creating offers so perfectly crafted to customers' needs and values creates powerful customer engagement—a momentum that obviates the need for expensive sales and marketing and the cost-cutting necessary to fund them. That is how momentum opens up the new efficiency frontier. Exploiting this frontier by moving from a compensating strategy to momentum strategy is the subject of several later chapters in this book. Now, as we head that way, the time has come to proclaim what we believe should be the single rallying cry of all momentum-powered businesses: *Less is more, more for less.*

Less Is More, More for Less

The key to the new efficiency frontier is to realize that less should be more for the customer, and that as a result the business will get more for less.

It's not at all paradoxical. For customers, *less* should mean that they get exactly what they need and nothing more, with no superfluous elements that create complexity and could destroy value. In a world where people are subjected to a geometric progression of pressures, time is a crucial resource and simplicity an increasingly valuable prize. The absence of unwanted features and complexity makes customers feel that they have been listened to and understood. This apparent personalization is why giving them less can actually provide them with more value. *For customers, less is more.*

This obviously requires a considered, confident understanding of human nature in general and one's target customers in particular. Firms that lack this understanding generally engage in a compensating strategy to make up for their deficiencies. To reduce the risk, they provide more—just in case. But this only increases costs to the firm and decreases value to customers.

In contrast, firms that are strategically focused on value origination develop a superior awareness of their customers' needs. This enables them to deliver exactly the offer that will resonate with them: nothing unnecessary, nothing wasted. By knowing that less is more for customers, they achieve *more for less for the business.* This is the essence of the new efficiency frontier. It is the road from compensating to momentum strategy.[13]

Unlock Your Unlimited Potential

Although efficiency drives, restructuring, mergers, and acquisitions can all help a company in capturing and extracting value, their potential impact on growth is limited, likewise, our obsession with acquiring and maintaining spending superiority. Pushing growth year after year through additional resources has obvious limitations that will one day catch up with a firm, its stakeholders, and its leaders.

The key imperative of modern business leaders must be to simultaneously achieve superior growth *and* superior efficiency—what we call exceptional growth. To achieve this ambition, they must seek not only to extract value from the business and capture value from competitors, but also, and more important, to originate new sources of value from customers. This is the unlimited potential of momentum strategy. The attention that momentum leaders give to the three drivers of a momentum strategy—customers, power offers, and mobilization— is what sets them apart from the rest. In the next chapter, we examine how to put this into practice through a systematic momentum process of eight specific steps. It is time to take the road to momentum and fulfill your unlimited potential.

3

The Road to Momentum

Vasella's Eureka Moment

What does it take to make a CEO jump? Dr. Daniel Vasella, chairman of Novartis, one of the world's largest pharmaceutical firms, found out in April 1999, when he was handed a report on a new drug developed by his oncology division. The results before his eyes were better than good—they were sensational. Vasella knew this drug would make a difference, not only to his company, but to cancer patients all over the world.

The report that electrified Vasella covered the first phase of research on a product then known as STI571, later renamed Gleevec, developed to treat a form of cancer called chronic myelogenous leukemia, or CML.[1]

At the time, there were about forty thousand known CML sufferers worldwide, with a life expectancy of just four or five years after diagnosis. Given the high costs involved and the small patient population, a purely financial calculation would have shown that it was not worth developing and producing the drug.

Set against this, the results on Vasella's desk showed an astonishing 100 percent efficacy. The drug had real potential to prolong patients' lives.[2]

Despite the seemingly small business opportunity provided by the restricted patient population, Vasella made Gleevec an urgent priority. He knew that every day before the product was brought to market, lives would be lost. Normally it would take more than a decade to move a new drug from phase-one research to launch—ten years in which patients would continue to die. By engaging employees, customers, and important stakeholders to share his passion, Vasella managed to build an internal and external momentum that powered a record-breaking performance. Driven by the power of this momentum, Gleevec came to market in less than three years.

The story of Gleevec is the story of how the value originated by that drug set Novartis Oncology on the path to becoming a momentum-powered firm.

The Momentum-Powered Firm in Action

As discussed in Chapter 2, "The Source of Momentum," momentum can be created by following a momentum strategy—a coherent set of actions focused on creating the specific conditions needed to produce momentum. But how exactly is that phenomenon brought about? The unique combination of factors that creates exceptional growth is too important to be left to entrepreneurial Darwinism or corporate chance. We need a systematic process to implement a momentum strategy. But what would such a process involve? The story of Gleevec gives some clues.

The key point for Gleevec was the "Eureka moment" when Dr. Daniel Vasella realized the value potential of this new drug and resolved to follow it all the way through, despite what appeared to be a limited patient population. The value he perceived was wide-ranging: for patients, their families, and caregivers, for the medical community at large, and for Novartis. Although apparently small in terms of economic potential, it was great in terms of social responsibility and employee pride.

This is a crucial point. Momentum-powered firms focus on key stakeholders and understand that the concept of "customer" is much wider than simply the product purchaser. Vasella knew that the customers were not just the people buying the drug. Several stakeholders were involved, each offering something different to the firm. Because he understood the different value Gleevec offered to a wide range of concerned persons, as well as the value each group offered the firm, he knew that it was his task to engage all these different customers. Great leaders balance and juggle differing demands by originating value targeted at each separate group in such a way as to engage them all.[3]

When Vasella sprang into action, his leadership over the following days and months built the conditions that set the momentum effect into play. He made sure everyone in the company was aware of the new drug's importance. The message got across: The Novartis Technical R&D team committed itself to beating senior management's deadlines, many of them volunteering to work overtime. This was internal momentum at work. "We were working day and night with great enthusiasm to exceed our already-ambitious production targets," one of the team members explained. "We knew patients were waiting for the drug to be available. They were even writing letters to the chairman. Several of them were dying every day. We were their only hope."[4]

Now momentum from within was joined by momentum from without. End consumers—CML patients condemned to death from an incurable cancer whose only available treatment was ineffectual and unpleasant—began writing to Vasella in masses begging to take part in clinical trials. With such a rare condition, it would normally take more than three years to recruit enough patients for large-scale trials. Novartis did it in four months.

Key stakeholders helped build more external momentum. Novartis kept the press constantly informed on the story of what inevitably became known as a new "wonder drug," although Vasella himself was reluctant to use the term, lest it raise false hopes. The U.S. Food and Drug Administration approved the drug in just ten weeks—the FDA's fastest-ever sanctioning of a new cancer drug.

By focusing on the needs of key stakeholders, understanding what each valued and what each offered Novartis, Vasella targeted and engaged significant groups beyond company walls to help him harness the full power of momentum. It required focus and drive, but most of all, it required ambition.

The Results Momentum Can Deliver

The power of momentum fueled Novartis Oncology's drive to fulfill Gleevec's potential. Its momentum gave it a reputation as one of the most exciting places to work in the field of cancer-treatment research.

The brightest and best flocked toward the firm where the action was, adding more momentum. For Gleevec customers, the value was even greater: They can survive for longer, with a treatment that is more effective and less unpleasant than chemotherapy. In addition to the obvious relief from suffering, this greatly increased the number of patients under treatment. The longer patients survive, the longer they will be buying the drug. On top of that, Gleevec was approved as treatment for other forms of cancer, too.

Chapter 1, "The Power of Momentum," presented the results of our research into the impact of momentum over groups of large firms, but what about its impact on an individual business? In 2002, analysts had estimated that sales of Gleevec would reach $800,000 by 2006. In fact, by 2005, they were already in excess of $2 billion. At the same time, a patient-assistance program was put in place that by 2006 had helped 18,907 needy people in different parts of the world. In India, 99 percent of patients receive Gleevec at no cost.

This wonderful story began with the value that Novartis had originated with the drug and the ambition to realize its full potential. That value and ambition was so strong that it engaged customers, employees, and stakeholders to share the passion that pulled Novartis to record-breaking performance with no need to push the drug or spin press releases to a skeptical media. That's how momentum works. Momentum-powered firms are propelled toward the new efficiency frontier by first gaining traction through powerful momentum design and then boosting their progress through momentum execution. These are the twin engines of momentum. Once these are understood, we can map out the road to momentum.

The Twin Engines of Momentum

In a car, regardless of how powerful your engine is, you need traction before you can start to turn that energy into momentum. Furthermore, your speed and fuel efficiency are hugely influenced by the conditions in which you are traveling.

If driving along a bumpy road, you'll never maintain the speed you would on a good one because the jarring vibrations will constantly check your progress. You'll burn a lot more gas trying to get to where you're going because you have to compensate, both for not having enough grip and for the resistance you encounter. You spend more energy making less progress. You have no momentum.

It's the same with business momentum. When a firm's offerings lack power, it must compensate for their lack of instant appeal, for the resistance they encounter. Its managers compensate with extra resources to make up for the offerings' lack of traction and for the rough surface they encounter.

For a business to take the road to momentum, two factors must be in place: traction and movement. These are the conditions under which the momentum effect arises. The first needs a method of designing a product that is so compelling to customers they will adopt it without having to be convinced with stupendous marketing or sales resources. The second requires all sources of resistance to be removed and all sources of energy to be brought into play, creating a vibrant buzz that keeps the momentum going. The first component we call *momentum design* and the second one *momentum execution.* These are the two engines of momentum strategy set out in Figure 3.1.

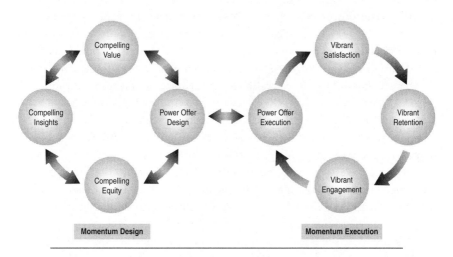

Figure 3.1   The twin engines of momentum

But how are these two engines linked? What is the connection that turns traction into movement? Through what we call *power offers.* We introduced the idea of power offers in Chapter 2: those offers that are so carefully crafted that customers find them irresistible. The twin engines of momentum strategy are linked at the point where the process of designing a power offer merges with the process of executing that power offer. It is on the strength of the power offer that momentum starts or stutters. That is why great power offers such as the iPod, the Wii, the Prius, and the Scion create so much momentum. Because they are the core of the twin engines of momentum design and momentum execution, they ignite momentum. The eight elements set out in Figure 3.1 are the conditions that must be in place for the momentum effect to take hold. They contain the power that will produce momentum growth. The procedure of aligning and intensifying them forms the eight steps of the momentum process.

Momentum Design

"Chance favors the prepared mind," said biologist Louis Pasteur. Leaders of firms that build momentum are skilled at preparing a corporate mindset that picks up *compelling insights* that in turn lead to developing great products. Daniel Vasella and the Gleevec story are an example of that. The word *compelling* is central to momentum design. It describes the powerful and irresistible force that the process generates, and it sets the bar ambitiously high. For example, the process of discovery that reveals compelling insights is much more ambitious than the detailed analysis of masses of data that traditional firms carry out. Analysis is good, but an overreliance on rational calculation—as opposed to exposure to the subjective reality of an individual customer's world— is deeply limiting and risks missing valuable insights.

For a number of years either side of the millennium, BMW excelled at discovering compelling insights about what really attracted customers. The service levels, design, and integrated marketing that marked its customer offerings were the result not only of the glamorous and visible superb engineering but also of the less visible and simple act of paying attention to customer needs and spotting trends.[5]

A prime example was the integration of Apple's iPod into car stereos. BMW was the first car manufacturer to understand the potential of the iPod, the hottest new music gadget in a generation, introducing it into its new cars in June 2004, a full six months before its nearest competitor. BMW drivers could simply place the iPod in a docking station and operate it through the standard steering wheel and dashboard stereo controls. Many other car manufacturers followed suit throughout 2005, including Volvo, Ferrari, and Honda. Significantly, however, it wasn't until August 2006 that Ford and General Motors caught up and realized that their customers might like it, too. Two whole years! How is that possible?[6]

Such lags occur because firms without momentum tend to rely excessively on analysis of market research. They never come up with ideas like this. Their forms probably lacked a box to tick asking, "On a scale of 1 to 5, how useful would you find an iPod docking station?" But executives in a firm open to discovery spend time with customers and notice people listening to iPods who ritually remove the earbuds when they get into their cars. That's when the lightbulb flashes over their head with a message: *If they like those little things so much outside, wouldn't they like them even more in their cars?* That is customer insight.

You can't just ask customers what they want. Smart companies must understand customers' needs better than customers themselves are able or willing to express them. The discovery of compelling insights allows us to better comprehend what drives *compelling value.* When exploring what customers value, you need to go far beyond the obvious financial and functional needs and work at understanding the deeper human drivers that underlie that value. This touches on customers' dreams, fantasies, and nightmares, to reach the essence of their emotions. BMW's "Ultimate Driving Machine" campaign is a fine example of the impact these insights can have. By focusing on the pleasure of driving with slogans such as "measured in smiles per hour" and "live vicariously through no one," BMW connected strongly with its customers' self-image and aspirations. The value they presented to their customers was certainly more compelling than that offered by Ford's more functionally-focused "Designed for living—Engineered to last."

This investigation of customer value is a never-ending process. For instance, BMW and other car manufacturers now face the challenge of discovering the design elements that are becoming of greater value for customers in a new era in which a growing proportion of the population is increasingly concerned by environmental issues.

Using customer insights to better comprehend the deeper drivers of value cuts both ways. In addition to a deep examination of the value that the firm can offer customers, the process of strategic exploration should be applied to the value that customers offer the firm, in a search for what we call *compelling equity.* Again, this is much more ambitious than mere segmentation studies and other such analyses. Companies can acquire compelling customer equity by deeply understanding not just the obvious long-term direct financial contribution of different customer groups but also other dimensions of equity such as the potential of word-of-mouth recommendations and the impact that opinion leadership can have on employees. Returning to the two marketing taglines from BMW and Ford that we highlighted, ask yourself this: Which customers are likely to be worth more—those who see a car as a pleasurable status symbol or those who crave durability first and foremost?

The understanding brought by exploring compelling value and equity helps firms to craft targeted *power offers* that are much more than mere products. The word *power* here has a double meaning: power with customers and power to generate growth. Obviously, the two are connected. The power with customers provides the traction that generates superior business performance. They balance the compelling value offered to customers with a compelling equity for the firm in return.

Such power offers can be achieved only through an iterative process involving true interactive cooperation between business functions. BMW's "Ultimate Driving Machine" slogan is a case in point. At the heart of BMW crafting is engineering and design. It is the heritage of the firm, continuously nurtured and developed. But every aspect of BMW must contribute to reinforcing the compelling proposition and the compelling target, including pricing, distribution, advertising, promotions, and service. In America, one of the actions that crafted BMW as stylish and fun to drive was an innovative communication via product placement in the 1996 James Bond film *GoldenEye*. The British secret agent drove the new BMW Z3 in hair-raising chases. This initiative was in the context of the launch of the company's new model, the Z3 Roadster, but it had an impact on the perceived value of BMW's entire range. This communication resonated among the firm's supporters because it cemented the repositioning of BMW from a yuppie status symbol into the "Ultimate Driving Machine." Eight years later, adding an iPod dock to their cars was just one of many iterative improvements of the power offer. It contributed in increasing its value further by associating the cars with a cool and desirable innovation.

Momentum Execution

It is extremely rare, even in the context of a power offer, that a new product gets it exactly right the first time around. Offers must be constantly improved and tweaked in light of customer experience. It is vital for employees at all levels to have the ambition to continually seek improvement. This is feasible in smart companies because employees will have been made aware of or participated in the crucial early strategic-exploration phases of momentum strategy. These early stages are essential to establish the traction that builds momentum. Everything must then be aligned and coherent to create momentum boosters and eradicate momentum killers.

Momentum begins by delivering the power offer to customers, and its first signature is superior customer satisfaction. Firms with momentum create *vibrant satisfaction,* a state of mind that inspires customers to help boost momentum. This kind of satisfaction leads to *vibrant retention* and *vibrant engagement* by customers. Again, like the word *compelling* in the design engine, *vibrant* represents an essential element to the execution process. Momentum execution must vibrate with the resonance of the power offer. Momentum-powered firms set much higher and more ambitious goals for customer satisfaction, retention, and engagement than do their momentum-deficient counterparts. The vibrancy of the execution process is what continually boosts momentum.

We examine these concepts more deeply in later pages, but as an illustration of satisfaction, retention, and engagement, consider Apple's renaissance since the late 1990s. When the American Customer Satisfaction Index began recording data in the early 1990s, Apple was bottom of the rankings in the computer sector. The turnaround began with the launch of the iMac in 1998. With its smooth curves and iconic "Bondi blue" translucent casing, the iMac was a masterpiece of momentum design. But how effective was the execution of this power offer? Extremely: Just two years after the launch of the iMac, Apple's customer satisfaction ratings had shot up from rock bottom to number three in the sector. By 2004, buoyed by the iPod's halo effect, Apple had reached number one, where it has remained ever since.[7]

The customers that Apple targeted with the iMac were affluent and design conscious—people who by their very nature are difficult to retain because they constantly seek the next new thing. But the satisfaction that the iMac created drove exceptional levels of retention, and not just for new versions of the iMac. The iPod, launched in 2001, was snapped up by the very same trend-setting design-junkies who loved the iMac: people who gave the iPod a level of media visibility that helped propel it to a 70 percent share of the market for portable music players.

The iMac, iPod, and iPhone also neatly demonstrate Apple's excellence at the most powerful stage of the momentum execution process: vibrant engagement. Whereas some consumers simply enjoy music on their iPod, others are constantly buying the latest model and accessories, downloading the latest iTunes tracks, and persuading their friends to do the same. Likewise, some iMac and iPhone users just like them because they look cool, but for many others they symbolize something much deeper and more personal. The first group is just consuming. Those in the second group are using Apple's products as vehicles for self-expression and self-actualization.

These committed iPod, iMac, and iPhone users are part of a tribe. They take great pleasure in sharing their knowledge and experience—it is where they belong. More important, their vibrant engagement persuades others to convert to the Apple family.

Coherently executing a well-designed power offer is the basis of the customer engagement that firms such as Apple achieve. Momentum design starts with the discovery of compelling customer insights: learning about them and understanding them. The whole process of momentum design is iterative—return to Figure 3.1 and note how the arrows go both ways in a constant to and fro. Traction is transferred through the power offer, the spark that fires momentum. Momentum is then constantly boosted by vibrant levels of satisfaction, retention, and engagement.

Thereafter, momentum continually replenishes and reinvigorates the offer. It must be actively managed and maintained, but when it becomes systematic to the way a firm does business, each improvement of the offer creates more customer traction. On and on it goes as momentum flows. Firms that harness the twin engines of momentum strategy—design and execution—remain externally focused, not internally obsessed. It is a cooperative, interactive, and iterative process rather than a linear one. It is dynamic and constantly changing. It is never "game over."

Momentum Design at Skype

To illustrate our framework for the momentum-powered firm, let's look at Skype, the Internet telephony company created in 2003 by two young Scandinavians, Niklas Zennström and Janus Friis. After less than three years in business, Skype had 53 million customers. In 2005, it was sold to eBay in a deal worth in excess of $3 billion, an incredible sum to create in 36 months.[8] How did Skype manage to create so much value in such a short period of time? Because it originated substantial value for customers and was propelled by momentum. Let's examine how this happened.

Skype offered free voice communication from any computer with a broadband Internet connection to any other computer with a broadband connection. All that is required is for the caller to download and register a piece of software.

Skype's momentum first derived from its superior understanding of potential customers, in this case broadband users. These compelling insights were the starting point on the journey to vast potential. The key components of momentum design—compelling insights, compelling value, compelling equity, and power offer design—are illustrated in Figure 3.2, which is simply the left half of the twin-engines model in Figure 3.1, as they apply to Skype.[9]

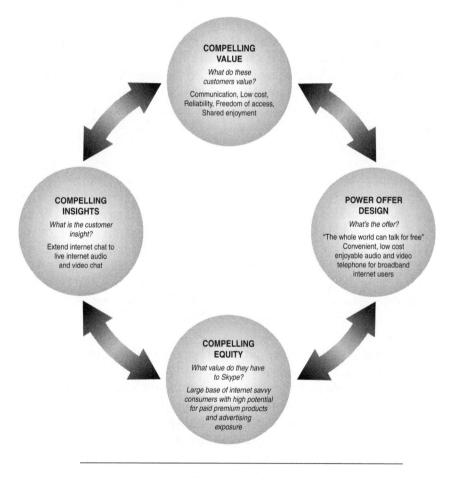

Figure 3.2 Momentum design at Skype

Skype's customers already have access to a higher-quality Internet connection to speed up their ability to send and receive information. They use keyboard chat services but also need to communicate verbally. Unfortunately, a landline telephone requires equipment and wiring and occupies additional desk space. And traditional telephony does not allow video transmission, which broadband does. This was the initial insight, the need for a single tool that integrated Internet chat, audio communication, and video transmission on the same PC that is used for other tasks.

What do Skype's customers value? Convenient chat, audio, and video communication is the starting point. In addition, as computer techies, they want reliability and, like all consumers, they value low costs. Intensive Internet users, they also feel connected with the culture of free exchange of information. The word *free* has emotional as well as financial resonance for them. Finally, as communicative people, they derive pleasure from sharing the fun of communicating. This is compelling value.

The equity that these customers offer Skype in return might be harder to spot. The product is offered free of charge, so where can Skype extract value? The most obvious way is that customers can be cross-sold additional services.

For example, not all their customers' friends and family will be willing or able to take calls through a computer. However, Skype's customers would still like to be able to talk to these nontechies. So in 2004, Skype launched its first revenue-generating service, called SkypeOut. This service lets subscribers place calls from their PCs to landline phones in a large number of countries for about two cents a minute, regardless of where the call is made from or to. Subsequent charged-for products have followed, and Skype has even established partnerships with the manufacturers of headsets and Internet-enabled handsets.[10]

But there is more than just cross-selling opportunity in Skype's customer equity. The company's brilliance in targeting heavy broadband users was in recognizing their special attributes: They are in regular contact with their network of friends, family, and colleagues; they are early adopters of new communication products; they are an extremely valuable advertising target; they have taken the power of word of mouth to a new level; and they have networking power. This is compelling equity.

The next step was to integrate that understanding into a superior business model—a power offer. In hindsight, the potential of a business that offers free voice communication, that harnesses customer networks for viral marketing, and that brings in profit by cross-selling charged-for products targeted to the same user group is blindingly obvious. But that is hindsight. It was detailed customer understanding and the ingenuity of Skype's founders that enabled them to create the power offer that everyone else missed.

The outside-in focus of the process of momentum design means that development of power offers is never-ending. The double-sided arrows in Figure 3.2 express the iterative and interactive nature of the process between its four components. Even when power offers have been created, customer reaction can tell an outside-in focused company more about what customers value and what they are worth. Skype is particularly good at capturing feedback from its users through blogs and web forums. This increased knowledge uncovers yet more compelling insights and the whole engine kicks off again—the value becomes more compelling, the equity greater, and the offer more powerful. Provided the firm remains focused on its customers rather than on itself, this becomes an iterative, never-ending process, building ever more customer traction. On the other hand, if it fails to learn these lessons and does not continue improving its offer, the firm is issuing an invitation for somebody else to build on its experience and develop a better offer. It will then lose its momentum just as a new competitor starts to build it.[11]

Skype's final piece of genius is in its marketing line: "The whole world can talk for free." What better way to connect with the Internet generation? The brilliance of that line—the communication of the offer—marks the point where the design of power offers, enabled by the traction that the firm has acquired, meets the execution that is needed to start momentum.

Momentum Execution at Skype

The execution of the power offer must first flawlessly unleash the customer traction built into its design. Then it must be on the look out for any opportunity to boost momentum. This vigilant power offer execution is the first step in a process that leads to vibrant customer satisfaction, vibrant customer retention, and vibrant customer engagement. This vigilance and vibrancy is essential, and a firm must set ambitious goals to analyze, monitor, and stimulate these four stages of momentum execution.

Skype's power offer was executed perfectly. First, the service was simple to use, easy to install, and robust. In short, it delivered on its promise—a telling advantage over many other new technology-based offerings. More important, Skype knew that users felt overcharged by traditional telecoms providers for years and would derive satisfaction from breaking free of excessive charges by using the very broadband connection that the telecoms were providing. Satisfaction is an emotional response, and for these people the enjoyment of besting a large corporation such as a telephone provider would be sweet. The cherry on the cake is that Skype is not limited to just a dumb handset—by donning a cheap headset, the user can simultaneously work or play on his or her PC, examine documents, or watch videos. It is fun. This combination offers more than normal satisfaction. It is a vibrant satisfaction, an emotion so strong that it leads customers to action.

However, customer momentum requires much more than satisfaction, even if that satisfaction is more vibrant than normal. Skype ensured that its customers remained active for a number of reasons. First, as broadband users, they spent a lot of time on their PCs. After the firm's software had been installed, what could be easier than dialing up a friend for a chat using Skype? Alternatively, a friend would be just as likely to initiate a call and prompt the user into remaining an active customer. The dynamics of human interaction keep customers actively using the product. This is vibrant retention, leading to further customer action.

The final step to attaining customer momentum is to secure the advocacy of customers. Because the offering was so good, Skype's customers actively engaged with it. The principal driving force behind their willingness to engage with it is built in to the offer. As soon as people became Skype customers, they had good reason to tell their friends about the service, spreading the news that they could all enjoy free calls together. Being heavy Internet users, they were almost by definition in regular contact with their personal networks. Within minutes of signing up, they were providing free advertising for Skype. In this manner, each newly signed person played a part in making the customer base grow. These combined boosts to the firm's momentum brought in approximately thirty thousand new users a day through word of mouth in May 2005. By November of the same year, it had swollen to around seventy thousand a day. Getting people to download software is not that difficult; ensuring that they keep using it is much harder. Here again Skype excels. It first reached one million online users in October 2004. One year later, shortly after its sale to eBay, that had grown to four million. Less than 15 months after that, the number had grown to 9 million—9 million people actively using a product at any one moment in time. This is more than just the result of casual recommendations. It is vibrant engagement—and momentum that creates exceptional growth.

The process is set out in Figure 3.3, which you will recognize as the right side of the twin-engines model of Figure 3.1.

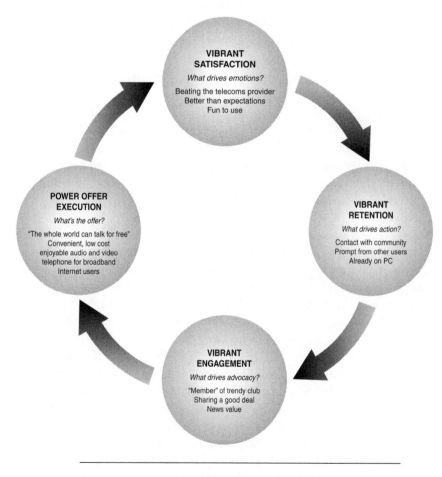

Figure 3.3 Momentum execution at Skype

Note that as opposed to the illustration of momentum design shown in Figure 3.2, the arrows in the momentum execution figure all go in the same direction. Whereas momentum design is an iterative process, with each stage feeding back and forth into those on either side of it, momentum execution is a one-way force that gathers pace as it builds. The force that momentum generates feeds back into the power offer—in this case, enabling Skype to improve the offer further and thus provide even more momentum boosters by increasing the vibrancy of the satisfaction, retention, and engagement. Each stage provides acceleration. Well-executed power offers can generate enormous momentum, giving firms profitable growth with fewer resources. Momentum execution is the second engine of momentum-powered firms.

Making Momentum Systematic

It's no coincidence that smaller entrepreneurial companies such as Skype are more likely to be fueled by momentum than large, established firms. There are several reasons for this, but if you work in a large organization you will probably recognize the two principle obstacles that stand in your path when it comes to building momentum: complex structures and sheer size.

That is no excuse, though, for a lack of ambition. As Microsoft, Wal-Mart, Nintendo, and Toyota show, even the largest of corporations can build and retain momentum for decades. But as Microsoft and Wal-Mart also show, those who have it can lose it if they forget the reasons for this momentum and fail to continuously nurture its source.

What large corporations need to do is systematize the processes that smaller firms manage intuitively. They need frameworks and tools to provide guidance and stimulation to employees in a wide variety of units, locations, and levels. They need to learn how to lift their heads, look beyond company walls, and connect with the outside world.

That is what we seek to offer in this book's remaining sections: a systematic approach to guide you, step by step, to momentum performance. Part II, "Designing Momentum," shows how firms that set the bar high can discover compelling insights that lead to compelling value, compelling equity, and the design of power offers. Part III, "Executing Momentum," starts with the moment of truth when the power offer meets the customers. You will see how ambitious firms can achieve the vibrant customer satisfaction, retention, and engagement that fuel momentum and create exceptional growth.

Momentum-powered firms come in all shapes and sizes, in all sectors, and in different times of business history, but the one thing they all have in common is a positive ambition. The Momentum League we encountered in the first chapter demonstrated that this ambition is realistic. To take the road to momentum, a firm must realize that unlimited potential for growth lies in originating value from customers. A firm that systematically places customers at the center of its thinking, and that strives to attain ambitious goals, will be able to harness the power of momentum and deliver the exceptional growth it provides.

The road to momentum is out there. The rewards along the way are enormous. Most important, the journey is not the exclusive right of lucky or gifted entrepreneurs—it can be systematically organized, even in the largest and most traditional of firms. It just takes guidance and ambition.

Designing Momentum

4

Compelling Insights

IBM Is Listening Again

"How could such truly talented people allow themselves to get into such a morass?" So asked Lou Gerstner in response to what he found when he joined IBM as chairman and CEO in 1993 with the brief of turning around the faltering company.[1] The story of Gerstner's revival of IBM has become hackneyed through admiring repetition, but that admiration is more than justified. Importantly for us, the story neatly illustrates the importance of the first stage of momentum design.

Almost immediately on arrival, he realized that IBM, which had always been famously customer centered, was no longer focusing on the external world. It was obsessed by internal processes and systems. Senior executives talked mostly to each other and made decisions based on lengthy reports and detailed analysis. Their overreliance on assistants distanced them from the heart of their business: their customers. It was the old problem of big-company inertia.

One story in particular encapsulates the phenomenon. Gerstner was meeting a senior executive responsible for a crucial part of the business.

When he arrived at the man's office, he was perplexed to see a dozen people awaiting him. Gerstner was told that staff frequently attended CEO briefings to ensure that "there's always someone who knows the answer."

Gerstner knew that to regain IBM's lost momentum, he had to get the company away from its own internal systems and refocused on the external world. In other words, it needed less analysis and more exploration. He asked his staff to organize meetings with customers all over the world, and he set out on an extensive travel schedule that packed his days with customer meetings.

Like a humble beginner, he started asking questions, exploring where IBM had gone wrong and seeking insights into how it could better serve its customers. Six months later, the message came back from the media: "IBM is listening again." Just four words, but they summarized the 80-year story of the company: IBM used to listen to customers; IBM stopped listening; IBM is listening again. These four words were worth billions of dollars in market capitalization.

Despite pressure from financial markets, Gerstner said he would not rush into formulating new strategies until he had gone around the company and its customers. So, although not much had tangibly changed at IBM in those six months, the outside world viewed the company more positively. External stakeholders gave the new CEO their trust because he had demonstrated that customers were to be at the center of everything that IBM did. Customer focus would replace internal focus.

Why did the market place so much importance on this? Because observers knew where the new orientation would lead. Gerstner was embarking on a voyage of discovery and exploring unsatisfied customers' needs. In terms of our framework, this discovery phase is the first stage in the systematic implementation of a momentum strategy. Its importance lies in its results, the compelling insights that fuel momentum.

The Value-Origination Blind Spot

For many years before this, IBM had been a momentum-powered firm. By focusing on customers and their needs, it had been able to uncover the compelling insights essential to the value-origination process that lies at the base of a successful momentum strategy. By the 1970s, the company had a 70 percent share of the global market in mainframe computers. It was CEOs' favorite supplier, with a price premium over its competitors that reflected its products' perceived superior value—the vibrancy of its offer. Then IBM strayed off course as it became more and more internally focused. It simply stopped seeing the things it used to see, because it wasn't looking anymore. Like many successful companies, IBM had become complacent. It no longer enjoyed the power of the momentum effect.

In IBM's case, it missed every single fast-growing development in its industry during the 1980s and early 1990s: mini-computers, microcomputers, application software, and services. These were not minor mistakes—they were huge mistakes worth several tens of billions of dollars each. They progressively undermined IBM's potential for profitable growth, and, eventually, they impacted the bottom line. In 1993, the company registered a record loss of $8 billion.

The answer to Gerstner's memorable question, "How could such truly talented people allow themselves to get into such a morass?" was quite simple: IBM's momentum had stalled when it shifted its focus away from its customers.

IBM in the early 1990s was convinced that it knew its customers. That's the problem, right there. A successful firm gets set in its ways of serving its customers and develops strong views about what they need. It believes it is customer oriented, but it has a tunnel vision of its customers, based on past experience. But experience is no substitute for constantly seeking new discoveries. It is useful, but momentum-powered firms also employ a systematic process of exploration. They are thirsty for new and compelling insights into customers' needs. This is why these firms see opportunities for originating new value, whereas momentum-deficient firms do not. Their origination blind spot is a brake slammed down, stopping momentum in its tracks.

Virgin Atlantic

This kind of blind spot in large companies is well illustrated by the story of one of the greatest discoverers of compelling insights, Richard Branson. He gave the name Virgin to his companies and products to signal that he knew nothing about the businesses in which he got involved. The message to the established competition was clear, "I know nothing, and this will be my strength. I will develop novel solutions. You believe your experience is a strong asset, but it is really your biggest liability—you are stuck in tradition." He proceeded to innovate in a variety of markets, including music, retailing, and airlines. In none of these sectors did Virgin's innovations stem from technology—they were all driven by superior customer understanding.

Of all the Virgin companies, the airline Virgin Atlantic stands out as one of the most complete examples of a momentum-powered firm. Because of its focus on customers, Virgin Atlantic has always stood out from the crowd by doing things differently. It created a new name—Upper Class—for a service with first-class standards at business-class prices. It was the first airline to offer a limousine service, check-in service in the parking area, and an unconventional passenger lounge. It was the first airline to offer all passengers a video-entertainment system.

But one of the finest examples of its customer orientation was the tailoring service it offered for a time on its London to Hong Kong flight. A tailor in Virgin's business lounge at Heathrow would measure passengers waiting for their flight, and then phone the details to another tailor in Hong Kong, who would make up the outfit while the plane was in flight. The Virgin Atlantic passenger could then pick up a brand-new, pressed, tailor-made suit upon arrival in Hong Kong. The company no doubt made a margin on the service, but its real value was the value it added for the customer—the intangible "coolness" inherent in stepping off a plane and into a new suit. A suit that only a few hours before had been nothing more than a series of measurements, taken six thousand miles away. That feels fun. That's a story you'll tell your friends, developing yet more favorable buzz for the company.

All these innovations, big and small, arise from a continuous search to bring more value to customers and thus to Virgin Atlantic. Its staff excels at the open exploration that constantly builds understanding of its customers and provides the compelling insights that fuel momentum. Like all momentum-powered firms, Virgin Atlantic realizes that its knowledge of its customers will never be perfect and can always be improved. These firms continuously explore the customer universe for the insights that create opportunities for profitable growth. These insights are the source of the traction to build momentum.

Customer Insights

Let's now take a look at three additional examples that illustrate how compelling customer insights are at the heart of a momentum strategy.

3M: Post-it Notes

The yellow sticky-paper reminders known as Post-it Notes, a trademark of 3M, are a great example of how customer insight can bring enormous commercial success. In 1968, Spence Silver, a 3M researcher, tried to make a stronger adhesive tape and ended up with a semi-sticky adhesive. Not exactly a storming success given what he was trying to do, but he suspected he had something valuable—he just didn't know what to do with it.

Six years later, Arthur Fry, another 3M scientist, stumbled onto the killer application. When singing in his church choir, he frequently dropped bookmarks from his hymn book. He needed something that would stick without being too sticky—something rather like the weak glue his colleague had created. With that, the Post-it was born.

This example highlights the importance of applying compelling customer insights to a technological innovation. 3M's "unsticky" glue was nothing more than an interesting curiosity from a scientific point of view, but it was the discovery of a compelling customer insight that enabled this innovation to create enormous value for 3M.

Alcoa Packaging: Fridge Pack

The aluminum company Alcoa has a packaging division that makes cans for soft-drink companies. Hunting for customer insights, its managers decided to visit the end users of their products instead of limiting themselves to talks with their direct customers, companies such as Coca-Cola.

Insight came from observing the career of a 12-pack of cans in an ordinary fridge. When full, the pack is highly visible, an invitation to the next person who opens the door to grab a can. As cans are taken away, however, the remaining ones are left hiding at the back. Alcoa looked for a way to make these orphan cans visible up-front. The solution was a cardboard package with the cans placed horizontally. Each time a can was taken, another rolled forward.

A Coca-Cola bottler in the Southeast was the first to apply the Fridge Pack. After one year, sales of 12-packs rose 25 percent, contributing a full point to the bottler's 2.8 percent total volume growth.[2]

Alcoa didn't just ask its engineers to innovate. It didn't just talk to its direct customers. It went outside and met the end user at home, examining its products with new eyes—and its solution was not even in aluminum but in cardboard, completely outside the company's normal line of business!

Dassault: The Falcon 7X Aircraft

Designing an aircraft is a long, complicated process that involves thousands and thousands of interdependent parts. Many problems are not predicted during design and have to be corrected during the first few years of production, which increases an aircraft's cost. Traditional design was a closeted, secretive process, but Dassault realized that involving its customers and suppliers at an early stage of development could create more value for all parties.

The Falcon 7X was the first plane designed using new software that allowed engineers to simulate the impact of every possible action. Dassault decided to use this virtual platform to involve external stakeholders, and it brought users, maintenance firms, and suppliers into the prototype discussions. A detailed online image of the virtual aircraft enabled these different parties to make contributions to the design before it was finalized.

Dassault reasoned that this approach had the potential to create more value for its customers, for its partners, and for itself. How right they were. The different stakeholders improved many elements of the aircraft's design, which led to much lower operating and manufacturing costs and a quicker delivery time. Assembly time was cut by more than 50 percent compared to earlier models, and tooling costs by 66 percent.[3] But the plane wasn't just cheaper to make, it was better. Word got around. Pre-orders swelled. The increased sales resulting from the aircraft's improved quality were the perfect vindication of the policy of customer focus.

The Systematic Discovery of Compelling Insights

These three examples demonstrate how the discovery of compelling insights builds momentum. They also show that there is no single path to exploring for new growth opportunities. What counts is for firms to realize the importance of taking a systematic approach to searching for insights, and that any genuinely compelling insights acquired must be translated into effective actions that generate momentum. As we will discuss in the next three chapters, this means investigating insights in terms of the compelling value and compelling equity that they reveal, and then using that information to design power offers. For the moment, however, let's consider how the process of discovering compelling insights can be made more rigorous and reliable.

In most companies, what activity there is in this area is usually marked out by the opposite of rigor and reliability. If insights arrive, they are the result of haphazard and happy chance. And yet if a true and systematic process of discovery aimed at uncovering compelling insights is installed, it can unearth a vast range of opportunities. We have organized workshops in which the depth of learning, the specific insights revealed, and the new attitudes created have surprised even the most skeptical participants. Most organizations are wells of knowledge, brainpower, and goodwill. The challenge is to mobilize all this to discover compelling insights.

Firms need tools to help them structure their exploration—instruments that set out and explain the different paths to discovery and suggest ways to uncover compelling insights. The *insight discovery matrix,* shown in Figure 4.1, is such a tool. It shows how four discovery paths are defined by the relative awareness of the two key partners: the firm and the customers.[4]

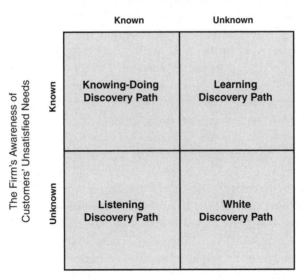

Figure 4.1 The insight discovery matrix

This matrix is divided into four separate discovery paths. Each path conceals unlimited opportunities for growth. Before describing them in more detail, let's illustrate them with software applications for personal computing.

The knowing-doing discovery path contains unsatisfied customer needs that both the firm and customers are aware of. In the case of PCs, this is repeated demands from users for greater simplicity, reliability, and support that are well-known to firms but which many do not resolve satisfactorily.

The listening discovery path contains unsatisfied needs that customers are aware of but the firm is not. For example, many applications have been, and could be further, improved following users' feedback and suggestions that developers could not imagine on their own.

The learning discovery path contains unsatisfied customer needs that the firm has unveiled but of which the customer is unaware. In this quadrant, we have all of those applications that users are failing to fully use because—due to the inadequate learning approaches that the firms offer—they are unaware of their potential.

The white discovery path contains unsatisfied needs that no one has yet discovered but which might represent tremendous future business opportunities. This unexplored white space represents the ultimate frontier, and it includes nearly all the most powerful applications we take for granted today. At one point, neither their potential users nor their future creators imagined the enormous potential of spreadsheets, Internet browsers, or online telephony.

We will shortly follow the exploration process and travel along these four discovery paths, but let's first illustrate them with an example to which we can all relate: retail banking, an industry generally guilty of a strong internal focus that frequently irritates its customers. The matrix for this industry is set out in Figure 4.2. Bucking that trend over the past decade or so have been the efforts of new and progressive financial services companies, including branchless banks[5] or innovative bricks-and-mortar institutions such as Commerce Bank. Calling itself "America's Most Convenient Bank," Commerce Bank grew from a single branch opened in New Jersey in 1973 to having nearly 470 branches, concentrated in the New York/New Jersey area, and 2.4 million customers in 2007, principally by offering better and more convenient service than traditional banks.[6]

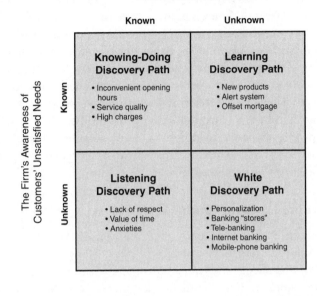

Customers' Awareness of
Their Unsatisfied Needs

Figure 4.2   The insight discovery matrix of retail banking

The Knowing-Doing Discovery Path

This box concerns opportunities that are known to both a firm and its customers. There are two principal and quite different reasons that explain why these unsatisfied needs are not exploited: unavailable technology and corporate apathy.

The first of these is excusable. At any point in time, many unsatisfied needs must wait for further scientific developments that can then be translated into business opportunities. The second is not excusable. Corporate apathy is the area to explore in the knowing-doing path, the morass that Lou Gerstner spotted at IBM. It is the swampland of the momentum-deficient league. It is also where the "low-hanging fruit"— the quick wins—are located. The problem here is not to discover the opportunities; they are already well known. Neither is the problem to develop technologies. This is not the issue. It is to discover the reasons why these opportunities have not yet been exploited, and then to find the ways to achieve change.[7]

In retail banking, apathy rather than technology has been the main barrier in the knowing-doing path. For decades, everyone knew that inconvenient opening hours, poor service quality, and high charges created customer dissatisfaction. Despite this, nothing was done until institutions such as Commerce Bank built enormous momentum by turning these givens on their head. Commerce Bank offered seven-day-a-week opening, extended opening hours, free checking accounts, and friendly staff. They offered free coin-counting machines in their branches that anyone could use to turn loose change into bills. They made it easier for busy people to bank. In doing so, they became the bank with the highest satisfaction rating in the New York area and generated exceptional levels of deposits.[8]

The Listening Discovery Path

The listening discovery path describes unsatisfied needs that are known to some customers but not to the firm. Many entrepreneurs enter the world of business as frustrated customers with unsatisfied needs who develop solutions aimed at others like themselves. Most often, these needs are perceived and expressed by only a small number of leading customers. The challenge for large firms is to detect the weak signals that this minority sends out through the static of the marketplace.

In retail banking, customer-oriented institutions such as Commerce Bank came to realize that customers felt frustrated with traditional banks—that they were treated with a lack of respect, that their time was undervalued and wasted, and that the banking experience was a source of anxiety. One indicator of Commerce Bank's excellence at listening is the fact that it resolves customer complaints two days faster than the average time taken by its competitors.[9]

The Learning Discovery Path

Many new products fall into this category at the beginning of their life cycle. A firm knows its customers have unsatisfied needs before they do. This was seen with past innovations such as automobiles, computers, and mobile phones. This cycle is ongoing, and the prospects for customer learning are unlimited.

These growth opportunities lie in a firm's ability to educate and persuade customers about the value of a new offering. Consider a story recounted in Malcolm Gladwell's *Blink:* the Aeron office chair.[10] This chair is now regarded as a design classic—there's one in the permanent collection of New York's Museum of Modern Art. And yet, as Gladwell points out, when it was introduced in 1993, it was so unusual that focus groups regularly scored its aesthetics as low as two and never higher than six on a one-to-ten scale. By the late 1990s, annual sales were growing by 50 to 70 percent, despite a hefty price premium. Today, focus groups score its aesthetics an average of eight out of ten. Customers had to be educated as to the ergonomic brilliance behind its unusual looks.

Returning to the retail banking sector, the learning path obviously includes the development of new products. Some of these financial products require more customer learning than others. It's easy to explain a simple product such as a mobile alert service that sends a text message to customers' mobile phone when their account balance goes into the red. But how about the "offset mortgage" that some innovative banks[11] in the United Kingdom offer customers? These offset all the customer's deposits with the bank—for example, the balances in checking and savings accounts—against an outstanding mortgage when calculating the monthly interest due on that mortgage. Interest is charged only on the net "balance," reducing the interest due on the mortgage without the need for any action by the customer. The full capital must be paid off within the term, obviously, but customers can save thousands in interest charges over the life of the mortgage and consequently repay the loan sooner. Customers fully appreciate this novel product—after they understand how it works.

The White Discovery Path

This quadrant represents the real unknown for both customers and firms. We call it white because its opportunities are like virgin land covered with snow. It represents the future innovations that neither party can anticipate. The matrix is fluid. As new technologies progress and customer needs evolve, these hidden growth opportunities will be unveiled and move to one of the other three discovery paths.

In the retail banking sector, this quadrant included growth opportunities from new technology that led to telephone banking, Internet banking, and mobile phone banking. It also included unexpected customer discoveries such as highly personalized banking through the use of customer relationship management (CRM) systems and the creation of "banking stores," as pioneered by Commerce Bank. The significant discovery was this: Customers had negative feelings about traditional bank "branches," whereas they were positively inclined toward visiting stores. Commerce Bank took McDonald's as a benchmark, designing its banking stores with large bay windows, and adding a drive-in. It created a welcoming experience superior to any traditional bank branch.

The Exploration Process

The previous examples show that discovering customer insights to drive momentum requires a kind of process different from the methods that large corporations traditionally use. Although analytical processes are one of the foundations of proper management, they can destroy opportunities to discover new and compelling insights.

The danger of an overly analytical approach is that it leads firms to improve what they're doing already, instead of investigating other, sometimes radically different avenues. Remember the value-origination blind spot? Genuinely compelling insights will be uncovered not through analysis but through exploration.

Guiding Exploration

Creativity is the only limit here. Usable tools include focus groups, think tanks, projective techniques, inspirational visits, and field trips, as well as video observation and other ethnographic methods. But they all have one thing in common: They encourage employees to meet customers, involve customers, and think in terms of customers. That is the only way to uncover the compelling insights that get momentum started.

The knowing-doing discovery gap is where we find the low-hanging fruit. These unmet customer needs could be satisfied easily but are being restrained by internal psychological, cultural, or organizational barriers. These barriers could include the defense of territories within the company, the specter of cannibalization, or the fear of failure. The exploration process for this path should involve an investigation of the low-hanging fruit and of the reasons why the firm is not exploiting them. In our experience, this is easily achieved through workshops led by a trusted external moderator. Such a workshop should conclude by identifying the top opportunities and building a commitment toward their positive exploitation. Systematic investigation and mobilization of management are essential to seize these low-hanging fruit.

The first cause of the listening gap is that, in many organizations managers remain distant from their customers, either consciously or subconsciously. Bank managers rarely do their own banking by standing in line. Airline executives never fly economy. Automobile managers are chauffeur driven in company cars. Consumer goods managers buy supplies discounted at their headquarters' store. These managers rarely experience their products or services in the same conditions as customers, and almost never at full price. For the same reasons, they seldom meet customers at all, or not for enough time to actually share their real concerns.

The most effective—and easiest—way to explore the listening discovery path is to spend quality time with customers. We have organized fruitful encounters between managers and customers that lasted 15 minutes, 1 hour, a full day, and even workshops of several days' duration. What is important is to have sufficient time to go beyond the usual business rituals and the superficialities of social encounters and build mutual trust and understanding.

As discussed later in this book, the concept can be taken further by having employees actually working on the customer's premises. This is what Procter & Gamble did when it sent a couple hundred employees to work in Wal-Mart's Bentonville, Arkansas, headquarters. In a similar fashion, Dell placed 30 maintenance engineers inside Boeing's commercial aircraft facility in Seattle. In cases like these, both parties win. The customer gains superior service, and the firm creates the conditions whereby its staff can discover untapped needs.

It is also useful to engage in qualitative customer research. This is likewise based on the principle of spending quality time with customers but involves specific techniques and professional staff. The purpose is to get information from customers that they would not share in simple surveys or casual conversations. One tool often used for this purpose is focus groups, which bring together selected customers to discuss a specific issue under a moderator's direction, while other professionals observe their behavior and discussion behind one-way mirrors. Like the anti-inflammatory gel applicator for the elderly woman's back, valuable ideas and insights frequently emerge from such approaches.

Bridging the learning discovery gap is very much like going to a foreign country: One has to measure the difference in culture and language and adapt accordingly. When a new product is ready for launch, the business teams involved are familiar with and enthusiastic about the innovation. At this point, it's easy to underestimate the gap between the internal momentum and the external inertia of the customer's perspective. Many new products have missed opportunities because of this misunderstanding.

In such a situation, the customer's state of mind should be explored thoroughly so that all potential gaps can be sealed. It is essential to understand all the blocks that could prevent customers from understanding that they have a need. This is particularly so in many medical situations where most patients do not realize the dramatic potential consequences of such conditions as obesity, hypertension, or diabetes. Unless diabetic patients understand that the complications of their condition can lead to amputations, blindness, and heart attacks, they do not realize how important it is to be treated. The key is to find the right approach that makes customers realize that a need they haven't yet fully perceived requires attention.

Often, development of a new approach to language—neologisms or euphemisms—is necessary to bridge the gap between customers and company in understanding needs. For example, during the launch of Viagra, Pfizer's appreciation of the stigma attached to the word *impotence* was critical. This led to the expression *erectile dysfunction* and the even more palatable acronym ED. This language enables patients to communicate more readily with their partners and doctors to discuss remedies.

The insight discovery matrix should sharpen a firm's understanding of its customers and help find new growth opportunities. Within this frame, it is the virgin, unexplored white space of the unknown-unknown box that represents the ultimate frontier. Navigation there is tricky, but certain different approaches can prove helpful. The challenge is to be ahead of both customers and competitors and lead future trends.

We have taken executives from Europe to Silicon Valley or Wal-Mart stores in the United States, executives from North America to fashion hot spots in Paris, and Western executives to the mushrooming cities of Bangalore and Shanghai. In all these instances, the culture shock resulting from witnessing different customer groups and different customer solutions led to new insights.

Another approach is to extrapolate customer and technological trends to the limit to detect possible growth opportunities with a plausible commercial future. Confronting consumer trends with technological trends should lead to potential growth opportunities. For example, in the IT and communications market, a think tank could investigate what needs might exist and be satisfied if the cost of chips and telecommunications became zero. Considering this hypothesis in light of the growing percentage of the population above retirement age could identify a large number of growth opportunities that could then be prioritized and further analyzed for their technological and economic feasibility.

In-depth consumer research is also a valuable tool in this unknown-unknown quadrant. The issue is to identify needs that customers have but cannot yet express or articulate. General projective techniques are well-known tools for this area. Ethnographic research is a promising trend that observes customers in their own natural environment. For consumer goods, this means in their normal lives, at home, while shopping, and so on. Alcoa used this approach in the discovery of the insights behind the Fridge Pack. In the case of business customers, these observations would be in workplaces, offices, plants, or construction sites. More sophisticated methodologies are constantly being developed in this field.[12]

To bridge the white discovery gap, the challenge is to identify opportunities that neither the customers nor the firms have detected. It is not easy. It takes time to develop empathy with deep customer trends. The leader who best exemplifies the ability to tap into such pure discoveries is Steve Jobs. He first played a central role in the personal computer revolution through his leadership of Apple. This led to the creation of the Apple I and II and the Apple Macintosh, which incorporated the graphic user interface and ball-mouse device originally developed by Xerox. Later, Jobs led the development of more successful products such as the iMac, the iPod, iTunes, the iPhone, and, separately, Pixar, which produced six of history's most successful animated films.

Enabling Exploration

Exploratory processes, essential for discovering customer opportunities, are simple to implement. Indeed, most entrepreneurs function with an exploratory mindset without any training or coaching. Employees welcome customer exploration; it can help to mobilize a work force.

So why don't large firms use these exploratory tools more often? The problem is that they conflict with the dominant analytical approach that traditional management favors. In our experience, the three most important areas of conflict between analytical and exploratory approaches to customers are concern about taking time out, resistance to external activities, and mistrust of small sample sizes.

Traditional management emphasizes efficient and effective use of time for productive activities. "Good" management behavior equates efficiency with busyness. In contrast, an exploratory approach to customers leads to investing time in tasks that might be unproductive in the short term, with the added perceived risk that they will lead to no concrete results at all. The odd thing is that in a crisis situation, such as Lou Gerstner encountered when he joined IBM, leaders often do take time out to reconsider the fundamentals. Why wait for a crisis when you could prevent one from happening?

Naturally, common sense should apply. As with R&D, customer exploration should not become a license for managers to gleefully run away from business pressures. Exploratory tools should be carefully managed to increase the likelihood of significant returns—but they must not be neglected. Our experience has shown that neglect of the discovery process by most firms almost inevitably guarantees positive results for those who have adopted a more exploratory approach. Creating time out is the first prerequisite to enable exploration.

Going out of the company premises and engaging oneself in external activities is the second crucial condition for exploration of insights. Traditional management largely takes place in the comfortable, familiar territory of office buildings and hierarchically supervised company sites. Managers might leave their secure offices on business trips, but they mostly visit familiar locations such as other offices, existing suppliers, or partners. Even salespeople rarely dip their toes into the waters of "missionary" selling by visiting noncustomers.

The usual working environment is a comfort zone, and leaving to investigate customers, ex-customers, and noncustomers is essential for exploring opportunities. This is particularly pertinent for employees who seldom have the chance to meet customers: marketers, engineers, scientists, finance, and HR staff. Go where Gerstner went—go and visit customers!

The third enabler of exploration is recognizing that the in-depth discovery of a few nonrepresentative customers is essential for unveiling compelling insights. This is, however, going against some of the sacred cows of professional management. For example, one essential guideline for market research is the importance of using representative customer samples, in terms of both quality and quantity. But exploration often works best when it first involves in-depth investigation of a single customer who is ahead of the crowd and therefore not representative at all of the mass. Remember Arthur Fry and the Post-it Note? Sample size: one.

Entrepreneurs are frequently inspired by the vision of one customer with an unsatisfied need—sometimes the frustrated entrepreneur himself, or a close acquaintance. Edwin H. Land was motivated to work on the concept of instantaneous photography not by scientific curiosity but by the naive gesture of his little daughter. After he snapped her picture while on vacation, she tried to open the camera to see the pictures inside. He had to explain the lengthy waiting process behind developing and printing film. His daughter's disappointment inspired Land to invent the Polaroid camera.

Investigating individual customers can be just as fruitful as "representative" samples. This deep individual exploration can then be validated by larger-scale studies. It is at this point that the analytical approach comes into play—but not until the full potential that these open, exploratory processes can reveal is uncovered.

The paradigm of the past was about who was big and who was small. Today's winners and losers are different. Now the distinction is between those who know their customers and those who don't, because this is how value is created. Momentum begins with the discovery of compelling customer insights, and such discoveries are possible only when firms are truly open to exploring their customers' world.

Explore the World for Insights

Firms that build momentum do it by constantly exploring, by going out and bringing what they discover back to the office. They are so focused on their customers that they feel they must understand everything about them. The reason they embark upon this constant, ambitious, and systematic voyage of exploration is that they are seeking new compelling insights into unsatisfied customer needs. Momentum-powered firms follow a never-ending quest to uncover the compelling insights that will shed light on new and untapped sources of compelling customer value and compelling customer equity.

A common weakness of momentum-deficient firms is the blind spot, the belief—probably not expressed and possibly not even conscious—that their products are pretty much the best they could be. Oh, maybe they could do with some tweaking, but, generally speaking, customers pretty much have everything they need. "We know our market" is a frequently heard claim. That lasts until someone who really *does* know their customer come along with an offer that shows just how much there was left to discover, how much more value could be originated.

The secret is exploration. Most managers would be embarrassed if they were asked how much time they spend engaging with customers, compared with time reading spreadsheets. The following guiding principles should help rectify the balance.

- Compelling insights are the launch pad of momentum. They are the first stage of the momentum design process that eventually ends in power offers and the momentum they generate. Everything that follows depends upon the quality of those insights.

- Compelling customer insights help create momentum for the firm in two ways: first, by revealing new and better ways of satisfying customer needs that lead to compelling customer value, and second, by uncovering new customers and new opportunities with existing customers, that will lead to compelling customer equity.

- The intense and revealing insights that drive momentum cannot be discovered through traditional management analysis alone. Managers must get out of the office and engage in genuine open exploration. Exploration is the biggest deficit in the management of large, established firms. It is essential for them to actively seek new growth directions if they want to generate the momentum effect. Momentum-powered firms have a deep understanding of their customers because they are externally focused rather than internally obsessed. They bring the outside in.

- The insight discovery matrix offers established firms a systematic way to achieve what entrepreneurial firms manage by instinct. It sets out four discovery paths to guide their explorations: knowing-doing, listening, learning, and white. The source of the greatest potential tends to lie in the virgin territory found along the white path—the needs that are currently unknown to both the firm and its customers.

■ Because the exploration process takes managers outside their comfort zones, firms must do all they can to encourage and enable their employees to make the step. The activities required to discover compelling insights conflict with the analytical approach most managers feel comfortable with. Managers must realize the potential benefits of taking time out from day-to-day activities to encounter the customer world. They must overcome their resistance to external activities and mistrust of small sample sizes.

Compelling insights offer the thrill of the "aha" moment. To paraphrase Isaac Asimov, the most exciting moment in discovery is not when someone shouts "Eureka," but when they mutter, "Now, *that's* funny." The dawning realization that you might be on to something marks the point when your compelling insights must be explored, fleshed out, and refined. These insights can fuel a momentum strategy only if they have the potential to make customer value or customer equity more compelling. The next chapter covers the first of these two avenues.

5

Compelling Value

What Women Want

Car shows have always been where "boys' toys" were shown off. It seemed as if the attitude of the men who designed and promoted the cars was that a woman's proper relationship to a car is to stand next to it and look pretty. And yet, around 80 percent of all decisions to purchase a car are either made or influenced by women. There is clearly huge potential for any manufacturer who understands what women want.

Volvo's answer was simple: a car designed for women, by women. The result was the YCC ("Your Concept Car"), a nonproduction concept car unveiled at the Geneva International Motor Show in 2004.[1]

Many of the prototype's innovative features were amazing: an indentation in the middle of the headrest for ponytails; gull-wing doors for better accessibility; storage space between the front seats; easy-clean paint; an exterior filling point for windshield washer fluid; run-flat tires; special compartments for umbrellas, keys, and coins; and magnetic seat pads that could be removed and changed according to the weather or color of the driver's outfit.[2]

The car got enormously positive reaction at the show and in subsequent press and online coverage. The insights the Volvo team discovered had clearly helped them create compelling new value for both female and male drivers.

However, one of the ideas hatched by the all-female design team didn't draw the same universal praise: The hood over the engine did not open. Reasoning that most drivers open the hood only to top up windshield washer fluid, Volvo's team provided a top-up point for the windshield washers on the exterior of the car and sealed the hood. In fact, the whole front of the car came away in one piece to give better access to the engine, but only a Volvo mechanic could open it. The car was programmed to automatically recognize any problems under the hood and send the information to the garage. Mechanics would then contact the driver and invite her over for the repair.

Although most women were happy with the idea that they need never lift a hood again, unsurprisingly, others felt insulted. They didn't want to be deprived of the choice of opening the hood if they so desired. Their perception, expressed on blogs and Internet chat rooms, was that this was an idiot-proof car, patronizingly designed for idiot female drivers.[3]

This example shows how the discovery of compelling insights can help create compelling customer value, but it also illustrates a crucial point: that different people will set different value on any given aspect of a product or service. It is this variation in value perception that creates opportunities for driving profitable growth by presenting specifically targeted compelling value.

What Does a Customer Value? That Depends

The focus of this chapter is on understanding how customers perceive value and how firms that understand it can create compelling offers for them. Contrary to appearances, a product does not really drive a company's success. It is the product's customer value that does. Products and services are only temporary vehicles to carry value from a firm to its customers. The only reason customers buy products and services is to obtain value.

This concept is best illustrated by imagining some of the different values underlying one industry. Let's stay here with the automobile sector. Imagine a young lawyer in San Francisco, newly offered a partnership in a prestigious firm, deciding to reward herself for her success. She decides to buy a BMW Z4. In doing so, she could be looking for a variety of different values, including transportation and prestige. In terms of transportation alone, she could buy a bicycle or motorcycle, or walk or use the trams or taxis. Similarly, in terms of gaining the value of prestige, she could purchase a luxury watch, a boat, or a painting. All these are competing alternatives to deliver some dimensions of value to this young lawyer. She has just decided that a BMW Z4 carries the most compelling value for her, given her needs at this point in time.

It's important to note that a product that some customers see as providing strong value will leave others indifferent. Some might even perceive it as offering negative value. Consider sport utility vehicles. A suburban mother of three who is also a keen skier might see SUVs as offering extraordinary value that combines important benefits such as safety, power, off-road capability, and prestige. She is willing to pay a high price to own one. At the other extreme, a Sierra Club member who organizes her employer's recycling program could well find them deeply offensive because of their high fuel consumption, level of pollution, and aggressive appearance. She wouldn't drive one even if she were paid to. Conclusion: A product or service has no intrinsic value. Its value is only in the perception of customers.

By using the phrase *"compelling value,"* we are not simply rebranding the commonly used term *"value proposition." Compelling value* is much more than just a value proposition. If an offer presents compelling value, it will have the potential to create customer traction and contribute to setting up the conditions needed for the momentum effect to take hold. Just how compelling the value offered is will always be relative: relative to expectations, to competition, and to what was offered yesterday. What remains constant is that the only thing that matters in determining whether the value is compelling is the customer's perception at that point in time. Returning to our young lawyer, for her and on this occasion, the value offered by a BMW is seriously compelling—more so than her other options.

This is why optimizing perceived customer value is one of the keys to building momentum.[4] It is crucial not only to ensuring the proper design and execution of products, but also to targeting specific customers who perceive the highest value of the offering. When it comes to customer value, firms must understand two things to be effective at compelling design. First, what is the value contained in the offer, as seen through the eyes of customers? Second, how can they increase value to targeted customers while simultaneously creating value for the firm?

Customer Myopia

Our experience suggests that the growth horizon of large, established firms is restricted by their very narrow view of customer value. We call this condition *customer myopia.*[5] This shortsightedness is caused by the incorrect and distorting assumptions that value is unique, functional, and rational. These firms mistakenly believe that truth is unique, that functionality is everything, and that rationality is reality.

A case in point is Coca-Cola's disastrous U.K. launch of Dasani—bottled water that the company had engineered as rigorously for taste as it had engineered the taste of Coke.[6] Yet in the United Kingdom, Dasani became a victim of these three customer myopia traps.

Is truth unique? Momentum-deficient firms believe that value is singular and absolute when in fact different customers make different evaluations of the same product. In other markets, customers agreed with Coca-Cola and took to Dasani—not so in Britain. Same product, different perceptions of value. Truth is not unique.

Is functionality everything? Momentum-deficient firms regard value as a bundle of functional benefits provided to customers at a price, and underestimate the intangible and emotional elements that actually drive customers' behavior. Dasani offered a quality drinking water in a bottle. It failed, however, to provide either the health imagery and positive emotions usually associated with bottled water, or the intangible uniqueness of a taste associated with soft drinks. There is more to value than functionality.

Is rationality the same as reality? Momentum-deficient firms extend the scientific concept of rationality to human actions, but in fact customers make decisions based on their perception. Their perception is their reality, and it might be quite different from the "rational" perspective of product-design engineers. Looked at rationally, Dasani offers extra value compared to tap water in several ways. But this was not the perception of the Brits. All they could see was a marketing ploy to repackage tap water at a high price, and they perceived it as an insult to their intelligence. They wouldn't touch the stuff. Rationality is not the customers' reality. Their perception is.

These three traps reflect customer myopia and limit the potential of momentum-deficient firms. If they could expand their vision on each of these three elements, a wealth of opportunities to increase customer value would come into focus. There is unlimited potential for companies prepared to correct their customer myopia.

The Customer Value Map

Customers develop their perceptions of value by intuitively trading off perceived benefits against perceived costs. The *customer value map* shown in Figure 5.1 is an effective visual tool to represent the strategic impact of this trade-off. It plots where products and services lie in terms of perceived benefits and perceived costs to customers. The map presents three distinct bands resulting from this trade-off process as indicated by the shading. In the middle, customers perceive that they are given fair offers, whereas at either extreme they feel either abused or delighted. Where firms place their offers on this map has a major impact on building or losing customer momentum.

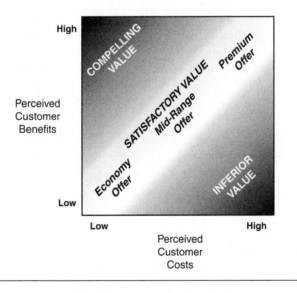

Figure 5.1 The customer value map

The upper-left corner of the map is the region of compelling value. It is where customers are delighted. Perceived customer benefits significantly exceed perceived customer costs. The compelling value on the offer is one of the key drivers of the momentum effect.

At the other extreme, in the lower-right corner, is the region of inferior value. Customers feel they are abused. They perceive that they are being offered low benefits at high costs. Such products tend to exist because of restricted competition—customers would not buy them if they had a choice. Obviously, these products have no momentum, and customers purchase them reluctantly. Companies with such products might make abnormally high margins for a while, but they run a huge risk. When the factors enabling their abuse disappear, as they inevitably will, they will miss the growth opportunities they could have enjoyed with better offerings.

The offerings that result from normal levels of competition are along the middle lower-left to upper-right diagonal of the map. They represent a combination of benefits and costs that is perceived as fair by customers, from a budget range that supplies customers with low benefits but at low costs, all the way up to a premium range that has high benefits but correspondingly high costs.

The customer value map can help gain a strategic perspective on how industries change through shifts in customer value. In many markets, the base for normal competitive operations sits along the central band. Then new offers appear and provide more perceived benefits with lower costs. They offer compelling value, delight customers, and are positioned in the upper-left corner. Established businesses lose customers until they react. Then, what was temporarily compelling value becomes standard, and a new equilibrium is found until the next innovation.

This is the story of modern business. The momentum effect that stems from superior customer value cannot be produced by a one-shot initiative. Sustaining it requires constant investment in a momentum strategy based on value origination.

Delighting Customers

The upper-left corner of the customer value map is the position that all new offers should strive to reach: compelling value that creates customer traction. It's where companies such as Virgin and Dell landed at their creation. They understood the strategic importance of delighting customers.

Nintendo is a company that has created enormous momentum by delighting customers. We've already mentioned the Wii. Before this breakthrough product, computer games were largely the preserve of students, sullen teenagers, or their noisy younger siblings—Mom and Dad were tacitly discouraged from picking up the other controller and joining in. Besides, the games, with their repetitive noises, flashing lights, and complex controls were unappealing or unfathomable to many parents and grandparents. To the moms and dads who usually end up buying them as gifts, they seemed antisocial, increasing the distance between them and their children. The Wii, on the other hand, with its emphasis on movement and togetherness—encapsulated in its slogan: "Wii would like to play"—has expanded the gaming market by creating a simple, fun, accessible product that the whole family enjoys. Many of the costs perceived by parents have been removed while a host of new benefits, ranging from family fun to moderate exercise, have been introduced. So much so that during 2007 the Wii was outselling its competitors by as much as six to one.[7]

The delight the Wii induces was very evident when we used the product to illustrate a point during a seminar we ran shortly after its release. Within minutes, the middle-aged executives on this program were throwing themselves into virtual tennis and softball, vigorously competing against their colleagues while laughing and whooping. At the end of the demonstration, they were all resolving to buy one, "for the kids."

And it is not just the Wii that is powering Nintendo's momentum. The handheld Nintendo DS is another success story. The console has been a big hit with the usual demographic for computer games but Nintendo has also managed to expand the market for computer games. The "shoot 'em up" or racing style of most computer games does not have widespread appeal with people over 40. If anything, the dexterity and rapid decision making these games require serves to highlight one's deteriorating mental and physical agility—something that no one is likely to regard as a benefit.

However, it was exactly this anxiety about failing mental speed and precision that Nintendo tapped into. The Brain Age[8] products, based on the books of Professor Ryuta Kawashima, offer a fun way of restoring those intellectual faculties that many feel have dimmed with age. A player takes a series of short mental agility tests[9] before the software analyzes his or her results and produces a score in the form of a "brain age." But how does the product delight a 55-year-old who it has pronounced to have a "brain age" of 87? By offering short, fun exercises that "train" the brain and by recording improvements in the player's score.

Perhaps the greatest customer delight is offered at the moment when players challenge their children and demonstrate that although they might no longer be able to hold their own on the tennis court, their brain is "younger." For the investment of a few minutes a day on simple and intuitive equipment, players feel they are getting sharper: lower perceived costs and enormous perceived benefit. The result? Brain Age is one of the biggest selling games for the DS, and the DS itself sold just short of 50 million units in its first two and a half years.[10]

Abusing Customers

At the other end of the scale are companies that provide perceived inferior value. Customers feel abused because they receive benefits that are too low relative to the costs they incur. In the worst cases, this can involve frankly illegal behavior. For instance, Marsh & McLennan, the world's largest insurance broker, has been scrutinized for fraud following revelations that its dominance in the sector allowed it to control pricing and the manner in which insurance premiums and payouts were disbursed. The firm was suspected of steering unsuspecting clients to certain insurers. Marsh suffered from a rising tide of defections by its brokers to smaller rivals who, they believed, treated clients more fairly. After New York Attorney General Eliot Spitzer charged Marsh & McLennan's insurance brokerage with fraud on October 13, 2004, the company lost $11.5 billion, or 48 percent of its market capitalization, over the next four days. Although customer abuse is often more insidious than in this publicly exposed case, it always ultimately destroys business value.

Such abuse often occurs when regulation, high switching costs, and other factors restrict competition. Consumers become captives while companies make abnormally high short-term profits. Customer abuse has been prevalent in regulated industries such as financial services, airlines, and utilities, but every industry faces the temptation. Market power is a key driver of profitability, and it is an absolutely correct strategy for companies to build market share through organic activities or mergers and acquisitions. If they exploit market power to abuse customers, however, they do so at serious risk to their long-term growth potential.

Many large, established companies, including icons such as IBM and Procter & Gamble, have found themselves in situations in which their growth stalled because they took advantage of their dominant position to extract abnormal profits. Customer abuse is inherently an unstable situation. It's only a matter of time before companies that enjoy its short-term rewards pay a high price for their misdeeds. When disaster eventually strikes, the only beacon that can guide an effective sustainable recovery is to re-create compelling customer value. Giving value to customers, by increasing their perceived benefits and decreasing their perceived costs, is the ultimate guide to creating more value for the firm.

What's It Worth? How Customers See Value

Customers make trade-offs between perceived benefits and perceived costs to develop a sense of value and come to an overall decision. The process is based on a subtle balance of factors whose outcome is often surprising.

It's important to examine customer value through the right lenses: to perceive value as a customer perceives it. Even leading companies renowned for marketing excellence can make massive mistakes if they fail to grasp the intricacies of how customers form their perception of value.

It is all a matter of perception. Fortunately for Coca-Cola, customer perception of Dasani, the bottled water that bombed in Britain, is more favorable in other countries. But its U.K. reception shows that customers regard value in a far richer, more rounded, manner than many firms imagine. Customers' perception of value goes beyond price and functionality, and involves a multitude of perceived negatives and positives. These can be organized in terms of *functional* elements (in the case of Dasani: taste, weight, minerals), *financial* elements (price, delivery cost), *intangible* elements (carrying pain, social status, storage space), and *emotional* elements (feeling of being taken advantage of).

In any situation, the systematic exploration of perceived customer costs and benefits must be done in terms of these four structural components: functional, financial, intangible, and emotional.

Cost and benefits are perceived by customers as mirror images of each other. The same element can be a cost or a benefit, depending on the value as customers perceive it. For example, the price of a product is usually perceived as a cost, but could be perceived as a benefit if it is much lower than similar offers—or, conversely, if it is much higher but this is perceived to add exclusivity. When selecting a laptop, lightweight could generally be perceived as a benefit, but beyond a certain point a customer anxious about the product's durability might perceived it as a cost.

Creating compelling value by optimizing the value the customer perceives is an essential aspect of creating power offers. A true and deep understanding of customer value enables a firm to unleash many hidden growth opportunities and prevent the sorts of mistakes made with many seemingly well-researched products. To develop this understanding, firms must embark on a systematic exploration of the depths of customer benefits versus customer costs. To do this, they need a tool that helps this exploration, a lens to correct their traditional, myopic vision of customer value. That tool is the *customer value wedge.*

The Customer Value Wedge

Remember the mistaken assumptions that lead to customer myopia: the belief that value is unique, functional, and rational. As we have seen, compelling customer value is broader, subtler, and more varied. To understand it, one must go deep.

The customer value wedge set out in Figure 5.2 is a valuable tool for creating the right mindset and for more thoroughly investigating the drivers of customer value. Whereas the customer value map is designed for strategic-level analysis of customer value, the wedge is a more active, everyday tool for building the deep understanding of customer value that will help design and execute a momentum strategy. Its shape evokes a metal wedge for splitting wood or stone to reveal what is inside. In a similar manner, firms need to crack the code of customer value. The wedge's sharp, downward-facing point contains the deepest emotional elements that are the real drivers of customer value. Ultimately, it is emotions that give rise to actions, even if the real trigger is not always manifest and might be explained away rationally. This is illustrated by the two lateral arrows.

The customer value wedge contains all four components of value, placed in a way that reflects their visibility from the top down. The financial and functional elements—articulated, rational, easy to see and comprehend—are at the top. In highly competitive markets, these often end up offering no competitive advantage because they are visible and obvious to all. But the wedge's cutting edge comes from the emotional elements that form the point at the bottom. Although easily overlooked or misunderstood, these are the elements that have most impact and bring the big payoff.

Three of the wedge's triangles have their points facing downward to indicate the need to dig deeper to find the hidden drivers where customer value lies. Even within the more visible financial and functional elements, some aspects of value will always be hidden and require exploration. The intangible element connects the other three. It points upward because as a general rule only a tiny portion or aspect of this element—such as, the peak of the "intangible" triangle in the figure—will be visible from the surface. But many broader and deeper ones lie below. Firms need to dig for them.

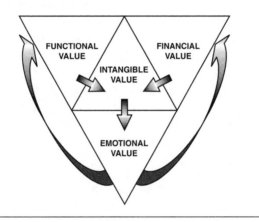

Figure 5.2 The customer value wedge

With the customer value wedge as a tool, you start with the more familiar financial and functional elements of value, move on to the intangible aspects, and then delve into the depths of the emotional drivers of value. The small arrows inside the triangles in Figure 5.2 illustrate this path. Typically, it is best to start by recapping what is known or anticipated about the elements of customer value of a specific product or market. Brainstorming activities and inspirational examples can be used to spark the discovery of less-obvious elements and develop a more complete picture.[11]

The process, which started at the top of the wedge, should become iterative as newly discovered items in one area help stimulate other ideas. Companies should further investigate questions or possibilities emerging from this process and then test them at the customer level via appropriate research. In a final stage, an important task is to translate the key emotional drivers of value into new financial and functional elements that can be communicated in a rational and socially gratifying way.

Using the customer value wedge as a tool mobilizes brainpower to systematically gather the broadest and deepest perspective on customer value for a given product. It builds on all the customer information that a firm has gathered from research and experience, and provides guidance to getting further customer information. Given the financial stakes, it is worth holding regular workshops to use the wedge, because it will uncover many insights and avenues of growth through new sources of customer value. These insights and new sources of value are the first ingredients required to fuel customer momentum. This approach is far removed from the dominant customer myopia that considers only the obvious financial and functional aspects of any offer—the superficial layer at the top of the wedge.

Before concluding with some key steps in the process of optimizing perceived customer value, we will share a few more helpful hints on each of its four components.

Financial Customer Value

One of the first symptoms of customer myopia is the belief that price is merely cost, and that this is what counts most in influencing perceived customer value. The myopia is understandable. Price is a highly visible, quantitative, and comparable item, and customers insist on its importance.

But the purchase price of a product is only one aspect of the financial element of value. Customers consider many other things when they evaluate an offer. For instance, when an airline has to replace part of its fleet, the price of aircraft is only one consideration. Financing facilities, fuel consumption, maintenance costs, price of spare parts, resale value, and training pilots and staff are only some of the multiple elements that must be scrutinized just on the financial front.

In the end, airlines want an evaluation of the plane's lifetime cost and the potential return on investment. The same applies to individual consumers considering the purchase of a computer printer. Many look at the price not only of the printer but of the compatible ink cartridges. Heavy users might calculate that the cost of the cartridges will quickly exceed the price of the printer itself.

Furthermore, in some cases the financial element of comparative customer value might be perceived as a benefit rather than a cost. Some firms sparked a strategic revolution by pioneering low-cost trends that gave them tremendous momentum. This revolution has already affected many industries, including airlines, banking, generic drugs, and telecommunications. At the other end of the spectrum, high prices can be perceived as benefits in the luxury goods market. Not only do high prices reflect quality and project social status, they guarantee exclusivity. If Louis Vuitton were to lower its prices, it would lose value for many of its customers. Wealthy consumers love luxury goods because they are inaccessible to the mainstream.[12]

One of the few infallible laws of business is that customers become smarter over time. Their perspective on financial matters grows more sophisticated and better adapted to their particular situation. The financial-value logic of one customer might appear stupid to another, but it is not—it is just different and specific to a different situation. Trying to reduce this richness of human nature to a simple formula is typical of customer myopia. Understanding this richness allows momentum-powered firms to exploit growth opportunities and build new growth momentum.

Functional Customer Value

The functional elements of value include physical properties, such as size, weight, and performance, as well as features offered. Like financials, functional elements are never totally absent when most firms consider an offering's customer value. However, three symptoms of customer myopia seriously reduce perspectives of customer value. All are quantifiable, and correcting them will create growth opportunities.

The first is the temptation to try to represent their impact on customer value in a rational way and to believe in set, universal rules such as "the lighter the better." In reality, different customers react differently to different properties and features. Great challenges and opportunities lie in understanding these differences.

The second trap lies in regarding functional features only as benefits when in fact customers might see their presence or absence as negatives—such as costs. Some customers, for instance, would never buy a mobile phone that does not include a camera. A product's most important negative aspect might be not its price but a functional deficiency such as this for which no price reduction can compensate.

The third trap is the belief that additional features will always increase perceived customer value. In fact, more and more customers perceive complexity as an important cost. For many of them, "less is more."

Intangible Customer Value

The importance of the intangible elements of value is increasing all the time. Out of the many intangible elements that could be relevant in different situations, let's briefly discuss three that are becoming crucial in a variety of contexts: risk, time, and innovation.

If customers perceive *risk* in a product, their perception of that product's value will certainly decline. Suppliers often underestimate this factor. Smart companies can create growth opportunities by providing mechanisms to reduce perceived risk. For instance, leading retailers today offer a no-quibble exchange policy, which reduces customers' hesitancy when purchasing gifts or clothing. Customers will often buy three identical skirts in different colors, secure in the knowledge that they can return two after they've tried them on at home. In a very different industrial setting, Cemex, the Mexican cement giant, grew from a regional player into a world leader by reducing risk to its customers. It guaranteed its customers delivery within 20 minutes, regardless of weather conditions, aided by satellite and web-based vehicle dispatch technology.[13]

Time is becoming an increasingly important driver of customer value, and it is perceived as both a cost and a benefit. Whether it is time spent lining up at an understaffed retail outlet or time on the phone waiting to speak to a bank's call center, many customers see it as an important cost. Well-planned new offers aim to reduce customers' wasted time by offering them better service, Internet access, or other solutions. In contrast, customers in other situations are prepared to spend more time to save money. The Swedish furniture retailer IKEA has reduced its products' price to a low level, so the perceived value increases for customers. IKEA's customers downplay as a cost the time they invest in assembling their furniture themselves.

Innovation also becomes an increasingly important intangible cost or benefit as customers become smarter and more discriminating. Some customers will pay a premium for an innovative offering because they enjoy change or wish to look trendy. Others are suspicious of innovative solutions, fearing the associated risk and time required to learn and adapt.

Emotional Customer Value

The emotional elements of customer value are often invisible to the analytical business world. And yet deep emotional drivers, such as fear and pleasure, are often the most powerful reasons behind customers' purchase decisions. Indeed, psychological research using brain-scanning technology has demonstrated that people presented with two options tend to make the wrong choice if the rationally right option is framed in a way that associates it with negative emotions.[14]

It is important to realize that these emotional drivers play a critical role even in the most rational business environments. For example, in an industrial firm run by engineers, a supposedly rational procurement officer could become an emotional customer if the factory came to a standstill because of delays in delivery resulting from his or her decision.

Lying at the sharp lower tip of the customer value wedge are the deepest emotional drivers, rarely expressed. It is generally easiest to elicit these deep emotional drivers from customers by focusing on the negatives. For instance, the following questions are more likely to elicit insights: What keeps you awake at night? What is your worst nightmare? What was your worst experience as a customer? In contrast, positive questions (for example, What is your ideal supplier or dream product?) are usually less effective, although they might bring forth revealing responses.

In most instances, these deep emotional drivers relate to personal issues. They are dictated by complex fears and convictions concerning self-image, trust, respect, and justice. In the case of commercial customers, they will also include the fear of being fired or the excitement and anticipation of promotion and success. In many business-to-business situations, the ultimate value that a supplier can bring to a firm is a way to help it outperform competition. Because of the intensity of competitive situations, this value is more than rational—it is emotional.

A company needs customers to have positive emotions about its product or service to achieve momentum: *Emotions drive actions*. This can be illustrated by a humorous legend circulated in a multinational firm specializing in pest control. According to this yarn, the head of international development used a simple research technique to test whether a country in which the firm did not yet operate was ready for the firm's services. Immediately upon landing, he would go to eat at a nearby middle-class restaurant. He would wait for the dining room to fill up before taking a cockroach from a box in his pocket and placing it on the floor. When the bug had reached the middle of the room, he would leap up from the table shrieking: "A cockroach! A cockroach!" Then he would observe how the other restaurant customers reacted. If people said, "So what, it's just a cockroach," then that country was not ready for the firm. If they were horrified, he knew the company was ready for a new expansion.

The basic value that this firm delivered was hygiene. The cockroach story demonstrated people's emotions about hygiene. Of course, the tale is apocryphal, but it makes a key point to the company's employees: The key driver of customer value is emotional.

The purpose of the customer value wedge is to find new insights into the financial, functional, intangible, and emotional drivers of compelling value by exploring as many avenues as possible. This is likely to be messy and confusing. If you are not confused at some point in your exploration, you are not doing it right! You have stayed in the comfort zone of your current experience and knowledge. Managers instinctively hate confusion, which is why they tend to stay in the comfort zone of tradition and not see all the growth opportunities out there. Getting confused is not only normal but essential for this process—you have to get confused through exploration. What is not normal would be to *remain* confused! After exploration, you need to sift through what you have discovered and focus on the most compelling elements that will be the base of your strategy.

Let the Customer See Better Value

The customer value wedge is an effective tool for deeply exploring the value drivers of different customer groups. In this exploration, we aim not only at a deeper understanding of these groups but at systematically identifying the many ways of increasing the value they perceive. This is basic stuff. Customer-value improvements unveil new growth opportunities.

Microsoft enjoyed the momentum effect for many years. It created superior value for its customers in financial, functional, and intangible terms. But it has lost its momentum despite being continuously innovative and bringing multiple new products to the market.[15] Why? We have used the customer value wedge to test the reactions of executive users of Microsoft products. We believe that Microsoft's problems stem principally from perceived emotional costs that, implicitly or explicitly, drive down the perceived customer value of its products and services. In terms of future growth, this has implications worth billions of dollars. The amounts at stake would certainly justify a major program to systematically identify the sources of these negative emotions in different customer groups, and to install an ambitious vision for injecting positive emotional benefits. It is the curse of many dominant companies to have their growth burdened by customers' negative emotions. For customers, these negative emotions add to the cost of doing business with the firm, and significantly reduce its products' perceived value.

A company can significantly improve its offers by exploring with the customer value wedge, gaining improvements in perceived customer value that it had not seen earlier. Providing superior perceived value is a fundamental driver of the momentum effect, and it is essential for an effective momentum strategy. The design of what we call a power offer will be addressed in its own chapter, but let's see here how the view through the customer value wedge maximizes customer value.

The Golden Pathway to Increased Customer Value

There are three tracks that together form a single broad pathway, glittering with tremendously increased opportunities for the smart company.

- **Decrease perceived customer costs.** Identify and prioritize all avenues to cutting and eliminating perceived customer costs, from financial to emotional ones.
- **Increase perceived customer benefits.** Identify and prioritize all avenues to increase perceived customer benefits, from financial to emotional ones.
- **Select customer groups.** Identify and prioritize the customer groups that perceive the highest value in the resulting offer.

These three paths are not independent or alternative courses of action. They must be explored together and iteratively to develop the best combination offer based on what has been learned from the customer value wedge. Care and reflection are required, though, because as we have seen, one customer group's negative can be perceived as a benefit to another. One customer's improvement can be reduced value for another. In any case, returning frequently to exploring these three paths will bring new customer value insights that might have been overlooked in previous investigations with the customer value wedge. Finally, although the emphasis at this stage is on optimizing customer value, we must also keep in mind the final objective of maximizing value creation for the firm. The key challenge is, obviously, to optimize both customer value and business value—not to increase one at the expense of the other.

Let's illustrate customer value optimization with an example. From its early days, the Dell computer company demonstrated that it had mastered the richness of customer value. Michael Dell built his company by going well beyond the basic, functional benefits versus price paradigm then dominating the PC industry.

Michael Dell first realized that the customer benefit of face-to-face interaction with salespeople was weak. The stores were often in inconvenient, out-of-town locations and were usually understaffed by poorly trained salespeople. The whole process was time-consuming and frustrating, but the retailers' high overheads meant that the computers were still relatively expensive. The low perceived benefits and high costs caused young student customers like Dell to feel abused. He searched for a better alternative. By selling direct, he was able to save the 40 percent retail margin with no noticeable loss in perceived customer benefits. In addition, customized assembly on order, fast delivery, and good service provided extra benefits. He had found the way to offer a compelling value to a certain population of customers. These customers went directly from a perception of being abused by other firms to being delighted by Dell.[16]

Now, consider some other aspects of Dell's strategy to see how they exploited opportunities for offering even more compelling value and creating momentum. Dell's business model allowed him to lower inventory from an industry average of eighty days to just a few days. Obviously, this saves working capital, but how could this create benefits to customers? The answer is speed. Customers like innovation and want to have the latest-available PC technology, so many companies invest huge sums in speeding up their innovation cycles—but the traditional distribution system eats up about eighty days of inventory time before new models reach their customers. So a low inventory level not only costs less but allows Dell to get innovations out faster. Again, more gain, less pain.

Dell discovered that its corporate customers incurred costs of around $200 to $300 per computer getting their IT departments to install customized software configurations on new PCs. Dell offered its key accounts a simple, valuable solution: Dell would install the customized company software during assembly. By direct connection to a customer's server, Dell could download onto each new PC's hard disk the relevant software for its future user at a fraction of the cost of the previous process—again, more benefits at lower cost.

These same corporate customers are an example of the evolution in the customer groups Dell selected. Initially, the target market was students like Michael Dell had been himself, with little money but not particularly demanding. As Dell expanded, its customers became more-demanding but more-affluent home computer users. Finally Dell began to target corporate customers who were yet more demanding but offered much higher revenue and lower costs in return. These demanding but highly attractive corporate customers ended up accounting for the largest proportion of Dell's business.

With these and other customer value-enhancing solutions, Dell stood as an exemplary momentum-powered firm, rising to top worldwide computer sales. It joined the elite Fortune 500 list of the world's biggest companies in 1992, and in 2005 *Fortune* ranked it first in its "Most Admired Companies" list. As always, though, the challenge for any company is to keep the momentum rolling.

An accumulation of challenges hit the company. Its PCs began to appear undifferentiated, customers reported increasing problems with its service support, and a number of lawsuits concerning marketing practices hurt customers' trust in the company. In 2006, two years after Michael Dell stepped down as CEO, the company lost its once-substantial lead in the PC business to Hewlett-Packard. Dell became momentum deficient because it became complacent and neglected to sustain a compelling value for its customers. In January 2007, Michael Dell returned as CEO, carried out a shakeup in top management, and embarked on a major turnaround.[17]

Go Deep, Be Compelling

Momentum-powered firms don't just offer good customer value to their customers, they offer compelling value—a value so intense and personal that it resonates with those customers' needs in a grippingly powerful way.

Going beyond the limits of the standard, the acceptable, and the average enables momentum-powered firms to uncover insights into customers' perceptions, and this is what builds compelling value. The only way to create compelling customer value is to transcend standard financial and functional value calculations and truly understand the drivers of perceived customer value, especially those that are veiled, emotional, and intangible.

Momentum-deficient firms cannot see the true nature of customer value because they suffer from customer myopia. Their view is restricted and distorted. We have established five guiding principles of compelling customer value to serve as lenses to correct this myopia and uncover growth opportunities:

- Customer value drives business, not products. Customers buy products only to obtain the value they offer. Products are only transitory, temporary vehicles to carry value from a firm to its customers.

- A product has no intrinsic, absolute value. Different customers perceive different value from the same product. For some, a product offers immense value. For others, the same product has no value at all or even a negative value. As a result, customer value must be explored from many different perspectives.

- Customer decisions involve a constant trade-off of perceived costs and perceived benefits. Achieving compelling customer value requires a deep understanding of the pain and gain as perceived by customers themselves.

- Perception of value does not follow a universally agreed rationality. Customers might explain their choices in a socially acceptable rational manner, usually in terms of the financial and functional aspects of value, but true customer reasoning is internal, personal, and hidden. And its most powerful drivers are often the deep intangible and emotional determinants of value.

- Perceived customer value must be continuously optimized by systematically decreasing customer costs, increasing customer benefits, and exploring alternative customer groups.

The customer value map and the customer value wedge are two visual tools that help implement these principles. They provide a framework to systematically discover opportunities for increasing perceived customer value. The objective is to energize the value delivered in the firm's offers, as its targeted customers perceive it.

In addition to optimizing perceived customer value, a profitable growth momentum requires simultaneous optimizing of the value of the targeted customers to the firm. This is the focus of the next chapter.

6

Compelling Equity

The Man Who Taught an Old Dog New Tricks

Put yourself in the place of someone who has just been appointed CEO of a long-established, low-tech firm with a dominant share of a very low-growth market. Your potential customers fervently hope they will never need what you sell. If they do, they are "high-maintenance" clients who delay your agents, bombard them with questions, and snoop around their work. They have to be serviced on location, but they tend to be unavailable when you need them during normal working hours, and their addresses are often difficult to find. They are hard negotiators, always looking for special deals. Your new business? An 80-year-old residential pest-control company—about as unlikely a candidate for momentum as one could imagine. How confident would you feel about delivering 20 percent annual growth for 12 years?

That's what Clive Thompson achieved in the 1980s and 1990s as chief executive of Rentokil, the U.K.-based international pest-control company. When he joined in 1984, he took a look at the business from a fresh perspective. He quickly saw that he could get better value from business customers than Rentokil's traditional residential market. Rentokil could charge businesses more for one-off treatments against rodents because of the larger sites and companies' readiness to pay the right price for a quality service. Moreover, business customers were easier to serve because people were present during working hours and more reliable than private customers.

They also offered more long-term potential. A business was more likely to hire Rentokil on a repeat basis to protect its facilities regularly on a yearly or multiyear contract. Large client companies often had several locations, and Rentokil could extend a contract across its different sites. Once accepted as a trusted supplier for pest control, Rentokil could expand into many other services that business customers required, including cleaning, gardening, and security. Financially, compared to the one-off fee of about $1,000 to private customers, revenue per business customer could be tens of thousands for a larger location, hundreds of thousands for annual contracts covering multiple sites, or even million-dollar, multiyear contracts for multiple services to a large global customer.

This is what customer equity is all about: a keen eye on the strategic value of customers and taking steps to optimize their value to the company. In Rentokil's case, this dramatic shift in customer equity generated amazing growth momentum. During Thompson's tenure, the company was at the top of the Momentum League on a global scale. It became a multi-billion-dollar outfit and the darling of the stock exchange, and Thompson earned the admiring title Mr. 20 Percent. It was so profitable that it eventually acquired a firm twice its size in a hostile takeover, to become Rentokil-Initial.[1] All this was driven largely by the shift in focus to a more valuable group of customers.

The Concept of Compelling Equity

Although firms do not own them, customers are a company's main asset. Indeed, they are more important to a firm than its factories, personnel, or brand, because they are the point of origin of most of its firm cash flow. In the Rentokil example, a client company will bring to the firm a stream of revenue, year after year, as long as the business relationship is maintained. Over the length of this relationship, it will also contribute other benefits, including reputation, references, collaborative product development, and the purchase of new products.

There will also be various costs involved in serving that client. What this customer is worth in total to the firm, taking into account all benefits and costs over the course of a business relationship, is called customer equity.[2] Momentum-powered firms are able to extract superior equity from their customers. They find customers who offer *compelling equity*—equity that induces the momentum effect.

Again, as with compelling value, the term compelling equity is not a meaningless rebranding of other well-known concepts. Compelling equity is about maximizing the value of customers to the firm. Of course, it has to be based on customer targets and market segments, but it has a much stronger intent and meaning. The word *equity* puts the emphasis on what the firm gets from the customers. The word *compelling* expresses the fact that this equity is so powerful that the firm will have the incentive, and potential means, to create a power offer that will have customer traction. A compelling equity is thus one of the conditions that is necessary for the momentum effect to take place.

Managers are naturally expected to have a complete and objective understanding of their firm's assets. Unfortunately, most managers' understanding of customer equity—the value of a customer to the company—is incomplete and based on subjective perceptions rather than objective reality. As a result, many companies fall into the trap of allocating more resources to demanding customers than to those who represent the highest equity or the greatest potential.

Remember that the process of momentum design involves two interconnected explorations: customer value, what the company offers customers; and customer equity, what it gets back from them. The point of the first is to create compelling value by increasing the attractiveness of the firm's offer to the customer. With customer equity, we are striving to increase the worth of customers to the firm. We want compelling equity. Stated simply: getting more back.

A product becomes a power offer when it is the source of both compelling value to customers and compelling equity to the firm. A power offer generates exceptional growth because of this combination. It is therefore important that the perceived value delivered to a group of customers should be balanced by the equity they return to the firm. If a company does not provide enough value to customers in line with what these customers are worth, a competitor will eventually see the opportunity to serve them better and will poach them. Similarly, offering customers too much value relative to their worth, will impact the profits the firm could be making from the relationship.

This balance is easily destroyed if management's perception of customer equity is incomplete or biased. As perception drives action, if the perception is wrong, the corresponding actions will be wrong, too. Chapter 5, "Compelling Value," made the point that when it comes to customer value, perception is reality. When it comes to management, it is a different matter! Managers must base their decisions on *facts*. They must ensure that their perceptions reflect a clear, undistorted understanding of reality.

Transaction Myopia

In most firms, management knows all about product profitability but rarely about *customer* profitability. Even with sensible customer-profitability information, management often falls into the trap of *transaction myopia* when attempting to understand customer equity. This ailment resembles the customer myopia that afflicts most firms when viewing customer value. It occurs because we are biased toward the short-term financial aspects of specific transactions with a customer. Our perception is driven by repetitive events that our memory registers automatically into our subconscious.[3] In the case of customer equity, these repeated events are the regular *transactions* with customers. But the reality of customer equity requires us to appreciate a customer's worth over the entire length of a *relationship*. To do so, we need to consciously reflect on and weigh several factors. A perception of customer equity based solely on transactions is inevitably myopic. To comprehend customer equity in depth, we need a broader perspective on the relationship.

Transaction myopia presents several dangers. First, it leads a business to run after any opportunity it can snatch, so long as the anticipated transactions, deals, or margins are attractive or, sometimes, even if they are not. This is because financial and psychological incentives are usually transaction based. Running after individual transactions usually ends up acquiring the exact opposite of compelling equity: *dangerously subsidized equity*. This is because less-profitable customers are inevitably pulled in to drive top-line growth, at the expense of overall profitability.

A simple example of this phenomenon is provided by one of our clients, a leading automobile manufacturer. In an effort to increase sales volume, the company had developed the practice of allowing deep discounts to car rental companies. This was having a doubly negative effect on profit—first by cutting the margins made on these sales, and then by reducing sales of other new cars in six months' time, as large fleets of lightly used vehicles were released into the market after the rental companies had finished with them. The company decided to progressively cut the number of cars it sold to the rental sector through the simple expedient of reducing the discount. In the space of two years, although the number of cars it sold to this sector dropped by 20 percent, the overall margin extracted from those sales increased by more than 50 percent. Correcting the company's transaction myopia had increased their customer equity.

Second, transaction myopia causes firms, managers, and employees to underestimate customer equity. As we shall see throughout this chapter, customer equity is a fertile mix of functional, intangible, emotional, and financial elements—exactly like customer value.

The Rentokil example illustrates how attractive nonfinancial features significantly increased the firm's customer equity. Rentokil's traditional private clients often required the service to be offered outside standard office hours and could be difficult to deal with because of the stress of vermin infestations in their homes. Business locations are always open in the daytime, so Rentokil's agents could access the sites easily. Business customers were busy with their own work, so Rentokil agents could get on with their job undisturbed. If they needed help, on-site workers were more likely to pitch in than squeamish homeowners. Business customers are more likely to be concerned with results than costs, so Rentokil agents were less likely to get stuck in petty negotiations. Various legal requirements often made services like Rentokil's mandatory for business concerns. Business addresses in commercial districts were generally easier to find than private homes, so driving time and frustrations were reduced. Commonly, several other potential clients were located in the same business district.

Altogether, therefore, it was win-win for Rentokil and its newly targeted customers. All the elements of customer equity it experienced—financial, functional, intangible, and emotional—form a mirror image of the customer value we discussed in Chapter 5. This symmetry between customer value and customer equity is a constant in momentum-powered firms. Transaction myopia leads to a fixation on just one of these elements—the financial—and even then in a limited and incomplete way. If a firm wants to seek out compelling customer equity, it must correct its transaction myopia and acquire a clear view of the relationship with customers over time and across all four dimensions of customer equity.

However, let's follow the advice set out earlier and proceed to first pick some low-hanging fruit. Transaction myopia causes firms to fixate on the financial elements of customer equity, but even here, in most cases managers and employees grossly underestimate the true value of a customer. Before investigating the deeper levels of compelling equity, let's look at a basic perspective that can be used to begin to correct transaction myopia: the concept of customer lifetime value.

Lifetime Value: The First Step in Correcting Transaction Myopia

How can companies begin to determine the worth of their customers? How to estimate equity? Even if incomplete, customer lifetime value can provide an initial estimate. It is the first step in correcting transaction myopia.

The idea of customer lifetime value is very simple. It involves adding up the worth of a customer's transactions over a lifetime—for example, the period of time we expect to retain him or her. If a customer in a pizzeria spends $10 on a pizza and a Pepsi, what is the equity of offers to the firm?[4] What if he's a regular and visits every week? What if he continues to visit the pizzeria for ten years before he moves away or stops eating pizza? He's not worth $10 to the pizzeria. He's worth $5,000 over ten years! This process is simple, fast, and has solid impact. Note that we rounded off the numbers—a simple average transaction, a simple weekly visit, and 50 weeks per year rather than 52. This is deliberate, acknowledging the uncertainties inherent in all estimates, but the emphasis remains correct in terms of the purpose of the estimate. Spending too much time on the fine detail provides a false sense of accuracy and loses sight of the purpose.

Like any idea, customer lifetime value can be made much more complex by adding more considerations to improve its accuracy. The most important ones are these: Should we consider revenues or profits? What is the right time horizon for the "life" of a customer? Should we adjust for the fact that $1 today is not the same as $1 some years from now? These are all excellent questions, and they have technical solutions. But what we suggest as a first stage is to consider revenues over a relevant time horizon of five to ten years and simply add up the numbers.[5] Starting from a simple but robust base, you can later refine the process depending on the accuracy needed for any decisions under consideration.

The key purpose of customer lifetime value is to shift from a transaction-based mindset to a customer equity mindset, an essential element for building sustainable, profitable growth. For this purpose, we need a rough estimate of the financial worth of different groups of customers over time. Obviously, the real equity in a customer will depend on our ability to retain that customer, and we explore this further in Chapter 10, "Vibrant Retention." For the time being, we are interested in knowing a customer group's *potential* equity, assuming that we will deliver the proper value and take other actions to retain them.

Using customer lifetime value as the first estimate of customer equity always provides a new business perspective. It helps escape from the usual focus on transaction size and evaluate the real business opportunities stemming from different customer groups. The small transactions that we tend to neglect can represent enormous opportunities when they are made repeatedly by the same customers. This is how certain firms have corrected their vision of customer equity, made big gains, and even transformed their whole industry.

Low-cost airlines are a case in point. Their strategy is usually explained by highlighting the efficiency of their operations. While this is obviously a crucial aspect of their success, they have also exploited the transaction myopia of established airlines that traditionally gave most importance to first-class and business-class passengers, because of the higher prices and margins.

Consider the success of Southwest Airlines. In the 1970s, when Southwest unveiled its low-fare strategy, the idea seemed at odds with the industry's conventional wisdom of concentrating on big tickets and long routes. Thirty years later, it is one of the world's most successful airlines. A short Southwest hop between two intrastate cities might cost about $50, a price that enables people to change their transportation habits and fly much more frequently than before. They will fly to local business meetings, to visit family, to watch a sports event, or even to commute between home and office. A commuter on such a route who flies once a week will represent an equity to SWA of about $50,000 over ten years. Suddenly the numbers begin to look pretty big despite the small value of a single transaction. This compelling equity is one of the drivers behind Southwest's momentum growth. Airline executives who never took the time to consider this issue would have totally underestimated it. Without such compelling equity, a low-cost airline like Southwest could not survive.

Customer lifetime value is the first step in the journey from transaction myopia to achieving 20/20 vision on customer equity. When kept simple, it is an excellent tool for engaging a wide variety of employees, from top management to the front line. It addresses important questions. Its outcome can be put in simple numbers that can be communicated effectively and strike the imagination. It can create desirable shifts in mindset and in behavior. But, admittedly, it is incomplete. It needs to be enriched by other considerations to reach the total perspective that will build compelling customer equity.

The Customer-Equity Wedge

Any customer relationship involves a variety of costs and benefits to business. They must all be fully appreciated before a properly rounded view of the relationship's worth can be formed. Taking a blinkered view, one that focuses solely on the financial aspects of the relationship, will cause management to underestimate the equity that some customers, such as key opinion leaders, represent and overestimate the worth of others, such as more arrogant, established customers. Customer equity is the net balance between the benefits customers bring to a company and the costs of serving them.

As with customer value, the business costs and benefits that must be considered in forming a view of customer equity include functional, intangible, and emotional aspects in addition to the more obvious financial ones. A useful tool for systematically investigating the elements that influence customer equity is a wedge similar to the one we first encountered in our examination of customer value—in this case reconfigured to form the *customer equity wedge,* set out in Figure 6.1. It cures transaction myopia in the same way the customer value wedge cures customer myopia.

The customer value wedge helped us to explore the different costs and benefits that products and services offer to customers. The customer equity wedge applies the same approach but from a mirror perspective. It helps investigate the different costs and benefits that accrue to a business in a customer relationship. With the wedge as a tool, the natural way to start is with the financial and functional elements at the top and then to go deeper into the intangible and emotional elements, as indicated by the small arrows. As with customer value exercises, brainstorming activities and inspirational examples can be used to elicit a large number of elements until you are satisfied that a complete, in-depth comprehension of the compelling customer equity picture is in place. The larger arrows indicate that in a second stage, one must try translating the emotional and intangible elements into financial and functional ones to better communicate their business impact. In the end, all these elements must be integrated into the two fundamental questions of the business model to serve the considered customer group: How do we serve them best? What do we gain from serving them?

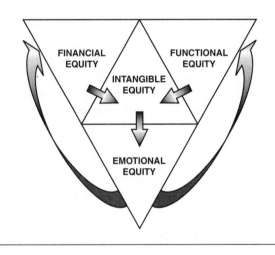

Figure 6.1 The customer equity wedge

The customer equity wedge does not require us to explore the uncharted territory of customers' hidden mental processes as was the case for customer value, but it does need a dual knowledge of the firm's operations and customers' behavior. The outcome of this process should be the discovery of some insights that will help us uncover compelling equity.

Financial Customer Equity

Customer lifetime value is the most appropriate tool for exploring the financial dimensions of customer equity. In the previous pages, this tool was described merely in terms of revenues because this is simple and sufficient to pull members of a team away from transaction myopia and encourage their commitment to building growth through momentum.

To have a more complete financial evaluation of customer equity, however, this must be complemented by an evaluation of customer lifetime costs and of the net customer lifetime value: the net profits expected over the customer's lifetime. Other financial considerations can be added depending on the situation, including customer sensitivity to price, payment conditions, and other relevant dimensions.

In the Rentokil example, shifting from residential to business customers resulted in a customer lifetime value revenue leap from a few thousand dollars to millions. Furthermore, business customers were relatively less costly to serve and less price sensitive. They presented compelling financial equity on all fronts.

Likewise, although the customers targeted by Nintendo's Wii are more affluent than traditional gamers, their greatest advantage in terms of financial customer equity is that, unlike dedicated younger gamers, they do not demand cutting-edge performance in speed, graphics, and other components. This has enabled Nintendo to make its hardware much more profitable than competitors', competitors who often sell their equipment at cost and make the profits only on the software.[6] The combination of its low manufacturing cost and a new more affluent profile of its gamers results in a significant increase in its customer equity.

Functional Customer Equity

The functional elements of customer equity lie at the point where the capabilities of the firm intersect with the needs of its customers. Higher financial equity—in the form of higher prices, higher consumption, cross-selling, and higher loyalty—will come only if a firm delivers compelling value to the relevant customers in a cost-effective fashion. However, the necessary adaptations to the requirements of those customers might have cost implications that negatively effect customer equity. So the question is this: Where is the best fit between the firm's capabilities and the value delivered to customers?

SKF is a global leader in ball bearings. A team of SKF managers was searching for industrial customers that might present new growth opportunities. Their insight was to leave behind the mindset of simply peddling more tons of standard ball bearings and to reconsider the fundamental customer need that their product satisfied. They concentrated their reflections on rotary friction and investigated potential customer groups who were especially concerned with energy wasted through this specific kind of friction. They identified the pulp and paper industry, which uses huge rotating machines to grind wood into pulp, and then pulp into paste, and then paste into paper. Energy is wasted not only because of normal friction in the machinery but also through the secondary operations required to dissipate overheating. Improved ball bearings custom designed for these heavy machines would allow significant cost savings in both their primary tasks and the secondary cooling. In addition, understanding the enormous cost of downtime in such operations, SKF developed new services such as machinery maintenance contracts with associated performance guarantees. And shifting the perspective from just supplying ball bearings to providing specific customers with a real competitive advantage created growth opportunities for SKF in the pulp and paper sector. The company's service business became its fastest-growing and most profitable division. By reexamining the functional elements of customer equity in relation to specific clients, SKF was able to increase the equity derived from these customers in a sustainable fashion.[7]

Intangible Customer Equity

The intangible elements of customer equity are those that cannot be appreciated as objectively as the financial or functional ones. For instance, some customers might represent different forms of risk that have to be considered because of their financial situation, their geographical location, or other reasons. Two examples are automobile manufacturers and construction companies, both subject to economic cycles that create instabilities for their suppliers. A glass manufacturer producing windshields and windows must take this into account to adjust the estimation of equity. The same glass manufacturer should realize that the food industry to which it supplies bottles is less cyclical, and this should influence its potential equity positively.

Being a supplier for companies with a reputation for excellence can help in gaining new customers or justifying a price premium for one's products and services. These special customers have such a reputation of expertise in their fields that their purchasing decisions are observed by others.[8] If companies such as GE, Procter & Gamble, FedEx, or BMW buy from you, it means you must excel in your field. This represents additional equity beyond the financial and functional elements.

This is equally true of customers who are loyal, easy to serve, or key opinion leaders. Malcolm Gladwell emphasizes this last element in his remarkable book *The Tipping Point.* He distinguishes between the "mavens" who have influence and the "connectors" who have access to a network. In the pharmaceutical industry, for instance, leading professors of medicine have a great impact through their research, their presence at conferences, and their training of generations of doctors. In a different way, doctors who socialize actively with their peers will also spread the good word when they are impressed with a treatment. They represent equity beyond the financial value of their prescriptions.[9]

Emotional Customer Equity

The deeper, less-explicit elements of customer equity are emotional. They can create an important gap between the perceived and the real worth of a customer. There are customers who bring important emotional benefits to other customers or to employees, and this should be acknowledged in the way we treat them. On the other hand, sometimes serving certain customers creates such emotional costs that one might consider dropping them.

Figure 6.2 shows some frequently encountered emotional elements of customer equity. In the case of Rentokil, for instance, employees found business clients less difficult to work with than residential customers. In addition, working for business customers was more prestigious and stimulating.

An anecdote involving Virgin Atlantic can illustrate several dimensions of emotional equity. One day at Sydney Airport, the airline was forced to cancel a flight to London because of mechanical problems. The announcement was made, and passengers lined up for transfers to other airlines or the next day's Virgin flight. A passenger near the end of the line began fretting loudly, making noises and generally creating tension. Unable to contain himself, he forced his way to the front of the line and screamed at the desk attendant, demanding an immediate transfer to the next flight. The attendant politely replied that every passenger in line would be served and that his turn would come. Predictably, he resorted to the ancient line of all self-important persons expecting special treatment: "Do you know who I am?" The attendant calmly took the microphone and ad-libbed a public announcement: "There is a gentleman here who does not remember who he is. If anybody knows him, please come to Gate 14." The entire hall broke into laughter, and the irate passenger retreated to the back of the line.

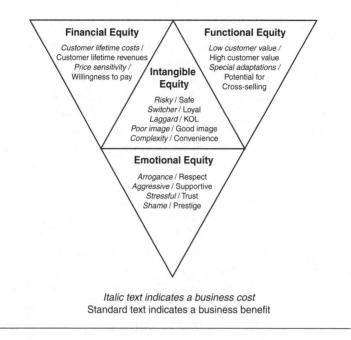

Italic text indicates a business cost
Standard text indicates a business benefit

Figure 6.2   Equity enhancers and equity destroyers

This incident is rich in learning material about the emotional aspects of customer equity. Although this one was exceptional by its public nature, similar situations arise regularly in more discreet fashion. This passenger was creating emotional costs to other passengers and to the staff, and the impact was amplified by the stressful nature of the situation. Satisfying this line-jumper ahead of the others would have caused resentment among dozens of other passengers. The attendant's spontaneous, witty response satisfied hundreds of passengers at the sole cost of, most likely, one future client. In total, she created customer equity for Virgin.[10]

An exploration of these four elements—financial, functional, intangible, and emotional—opens many avenues that are otherwise hidden by transaction myopia. The concept of customer lifetime value leads the way to this discovery process, but it doesn't stop there. Firms that examine the deeper reaches of customer equity will be able to target customers that offer compelling equity more effectively and, just as important, avoid customer groups that are potential sources of the friction that slows momentum. As with the exploration of customer value, the process of exploring customer equity should be messy and confusing. Done properly, it should result in long lists of positives and negatives, some of which might initially appear contradictory. The process only really begins to become clear when the results of this exploration are merged with those of the examination of customer value during power offer design. But that is getting ahead of ourselves. For the moment we must, temporarily, accept some uncertainties.

When working with this wedge, note that the location of pertinent factors within each triangle can be somewhat arbitrary, and that these factors can migrate into the space of another element. For instance, if an intangible factor such as risk or the presence of a key opinion leader can be quantified, it could be considered either functional or financial, depending on the case. Having a key business leader as a client could be regarded as the equivalent of a $2,000,000 communications budget. That would move this factor from the intangible triangle into the financial. But precise categorization of location is less important than uncovering the various elements that can enhance or destroy customer equity.

The Customer-Equity Map

Although the customer equity wedge is an in-depth exploration tool for figuring out the benefits that different types of customers bring to a firm and the costs of serving them, companies also need a broad, strategic view of the relative equity of these different customer groups. The *customer equity map* provides this.

The map, shown in Figure 6.3, is a tool for visualizing the total equity that customer groups bring to the firm. Its vertical axis corresponds to the business benefits brought by different groups of customers, and its horizontal axis corresponds to the business costs associated with serving them. The positioning of particular customer groups on this map does not need to be absolutely precise, but it should act like a spotlight to illuminate areas requiring attention.

Customer groups that are on the diagonal that sweeps from lower left to upper right offer a firm normal equity. This means they represent a mix of benefits and costs that brings the firm returns in line with expectations. Along the diagonal, they represent balanced combinations that make sense for the firm: Increasing business costs are matched by increasing benefits brought by customers. In the lower-left corner, "economy" customers offer limited benefits but cost little to serve. For Southwest Airlines, for instance, these would be the occasional passengers on the short routes. The "mid-range" customers provide average levels of benefits in return for average business costs. At the top of the diagonal are "premium" customers, those who bring high benefits but are more expensive to serve.

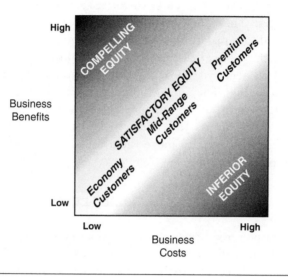

Figure 6.3   The customer equity map

Given the forces of competition and levels of professional management, you might expect all customer groups to be on this diagonal, but this is obviously not the case. One of the objectives of momentum strategy is to attract customers who bring compelling equity. They would be positioned in the upper-left corner of the customer equity map, bringing high benefits at relatively low business costs.[11] In the case of Southwest, these would be the regularly commuting passengers. In the case of Rentokil, they would be corporate customers in dense business centers. These are the customers who help create momentum. Competitors will eventually discover the attractiveness of these customers, so the firm must also offer them adequate value to retain their equity.

In the lower-right corner of the customer equity map are customer groups whose cost of service is disproportionate to the benefits they deliver to the firm. Their equity is poor—and possibly even negative—relative to other customer groups. Why do companies continue to do business with them? Because of transaction myopia and an ignorance of the real equity of customers. These customers act as leeches, draining the firm's resources. They are likely to be attached to the firm because competitors will not make efforts to attract them away. They are, in fact, subsidized by the profits that the company is making from higher-equity customers. The negative impact on momentum of these subsidized customers is double: They are a burden on the firm, and they draw resources away from other customer groups who are of strategic importance for the future. It is thus crucial to identify them and take appropriate actions either to move them toward an acceptable level of equity or to phase them out.

Optimizing Customer Equity

Momentum-powered firms constantly seek to optimize their customer equity to make it truly compelling, to load it with power. To help us in this mission, we have two tools. The customer equity wedge gives us *depth* to discover the various elements that influence a customer's contribution to the firm. The customer equity map gives us the *strategic perspective* on alternative customer groups. The discoveries stemming from the use of these tools are the ingredients that help optimize customer equity.

The Three Paths of Customer-Equity Optimization

There are three paths to optimizing the equity inherent in a firm's customers:

- **Chase equity destroyers.** Identify and prioritize ways of eliminating or reducing the total business costs of serving customers, from financial to emotional ones.
- **Build up equity enhancers.** Identify and prioritize ways to increase the total business benefits from existing or potential customer relationships, from financial to emotional ones.

- **Shift customer targeting.** Identify and prioritize the customer groups that can contribute the highest equity to the firm.

These three paths are not independent. A change in one is likely to impact the other two. This process of iterative exploration is likely to lead to new insights that will reveal previously overlooked sources of customer equity. As mentioned earlier, an important consideration is to avoid immediately focusing on financial issues, because doing so tends to limit the scope of reflection and the resulting insights. The goal is to uncover the less-visible dimensions that have escaped the attention of the firm and of its competitors. The most sustainable advantages will be the ones that are most hidden.

One must not lose sight of a basic fact: Ultimate customer traction, and hence ultimate momentum, is achieved when an increase in customer equity is balanced by an increase in customer value. The two elements are synergistic—the more equity that can be extracted from the customer, the more resources the firm will have to invest in delivering greater value back to that customer—the more value delivered to the customer, the greater the equity the firm will be able to extract and so on. Chapter 5 described how, over two decades, Dell managed to continuously increase the perceived value it delivered to customers. Let's now see how the company also exploited the three paths of optimizing customer equity to generate momentum—and how it missed a big opportunity.

Dell started with individual customers but, like Rentokil, soon recognized that developing a presence among business customers could have a positive impact on customer equity. A less-visible action was Dell's decision to move maintenance engineers into key account sites. This increased both the value the company delivered to its customers— better and faster service—and the equity of these customers to Dell. It eliminated the equity-destroying business costs of time and money wasted in transportation, while at the same time lowering demand on its own office space. It also built equity enhancers by increasing total business benefits that were often nonfinancial: Resident engineers were spending time with customers and identifying new opportunities. Companies receiving these services became more satisfied, bought more products and services, and spread the good word. A significant illustration is Boeing. In the late 1990s, Dell placed 30 engineers in the aerospace company's commercial division in Seattle. The perceived value of the services they delivered was so great that five years later Dell won a lucrative three-year contract to take over technical support for the computer systems of Boeing's defense division in St. Louis. The division employed 78,000 people—that represents fairly compelling equity!

But Dell could have done even better. It took the company two decades to realize that it missed a golden opportunity in terms of customer equity—and Michael Dell even made a public mea culpa for the oversight. It concerned printers. These machines aren't necessarily very profitable themselves, but the cartridges they repeatedly churn through are. Selling printers and, more importantly, cartridges would have substantially increased the equity of these customers over the whole life of the printer. Instead, Dell left the field wide open to its archrival, Hewlett-Packard. Dell lost out twice—in revenue for itself and in the customer equity that HP extracted from printers and peripherals to fund its competitive position in PCs.

These selected elements of Dell's strategy illustrate the three paths for customer equity optimization as well as the underlying dimensions of the customer equity wedge and the customer equity map. Note in particular the variety of ways in which customer equity is impacted by just the few actions described previously: shift to large business customers, resident engineers, service quality, cross-selling, maintenance contracts, and the late entry in printers. All these actions were on the top of the core activity of developing, selling, and manufacturing PCs, and they contributed significantly to its growth momentum. The challenge, again, is to keep up this momentum. And the solution is to continuously explore the customer equity wedge and the customer equity map to identify new growth opportunities from new or existing customers.

Zero-in on Customers Who Drive Momentum

Offering compelling value to customers is only half the story. A firm must also be able to extract sufficient equity from those customers to secure a profit. A key driver of momentum is ensuring that the right customers are being served, and in the right manner. Most businesses understand that all customers are not created equal. Momentum-powered firms go beyond that and understand what determines the value of customers to them. They are able to extract compelling customer equity. Momentum-deficient firms are blinded by a transactional myopia that limits their understanding of value to the obvious financial scale of their relationship with customers.

Momentum-powered firms use their broader understanding of customers to take actions that increase the equity of the customers they serve. They build superior customer equity—compelling equity. The following five guiding principles will help you do the same:

- Customers really are a firm's most important "assets," although they are not the traditional balance sheet assets of company property. They must be won and held, and their value must be understood as clearly as that of any other asset.

- Transaction myopia results from the routine of business operations. It affects whole organizations, from top management to the front line. It tends to generally underestimate customer equity and creates a bias toward the most vocal or visible customers, instead of those most important to the firm.

- Average customer lifetime is a first estimate of customer equity. It can help correct an organization's transaction myopia if used as a leadership tool rather than just as a financial one.

- Acting on customer equity requires a deep understanding of the total business costs and benefits related to serving customers. This will uncover many more growth opportunities hidden by the traditional paradigm of focusing on the financial aspects of customer transactions.

- To remain compelling, customer equity must be continuously optimized by systematically chasing down and eliminating equity destroyers, building up equity enhancers, and exploring alternative customer groups.

Different customers, and different ways of serving them, offer differing returns. Building momentum means that those returns must be optimized to build compelling customer equity. You have to find the customers that offer the best chances for momentum.

The process of momentum design involves discovering compelling insights that lead to new and unfulfilled sources of compelling customer value and to new and untapped sources of compelling customer equity. These three elements—compelling insights, equity, and value—are complementary, interactive, and synergistic. These have to be exploited fully to craft products and services that are perceived by customers to be *power offers,* the focus of the next chapter.

7

Power Offer Design

A Bank That Doesn't Like Banking

For most day-to-day clients, recommending one's bank is something like recommending the local tax collector. The easy joke is that they're both unavoidable, they want your money, they gobble it like Pac-Man, and they leave you with the vaguely disquieting feeling of having been used as a disposable cash cow. Oddly enough, however, there is one bank whose customers like it so much they have become unpaid cheerleaders: 70 percent of them recommend it at least once a year. That's the highest, most enthusiastic approval rate you'll encounter for a bank anywhere in the world.

Its name? First Direct. This exceptional bank is a remarkable example of momentum created from a standing start. It is a division of HSBC, the leading global financial services company, and was formed in 1989 as a branchless "direct" bank offering telephone-based retail banking services. In an industry as conservative as the British retail banking sector in the 1980s the idea that people would trust their money to a bank they couldn't visit, staffed by people they couldn't see, seemed absurd. Yet, less than two years after its inception, it had become the most recommended U.K. bank—a position it hasn't lost in the many years since.[1]

The innovative banking experience that First Direct developed is a demonstration of creating a power offer through the process of momentum design. It is an experience so convenient, easy, and enjoyable that it doesn't seem like banking at all. That's deliberate, of course, and the company plays on it in its advertising. One recent campaign ran this slogan: "Funny. We're a bank but we don't like banking. Luckily for us, you probably don't either. Give us a try."

First Direct's power offer, like most others, looks obvious in hindsight, but when it was launched very few people in the industry saw its brilliance. They failed to grasp that it was based on a profound understanding of what certain consumers wanted from a bank and the potential equity they represented in return. Everything was perfectly lined up for success: a *power offer* that presented *compelling value* for a specific customer group that represented *compelling equity* for the bank—all based on *compelling insights*.

"In the U.K. in the 1980s, to most people banking was tiresome and troublesome," explained Alan Hughes, the bank's CEO from 1999 to 2004. "First Direct realized that a bank you could access anytime, without paperwork, lines, or hassle, was possible, but that alone was not enough: It had to appeal to confident, busy, savvy people intolerant of poor service and inconvenience. So First Direct had to make banking easy *and* fun. The first First Direct person the customer spoke to had the knowledge and capability to do almost any transaction and they had the self-confidence and the will to make it enjoyable. Of course, that made working there fun, too."[2]

This chapter lays out the process that will help firms turn the insights they have acquired into offers of the sort that First Direct generated—power offers that contain within them the energy to ignite the momentum effect and exceptional growth. These offers are designed with "power inside."

What Is a Power Offer?

We know that power offers are at the heart of momentum. They deliver compelling value to customers, who in turn offer compelling equity to the business. Table 7.1 lists some recent ones. As different as these products and services are, they are all linked, because all power offers share one trait: resonance. They resonate with their customers' needs, wants, and emotions while offering their creators superior profit. That grip between compelling value and compelling equity provides the traction that starts momentum.

Table 7.1   Recent power offers

BlackBerry	Lexus
BMW 5 Series	Nespresso
Boeing 787	Nintendo DS *Brain Age*
Cemex	Nintendo Wii
Commerce Bank	Novartis Gleevec
Corona	Red Bull
Dassault Falcon 7X	Skype
eBay	Southwest Airlines
Facebook	Swatch
First Direct	Tetra Pak
Google	Tom Tom Navigation System
Harry Potter	Toyota Prius
iPod and iPhone	Virgin Atlantic

It is a power offer's ability to find traction that enables momentum-powered firms—the Pioneers—to surge ahead of their competitors. Their goods and services sell themselves with relative ease. The role of marketing is just to help them reach their full potential. Remember that more than a third of First Direct's customers joined up on the strength of a 70 percent recommendation rate.

Power offers are the defining characteristic of momentum-powered firms. They set a whole new benchmark for business. Customers targeted by a power offer perceive it as offering such unquestionable value that they are magnetically drawn to it. The value it carries is so immediately apparent to them, so personal, so resonant, that they feel as though it was designed especially for them. They don't need to be convinced, persuaded, or pushed into making a purchase.[3]

Power offers are highly efficient. An average, run-of-the-mill offer can, for a short time, be compensated for by high promotional investments, but this is an inefficient way of doing business.[4] First Direct's marketing is excellent, but it is secondary to the offer itself. The marketing and communications behind a power offer support the value that the offer delivers but can never substitute for it. Consider the BMW 5 Series. It was named *Management Today*'s Executive Car of the Year, because, as the magazine wrote: "BMW's chief designer, Chris Bangle, has given executives who do not wear ties a car to represent them."[5]

The article went on to suggest that the car showed an understanding of customer psychology. It expresses class, quality, achievement, and prestige—all aspirations of its core business customers. The BMW 525 is a power offer because of the perception that customers attach to it, and that is the source of its momentum.

Beyond the recent examples in Table 7.1, every positive story in this book has a power offer at its heart.[6] The Walkman, Wal-Mart, Microsoft, IBM, IKEA—all, at some point in time, have been power offers. They were successful because they were appealing to customers and created momentum, pulling their companies to extraordinary, efficient, profitable growth.

Power offers share another characteristic: They look deceptively simple. This is part of their power. All elements of the offer have been carefully crafted, specifically for a targeted customer. They are aligned harmoniously to ensure that nothing jars and that everything is coherent. But coming up with such power offers is not easy. It is the result of long, messy, iterative explorations converging on tough decisions.

Exploring for Customer Traction

Obviously, power offers aren't just lying around fully formed, waiting to be found at your feet. Not only must they be assembled with care, but even before that process can start, their components must first be uncovered. This can be done only by firms willing to journey in search of them. The voyage starts with the discovery of compelling insights into unsatisfied customer needs and then plunges into a deeper exploration, searching for further insights into compelling customer value and compelling customer equity. This exploration can be arduous, but it is exciting, eye opening, and fun.

It leads to two parallel and in-depth investigations that reveal how compelling value and compelling equity can be enhanced or destroyed. These insights enable firms to optimize both the value that a customer group will perceive in the offer and the equity the firm can extract from the customer group being served.

The development of a power offer is a dynamic and iterative process. Like the creation of a sculpture or a poem, the idea for a power offer evolves and is refined over time. Figure 7.1 illustrates this essential dynamism. The double arrows emphasize the iterations required between the phases of compelling insights, compelling value, compelling equity, and power offer design. The process emphasizes exploration centered on the customer and focuses on the value and equity to be transferred by the product rather than the product itself. It is iterative, constantly oscillating between phases in which different functions of the firm collaborate. The net result of this process is the design of a power offer that has sufficient customer traction to produce momentum growth.

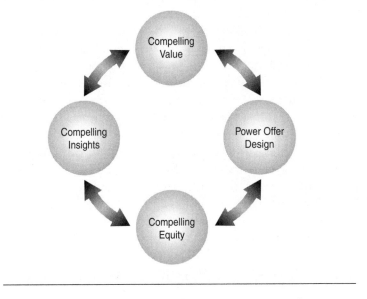

Figure 7.1   How momentum design generates customer traction

Power offers are usually the result of a messy, organic maturation quite unlike the orderly, linear pathways between silos that characterize the traditional product-design process of large, established firms. Business success stories rarely dwell on the haphazard stumbles of the early stages of gestation. The success might appear simple and logical, but the reality behind it is usually complex and chaotic.

Swatch, the Swiss watch manufacturer, is certainly a power offer. Simple accounts of its history often omit the disorderly elements of its evolution and the lessons painfully learned. Swatch as we know it today has evolved from the original idea that launched it. The initial intent was to design a high-quality but low-cost watch made in Switzerland, to fight low-cost competition from Asia. Total automation was needed in the manufacturing process because labor costs were much higher in Switzerland than Asia. This economic necessity led to a simple design and the selection of plastic molding.

The first Swatch collection was exactly what it was supposed to be: high-quality analog watches at a low price. They were black or brown only, because those were the established colors for watches. Only later, after the first collection, did Swatch come up with the idea of adding color. Red, yellow, and blue Swatches gave the mass market new variety in timekeeping at low cost.

Consumers loved these bright new timepieces. They were innovative and fashionable. Swatch maximized the potential of this favorable reaction, introduced more designs, and eventually recruited professional designers. The watches soon became a "fashion item that happens to tell time." With that, the firm changed track from concentrating on production costs to a focus on design and communication. They switched their initial customer selection: Swatch now targeted not the mass market but, rather, a large group of fashion-conscious younger consumers. This continuous evolution in strategy exploited the progressive discovery of customer insights, customer value enhancers, and new sources of customer equity. This unplanned but well-managed iterative discovery process propelled Swatch to its number-one position. That's the power of momentum.[7]

From Exploration to Design of a Power Offer

The exploration phase of power offer design should be inspiring and rewarding, but managers accustomed to the world of rational analysis can feel uncomfortable with its lack of structure. Working outside the comfort zone of established management practice is something most managers are reluctant to try. This explains why large, established firms miss so many opportunities that entrepreneurs with smaller resources uncover. And this is why the discomfort is necessary—it is the only way to build momentum.

To help managers feel more in control, a simple process is needed to make the transition from the messy, free-form world of exploration to the focused choices that must be made in the final design stages of power offers. Here, the mass of information that the discovery and exploration process uncovers must be distilled into a few key findings. There are two separate but similar paths to be followed. They eventually converge at the point of power offer design but come at it from different angles. The first concentrates on insights that have the greatest impact on customers' perceptions of value, the second on the ones that relate to the equity those customers offer the firm.

The Compelling Value Path to the Power Offer

The choices that managers need to make in the design of a power offer can be systematized to a certain extent. Our experience has shown that when managers are exploring—searching for the compelling value inherent in all power offers—opportunities can be easily crystallized by focusing on the four key goals of the process:

- **Customer value enhancers.** Where is the greatest potential for creating value for customers by *increasing* their perceived benefits?
- **Customer value destroyers.** Where is the greatest potential to create value for customers by *decreasing* the perceived costs that might lower that value?
- **Compelling proposition.** What is the value proposition with the greatest resonance?
- **Compelling targets.** Who are the potential customers for whom this value proposition is the most compelling?

These four questions can be integrated into an action tool, the *compelling value path* set out in Figure 7.2, building on the insights stemming from the customer value wedge in the exploration phase.[8] The two top boxes under Compelling Value Insights are the results of optimizing compelling value, as discussed at the end of the previous chapter. They should contain a short list of customer value enhancers and destroyers, prioritized for action that will optimize the value perceived by customer groups.

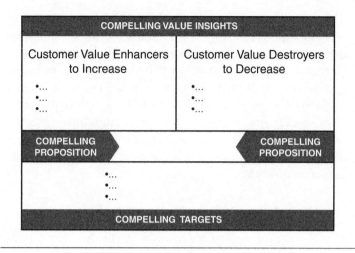

Figure 7.2 The compelling value path

Of particular importance among value destroyers are elements in the design of existing offers that do not resonate with some customer groups but incur business costs. One must chase significant costs from the design of offers currently on the market. Without this ruthlessness, the ability to create value for customers will be limited. Note how Dell and First Direct created power offers by removing a major cost item from current offers, respectively retail trade and branches. In each case, this amounted to around 40 percent of total costs.

This is what we call *cost-out.* Almost inevitably, existing offers will contain expensive elements that do not add to perceived benefits for some customer groups. Removing underperforming elements can free up many interesting options in the design of existing offers by removing the consequent costs. Firms thereby give themselves the option of improving those parts of the offer that *do* resonate with the customer. This is one of the reasons why momentum strategy delivers greater profitable growth than compensating strategy. Remember: Less is more.

These insights—identifying value enhancers to increase and value destroyers to decrease—show the path to boosting customer value to the point where it becomes compelling for customers. Multiple combinations of these actions are possible corresponding to different value propositions. These value propositions are succinct ways of describing the key value offered to customers. For instance, in the case of a retail operation, alternatives could be "guaranteed lowest prices," "your friendly neighborhood shop," or "convenience anytime." These three alternatives have different implications, and the first consideration is how compelling customers will find them.

A compelling proposition is the one that has the potential to create a high level of customer traction. To be compelling, it must be significantly more attractive to customers than any existing value proposition. This is why it can result only from compelling insights followed by significant changes in customer value enhancers and destroyers.

The middle section of the compelling value path is where one has to select the compelling proposition that has the most potential. The other factor that will affect the perceived value of the selected proposition is the customer group at which it is targeted. The process of defining this target begins in the bottom section of the compelling value path.

The key here is to focus only on those customer groups for whom the compelling value offered has the greatest resonance. These are the *compelling* targets. The process is to actually visualize multiple customer groups and identify those for whom the perceived value is the highest. At this stage, do not consider the economic dimensions of different customer targets. This will come into play later under compelling equity. Premature concentration on the purely economic side can lead firms to disregard potential targets that might turn out to be more profitable than they first appeared.

To see how all this comes together, consider what the customer value wedge would look like if applied to Wal-Mart's small-town customers at the time Sam Walton was building the firm. The insights that his exploration of customer value uncovered would certainly have included basic financial and functional considerations. His customers valued greater choice, lower prices, and convenience. However, at the more fundamental, intangible, and emotional levels, he surely uncovered more than that: lack of trust in both big-town commercial centers with their deals that seemed too good to be true, and high-priced local suppliers taking advantage of the lack of competition. Further reflection told him that local people felt slighted that no one deemed their town worthy of a large retail store. In small towns, simple things such as trust and community spirit are alive and meaningful.

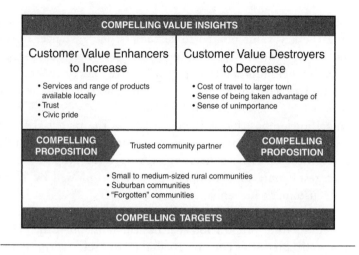

Figure 7.3 The compelling value path: Wal-Mart, 1960s to 1990s

Such are the insights that might be represented on the customer value wedge. But to turn those basic insights into actions that will build a power offer, we have to ask the four questions listed earlier, using the tool presented in Figure 7.2. This helps to map out the compelling value path to power offer design as set out in Figure 7.3. But we're not home yet. This is only half the story. The next step is to consider the insights gained from an exploration of customer equity.

The Compelling Equity Path to the Power Offer

The process of using the information gleaned in exploring customer equity for the design of a power offer follows the same steps as the search for compelling customer value. They're symmetrical, but because the exploration is conducted from a different perspective, the principal focus is different.

Whereas compelling customer value involves the trade-off of *customers'* perceived costs and benefits, compelling customer equity looks at the balance of the cost to the *firm* of serving a particular customer group and the benefits that accrue from serving it. Just as different products can either create or destroy value for different types of customers, so too can those different types of customers create or destroy equity for the firm. The point is to optimize the equity that the customers represent.

The four central issues here are as follows:

- **Customer equity enhancers.** Where is the greatest potential for extracting equity for the firm by *increasing* the business benefits from serving specific customer groups?
- **Customer equity destroyers.** Where is the greatest potential for extracting equity for the firm by *decreasing* the business costs generated when serving specific customer groups?
- **Compelling target.** What customer group offers the greatest equity to the firm?
- **Compelling propositions.** What value propositions have the potential to secure equity from the targeted customer group?

Let's revisit Dell's relationship during the 1990s with corporate customers already considered in the previous chapter and apply it to the compelling equity path leading to power offer design. Note that the layout of the compelling equity path in Figure 7.4 is similar to the compelling value path presented in Figure 7.2. The key difference is that the objectives of the central and bottom boxes are inverted. In the central box we must now concentrate on identifying the single source of compelling equity to be targeted, and in the bottom box our task is to reveal a number of value propositions that will be particularly compelling to that targeted equity, rather than the other way around.[9]

Dell's initial direct business model, addressed mainly to individual consumers, was a very effective power offer, but the firm soon identified potential growth opportunities with large business customers. The previous two chapters described some of the novel actions the company took in this market, including moving resident engineers to customer sites and preloading customer-specific software on the delivered PCs. To penetrate this highly competitive market, Dell's challenge was to find ways to provide superior customer value to generate superior customer equity. They succeeded. On the customer equity side, they found ways to increase the benefits derived from customers while decreasing the costs of serving them, as Figure 7.4 illustrates. Dell became perceived as a value partner to business customers who were particularly demanding about getting good value for money from the total cost of their IT equipment, including servicing expenses. Dell generated enormous equity and, with that, momentum-powered growth over many years.

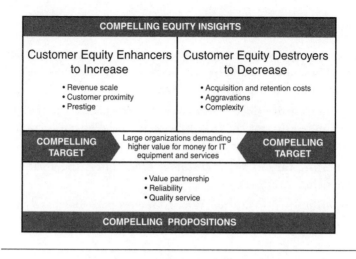

Figure 7.4 The compelling equity path: Dell and corporate customers, 1990s

Some observers claim that Dell was a one-trick pony and that the trick—innovative and effective supply chain management—has now been matched by competitors. This is a narrow perspective of a much more strategic problem. Dell's momentum stalled because it failed to continually reinvigorate its power offer both in terms of compelling value and of compelling equity. Dell took its eye off the ball in terms of reliability, quality, and service, all key drivers of value, and especially for the more-demanding corporate market. It also began to miss a number of emerging sources of compelling equity back in the consumer market, just two of which were digital camera owners and the gaming community.[10] Both customer value and customer equity require constant exploration, insights, and actions to remain at a compelling level and to fuel a power offer.

The Pillars of a Power Offer

The two paths that explore the rich spaces of compelling value and compelling equity meet at the point of the power offer's design. From different perspectives, each brings qualified options for two key aspects of a power offer: the compelling target and the compelling proposition that will attract them. These different options have to be compared, reconciled, and eventually integrated to develop the most powerful offer possible: the offer that simultaneously optimizes customer value and customer equity. Although we talk about a "power offer," we should really think of it as a *double* power offer—one that provides most value to the customer and most equity to the firm. It is the synergy offered by this double-sided character of power offers that makes them so efficient. The compelling customer value means customers buy more and for a longer period of time—hence compelling equity. The compelling equity allows the firm to invest more in increasing customer value. It is a virtuous circle that builds more and more momentum.

After the key elements stemming from the twin explorations have been reconciled, they must be subjected to the third component of power offer design: power crafting. The existence of this third component has been implicit throughout this chapter. We didn't make it explicit until now because focusing too early on a power offer's specifications has a tendency to stop the exploration before all the potential opportunities have been uncovered. This is exactly what happens in many large, established firms. The tendency is to be impatient, to want results fast, and to jump on the earliest glimmer of solutions to nail down uncertainties. But the whole process of exploration and convergence must be given adequate time. Only when this process has matured can it move to the power-crafting stage.

To appreciate the scope of power crafting, it is important to remember that a power offer is much more than a product or a service—it is the entire set of elements that influence the value that the targeted customers perceive. A central principle of momentum strategy is that a firm delivers to customers not just a product, but value. As a result, power crafting includes technological and operational elements (that is, possible product specifications), economic considerations (that is, pricing and the business model), and image (that is, communication, media, distribution).

An example of how the process differs from traditional design can be seen in the Opel Astra GTC, launched by GM Europe in 2005. The traditional design view was that the three-door model of a car should sell for less than the five-door version—after all, it's just a five-door car minus two doors and so should run about €500 cheaper. Not the new three-door Astra GTC. It was introduced with a sporty design, great communications, and at the same list price as the five-door version. In fact, the average transaction price ended up being close to €2,000 *more* than the five-door version.

Why? Because the crafting of the new design and associated communications created compelling value for a different customer target than had previously been attracted to three-door cars. Its buyers were no longer those people who couldn't afford a five-door car but a younger, wealthier customer group who liked its sporty looks and image. As a result, they were much more likely to purchase the versions with more powerful engines and additional trim such as alloy wheels and expensive sound systems. All three pillars of power offer design propelled an exceptional growth for the Opel Astra GTC.[11]

Compelling proposition, compelling target, and power crafting are the three pillars of a power offer. As shown in Figure 7.5, they are intrinsically interactive, and the process of designing a power offer involves aligning all three to form a coherent whole. The compelling proposition summarizes what makes a power offer attractive for customers. Its shorthand expression is an inspirational guide that should both connect with customers and drive everyone involved in crafting the offer.

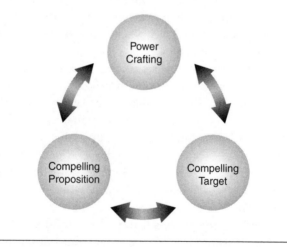

Figure 7.5 The three pillars of a power offer

The compelling target identifies the core customer group to be served to maximize equity. For the BMW 5 Series, successful business executives are a customer target group with high equity. Again, the customer target should be expressed in shorthand form to serve as an inspirational guide for customers and for anyone involved with the design of the offer, but the key is to remember that it is the compelling equity for which this shorthand stands that is vital.

Finally, power crafting translates the compelling proposition and compelling target into a tangible power offer: developing the intended offer, from its physical appearance to its price, image, delivery, and anything else that carries value to customers. Power crafting involves myriad details and can be successful only with the guidance of a clear compelling proposition and compelling target. But it is also the process that ensures the compelling proposition is delivered and that it is not really just a marketing slogan that leaves a sour taste in consumers' mouths. It is the process that ensures that the compelling target is truly captivated by the offer and not frustrated by an unfulfilled promise. And, it is the process that forces you to revisit the selected proposition and target and polish them until they are in perfect shining alignment—until they are truly compelling. The sign of excellent crafting is that the compelling proposition and target seem obvious to all those experiencing the offer. Its final objective is to simultaneously produce the superior value and equity that will create customer traction and momentum.

Let's now review in more detail each of the three pillars of a power offer.

Compelling Proposition

A power offer must deliver compelling value to its target customer. This value must be encapsulated in a compelling proposition. This should crystallize, in just a few words, the deepest emotional elements of perceived value—those that drive purchasing behavior. It might look like a slogan, a unique selling point, or a positioning statement, but it is much broader than concepts that focus on communication to customers. The compelling proposition points to the core of the offer. It must simultaneously be attractive to customers and inspire those who craft and deliver the offer. Both, however, must be aware that it is mere shorthand for the richer package of compelling value contained in the offer.

Be it *trust* or *community* for Wal-Mart, *fashion* for Swatch, or *togetherness* for the Wii, these words are seldom used in the brand communication of these firms, but they are at the core of their compelling value. And they are the key emotional drivers of purchasing behavior. Wal-Mart has long emphasized its "everyday low prices"—the financial element of the value it delivers to its customers. But behind this very pragmatic communication, the real emotional driver for its core customer group is trust. Beyond low prices, this trust has been established through systematic behavior demonstrating a genuine care for its customers' interests. This customer trust is the essence of Wal-Mart. That is its compelling proposition. As such, it is at the heart of the company's successful momentum growth, and it has to be protected at all costs. If Wal-Mart were to lose this compelling proposition, it would become a different and much less successful company, even if it were still practicing "everyday low prices."

Swatch is a "fashion accessory that happens to be a watch." As described earlier, this strong, resonant, and compelling proposition of fashion evolved progressively. It took Swatch a long time to discover and crystallize this value proposition. But it clearly marks which kind of customers will probably buy its offers and what the company should expect from them. It is not just a communication promise. It is supported by innovative designs that are being constantly renewed. More than twenty years after its creation, Swatch is still setting new trends and enjoying profitable growth.

Compelling Target

A compelling target has two dimensions that are present in all power offers, including those of Rentokil, Dell, SWA, Swatch, and First Direct. First, resonance: the fit between the compelling proposition and the compelling target, resulting in a superior perceived customer value, a compelling value. Second, the economic significance of the compelling target in terms of the contribution it can make to the profitable growth of the firm—the compelling equity they offer. The two are inextricably linked. If the resonance between the target and the proposition is weak, the economic significance of the target will be correspondingly lower; it will fail to be compelling.

The Swedish furniture firm IKEA is an excellent example of both aspects. Ingvar Kamprad, its eccentric, hands-on founder, has always been clear that IKEA targets people with "thin wallets," as he calls them. For IKEA's customers, money is more valuable than time. To save money, they are prepared to invest their time traveling to the store, getting sucked into its labyrinthine retail environment, and assembling their own furniture. A large proportion of them are young couples who are setting up their first home. This targeting is so effective that it has been estimated that 10 percent of all Europeans alive today were conceived in IKEA beds![12] This customer selection ties in neatly to IKEA's key proposition, which is all about democratic design: making intelligently conceived furniture accessible to the masses. The company creates value by passing on some traditional manufacturing costs to its customers—they must assemble their own furniture from flat packs.[13]

Compelling targets, like compelling propositions, should evolve. Power offers should always be led by economic significance and resonance, and as these change, so, too, must a power offer. Many traditional luxury names such as Gucci, Louis Vuitton, and Dunhill were established by catering to aristocrats and the very wealthy. The resonance between these customer groups and the original value proposition of exclusive quality established them as power offers. But the size of these customer groups eventually represented a limit for growth. The success of these luxury goods as power offers was obtained through a progressive extension of the compelling proposition toward fashion and social assertiveness. This caused the targeted audience to grow and become more compelling, offering more growth opportunities and a new momentum.

Power Crafting

Power crafting requires every possible design element to be integrated to deliver the highest possible value to targeted customers and extract the highest possible equity for the firm. These elements can concern any aspect, tangible or perceived, of a product or a service. They can be crafted through a variety of means, including technology, design, manufacturing, pricing, packaging, advertising, promotion, and distribution. It involves all aspects, both internal and external, that might influence the value of the offer as perceived by customers.

First Direct knew that as a virtual bank, the quality of its call center employees' interaction with its customers was critical. Part of the crafting of its offer was to recruit and train people who sound like human beings rather than automatons. They respond to their caller's tone of voice and strike the right balance between respect and friendliness. They may engage in spontaneous small talk if appropriate, but, if not, they project an air of calm professionalism and efficiency. Either way, the customer's positive feelings about the bank are reinforced every time they call.[14]

The following is a slightly edited transcript of a typical conversation between a First Direct customer we'll call Mr. Scott and a call center employee:

> *Mr. Scott*: I'm going skiing in the States. Can you tell me if there is a cash machine in Vail, Colorado, please?
>
> *Employee*: I'll need to ask you to hold the line for a minute while I find that information for you, sir.
>
> *Mr. Scott*: Thank you.
>
> *Employee*: Hello, yes, in fact, there is a Cirrus ATM machine at the First Interstate Bank at 38 Redbird Drive in Vail.
>
> *Mr. Scott*: In that case, I'll only take $500 in cash with me and use the cash machine at the resort.
>
> *Employee*: Right. I'll put in an order for $500. Shall I debit your checking account and have the currency delivered by registered mail to your home address?
>
> *Mr. Scott*: Yes, please.
>
> *Employee*: Thank you, sir. You should receive it within three days. We'll include a confirmation of the amount deducted. Have a nice trip!

A few weeks later, the same customer calls First Direct for another transaction. This time it is a different employee who takes the call:

> *Employee*: Hello, First Direct. How may I help you?
>
> *Mr. Scott*: Good evening. I would like to make a payment to British Gas, please.
>
> *Employee*: Thank you Mr. Scott. I'll be glad to arrange your payment to British Gas. By the way, were you able to find the First Interstate cash machine in Vail when you were on your skiing holiday in Colorado? I hope everything went well.

The bank's advertising states, "We always hire people who are naturally approachable and friendly and train them to become bankers. It's much easier than hiring bankers and training them to be approachable and friendly people."[15] It's not just a joke at their competitors' expense—it is an integral part of the power offer and just one example of the excellent power crafting that went into it.

The sheer vastness of the task of power crafting makes it essential that the compelling target and the compelling proposition are fully understood throughout a firm. The crystallized vision of these two elements forms the essential guide for the firm and all its stakeholders to craft a coherent and most effective power offer. This is what underlies the success of First Direct, and it is certainly not visible to the outsiders who visit its call centers, because they simply experience the outcome of the crafting. This is also what underlies all the firms discussed so far, across a variety of industries, when they enjoyed the momentum generated by power offers, including Dell, Rentokil, SWA, Wal-Mart, Virgin, IKEA, Swatch, and Gucci.

The Virtuous Circle of Power Offer Design

A compelling proposition, a compelling target, or strong power crafting can often be sufficient by itself to make an ordinary product successful. Frequently, one of these three elements lies at the origin of what eventually becomes a power offer. But what creates real momentum growth is the synergy that develops when these three pillars of a power offer are aligned and resonant.

The quality of First Direct's power offer stems from this level of resonance. Its targeted customers are time hungry, busy, well educated, financially aware, and in their early middle years. Apart from the obvious functional and financial drivers of customer value, they are also open to innovation, and they value convenience, service, and flexibility. They want a personalized and responsive service they can trust. At a more fundamental level, they expect to be treated with respect, and it is respect that is at the core of First Direct's compelling proposition.

The equity that customers of this sort offer in return is a high level of engagement with anyone who can meet their needs. When it happens, they tend to be pleasant people to do business with. Their high level of financial awareness makes them easy to sell to and unlikely to waste First Direct's time. Their age, combined with their financial and social profile, means that they are likely to be big consumers of high-ticket financial services such as mortgages, insurance, and investments.

Matching this compelling proposition with an equally compelling target required innovative power crafting across a vast array of components, including call center technology, employee recruitment and training, customer-focused corporate culture, low-cost operations, intelligent communications, branding, and, of course, attractive financial products.[16]

It is this convergence between compelling proposition, compelling target, and power crafting that makes First Direct's offer so powerful. The three elements feed on one another, and the synergy they create is dynamite. Plenty of other telephone and Internet services chewed on the same idea and failed. They weren't able to come up with a power offer that brought an enthusiastic response. But First Direct got the cocktail just right. Their customers find the bank virtually irresistible.

The almost-perfect convergence of a power offer's three pillars is what makes power offers look obvious after the fact: "Why didn't we think of that?" But the process of generating such a neat outcome is far from easy, and it is certainly not linear. As we have seen, it first requires exploration to identify new insights that will increase both customer value and customer equity. Compelling value and compelling equity must be contrasted and harmonized to refine a single compelling proposition and its matching compelling target. They then have to be worked through power crafting that will bring new insights for technological and economic realities.

Only an iterative process can create such a strong convergence. Each component influences the other. The selection of a customer target will influence the most appropriate value proposition, and vice versa. Each provides essential guidance for power crafting, which in turn informs, enriches, and refines the others. The power of these three components must be optimized, and all have to be mutually supportive, coherent, and aligned. This always takes multiple iterations, with each one getting more compelling and powerful. The idea of a clean, linear process in the development of a power offer is rationalization after the event of a richer and messier process.

Business cemeteries are packed with products that failed to be sufficiently attractive in any of the three pillars. More exploration and optimization on any of them could have saved many and built a strong base for growth. Even more common are products that need inflated marketing budgets to do battle in crowded markets. These products would have more power if their value proposition, customer target, and crafting were improved and fine-tuned to create resonance. And it is resonance that provides the power for new momentum.

Design for Traction

Momentum strategy is about developing power offers that get the customer traction to build momentum. This momentum delivers superior growth while requiring fewer marketing resources than less-compelling offers require. As a result, momentum-powered firms can grow with a level of efficiency of which their competitors can only dream.

The design of such power offers is the crucial phase in creating momentum. It is the culmination of the discovery of compelling customer insights, along with the exploration for customer value and customer equity. It stands or falls depending on the quality and coherence of the three pillars: a compelling proposition, a compelling target, and power crafting.

These are the guiding principles that we have established for the effective design of power offers:

- Power offers resonate with targeted customer needs so vigorously that they "sell themselves" while simultaneously offering superior profitability to the firm.

- The exploration of customer value should determine the single compelling proposition with the highest potential to deliver compelling value. It will also identify several potentially compelling targets for which that compelling proposition has the most resonance.

- The exploration of customer equity should determine the compelling target that offers the firm the highest potential to extract compelling equity. It will also identify several potentially compelling propositions that have the most resonance for this group.

- Power crafting integrates every possible design element to deliver the highest value to targeted customers and the highest possible equity to the firm.

- Maximum momentum is achieved when a power offer perfectly aligns the three pillars of a compelling proposition, a compelling target, and power crafting in such a way as to truly resonate with customers. To achieve this, the design process must be iterative and continuous.

No power offer ever arrives perfectly formed like Venus emerging from the sea. It takes a lot of tinkering and polishing. All three pillars must be continuously fine-tuned, improved, and better aligned: tweaking the value proposition, shifting the customer target, and improving the crafting. This is the perpetual process of removing any sources of friction that could negate the impact of the power offer and slow the momentum it generates.

The work is not over once the power offer is designed and taken to market. In fact, it has just begun. As we shall see in Part III, "Executing Momentum," execution of the power offer is itself an iterative process. The lessons learned as the offer is delivered and begins to generate customer momentum can be fed back into the design process to improve the offer's efficiency and add to the process of discovering compelling customer insights. This is how the perpetual motion of customer momentum begins.

PART III

Executing Momentum

8

Power Offer Execution

A Tape Recorder That Didn't Record

As shown earlier in this book, the iPod is a great power offer, but, interestingly, its success is built on a competitor's earlier power offer. It is well known that Sony originated the era of personal portable sound systems with the Walkman but missed the opportunity to do it again in digital music players. What is less known, however, is the genesis of the Walkman's huge success—it was due to a crucial course-changing decision made well after its design was completed. This innovative product was saved from premature death only by a brilliant change at the point where design hits execution.

Back in 1979, Sony was having trouble with the launch of its revolutionary new offer. The problem? The Walkman met skeptical resistance from potential users, retailers, and the press alike. Its portability was appreciated, but it had an important perceived defect: its inability to record. Consumers compared it with what they were familiar with, a tape recorder—they saw what it couldn't do rather than what it could do.

Sony thought of a way to change that. The company distributed the Walkman to young recruits in Tokyo, New York, and other large cities and told them to just stand on street corners enjoying the music. If anyone asked them what they were doing, they were to place their headphones over the enquirer's ears. With this, the perception of the Walkman was instantly transformed from a tape recorder that couldn't record into a portable personal sound system. The basis of comparison was no longer a tape recorder but a "ghetto blaster," the huge, (barely) portable sound system so frequently seen at the time being lugged on teenagers' shoulders. Literally, there was no comparison—the Walkman won the sound and portability battle hands down.[1]

The Walkman achieved tremendous momentum and contributed to making Sony an exemplary momentum-powered firm at the time. The click that changed everything was a brilliant initiative at the execution stage, one that corrected the perception of a noncompelling proposition in an otherwise technically innovative, well-designed product.

The Execution of the Power Offer

The principal difference between design and execution relates to where the two activities are conducted. Although design must, of course, be externally focused to be successful, the process is largely internal, where the firm has control over the variables. On the other hand, execution happens in the outside world, where unexpected reactions and events can make a mockery of the best laid plans and force rapid reengineering of offers that once appeared perfect.

The first step in execution is to ensure that the design is properly implemented as originally intended, but that's only the first step. To increase the intensity of the momentum effect, momentum-powered firms continually improve their offers by learning from the experience of customer reactions. Sony rapidly realized that something was wrong with the way the Walkman was demonstrating its value, so the company quickly searched to optimize the perceived customer value inherent in its offer through a clearer and more compelling proposition.

This interactive process between the design and execution of power offers is at the core of momentum strategy. It has implications for the underlying logic of running a business. It represents a new business model.

From Product Focus to Value Focus

Traditionally, firms' operations have been product focused. The emphasis has been this: Develop the product, make the product, sell the product. This is the easiest way to run a business. It corresponds to the specialties of separate departments of the firm. It is the natural outcome of how companies are organized.

Customer considerations, such as market research and customer product tests, are often added on top of this product-centered approach, but they are peripheral. Even if they use the tools and jargon of customer research, these firms are instinctively inward looking. This approach critically limits the growth potential of momentum-deficient firms. However, it still dominates the business world—it is the easiest way to manage.

A second business model, based on the concept of "value delivery," emerged in the late 1980s. As competition increased and customers became more demanding, more firms focused on customers and the value delivered to them. This approach clearly recognizes that customers do not purchase products for what they are but for the value they carry.[2]

A value-delivery-based model has three key phases: Select the value proposition, create the value, and communicate the value. In the case of Swatch, we could say that the value selected was fashion. This value was created through the use of professional designers hired from outside the watch industry, and this value was effectively communicated through advertising, packaging, point-of-sale displays, and public relations.

One of the direct implications of the value-delivery approach is that multifunctional teams are essential to encourage effective cooperation between departments, especially R&D, marketing, and operations. This is unquestionably a vast improvement on the traditional product-based approach. Firms that adopted it improved the quality of their offers and opened new growth opportunities for themselves.

Momentum as a New Business Model

As a business model, momentum goes much further. Its ambition is to create extraordinary growth through customer traction. It is impossible to achieve this through a traditional linear process. The momentum approach takes the value-delivery perspective into an interactive and iterative mode in two ways. We illustrated the first one in Chapter 7,

"Power Offer Design," in particular with the example of Swatch. We have seen how the design of a power offer follows an *iterative process:* Dynamic iterations are essential to achieve a compelling proposition, a compelling target, and power crafting that will create the resonance necessary for a power offer.

The second need for constant interaction is between design and execution—a permanent state of flux between the two that enables each to feed off, and improve, the other. For this to happen, one must recognize that continuous improvements, both in design and execution, are possible and necessary to make the offer more compelling and more powerful. These two phases follow exactly the same process, as shown in Figure 8.1. As the Walkman example demonstrates, new insights can appear in the field and dramatically increase a product's momentum and growth potential. These insights can either lead to ad hoc adjustments in the field or be fed back to design. Either way, they continuously improve the offer and its momentum potential.

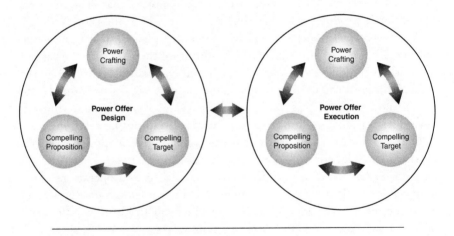

Figure 8.1 The momentum business model

This symbiotic relationship between design and execution requires humility—it is a recognition that, even with an excellent outside-in perspective, no design can be perfect. In addition, the competition will improve its own offers, and customers' expectations will keep increasing. Power offers must be constantly and rapidly reworked in light of new customer discoveries. A key strength of momentum strategy is the way that it encourages firms to learn from their external environment and to act swiftly on their discoveries.

The momentum business model reflects the story of great power-offer successes. These were not the results of tidy, compartmentalized, linear stages but, rather, of multiple, iterative interactions. Two of these interactions are particularly important. The first concerns the search for a continuous and ever more powerful resonance between the three pillars of a power offer, and the second deals with efforts to ensure an effective synergy between design and execution of the offer.

The Dynamic Evolution of Power Offers

A power offer's dynamic evolution means that its compelling proposition, compelling target, and power crafting must be adapted where needed. The order in which we present these three pillars, however, should not be considered as a prescribed sequence. Successful power offers have emerged from product, distribution, or communication innovations (power crafting); from the identification of a potential valuable group of customers (compelling target); or from an unsatisfied need (compelling proposition). Imposition of a dogmatic sequence would reduce opportunities for a free and aggressive entrepreneurial approach. You have to start from an insight with potential, whatever its origin, and build on it to transform it into a powerful offer. One might want to approach the design phase with an organized process, but the need for opportunistic initiative is especially strong in the execution phase, where direct customer experience will bring new inputs in a noncontrolled fashion.

In what order the process is conducted, and where each subsequent improvement of the offer starts, is *totally irrelevant*. What is important is to grab opportunities to improve the power inherent in an offer, to strengthen each of its three components, and to ensure that they are mutually supportive, coherent, and aligned.

Whatever the starting point, compelling proposition, compelling target, and power crafting must be continuously improved and aligned throughout the design and execution phases, and over the life of a power offer. This is true at all levels, from a specific product to an entire firm. Let's illustrate this point by taking a fresh look at an old story. How do the successes and misfortunes of IBM over 50 years of its history look when viewed from the perspective of the momentum model?[3]

Figure 8.2 shows a power-offer perspective covering more than half a century of IT in business. It is a simplified view, and it has its limits, but it highlights the crucial value drivers in terms of compelling proposition, compelling target, and power crafting. The first phase was the establishment of IT as an essential tool for managing a modern corporation.[4] Business computers were brought in to replace clerical workers performing repetitive tasks such as payroll, and to do them more cheaply and reliably. Typically, suppliers would contact computer managers and make feasibility studies and proposals for investing in these impressive new machines.

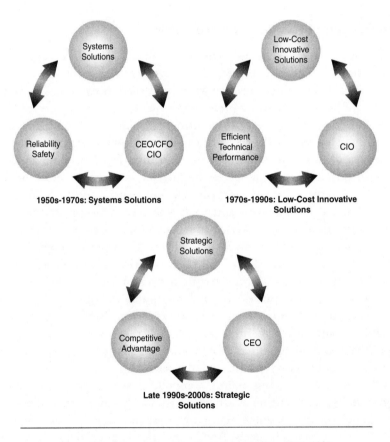

Figure 8.2 The evolution of business IT power offers, 1955–2005

Given the size of the investments and the potential impact on the business, IBM understood that the key decision makers were not the computer experts but the chief executives and heads of finance, CEOs, and CFOs. It also realized that because early generations of computers were unreliable, CEOs were kept awake at night worrying that massive computer failure could threaten the entire business. IBM understood who the key decision makers were and the deep emotional costs and benefits tugging at them in relation to their computer-purchasing decisions. Unlike its competitors, IBM systematically built relationships with CEOs and CFOs to create the compelling proposition of reliability.

IBM's whole offer was crafted to resonate with this compelling target and this compelling proposition. The company carefully built a reputation for high-quality service and rapid reaction to problems. Over the years, word got around that "Nobody got fired for buying IBM." Its price was generally set 15 percent higher than its competition.

IBM's power crafting, from R&D to service to pricing, was coherent and in line with the compelling proposition of reliability that resonated with its compelling target. A revealing example of this resonance was the dress of its salesmen: dark blue suit, black tie, and white shirt. Competitors made derisive remarks about IBM's dark blue "uniforms" but only half-understood that this dress code was the sign of a coherent, resonant strategy—and part of a power offer.

The company's momentum strategy had created a power offer that generated tremendous momentum, and it demonstrated continuous excellence in the design and adaptation of its power offer. IBM won a dominant position, with a global market share in excess of 70 percent in mainframe computers.

However, the situation evolved, and IBM's offer became less in tune with customers' requirements. Computer reliability increased to the point that it was no longer a salient issue—PCs became routine business investments. Technology progressed more rapidly, and competition developed new power offers with mini-computers and later with microcomputers. Purchasing decisions moved down the client organization. CIOs wanted low-cost innovative solutions providing higher performance.[5]

IBM had become so dominant that it was no longer listening to its customers, not understanding the strategic nature of the changes in its environment, adapting too slowly to a changing world. It failed to take its offer through the constantly iterative process of design and execution. Its power offer stagnated and lost its power. The company lost its momentum.

The impact was so dramatic that IBM entered a major crisis in the early 1990s that led to the appointment of Lou Gerstner as its new CEO. We look at Gerstner's style of leadership in some detail in Chapter 13, "Momentum Leadership," but what is important here is to understand how he designed and executed a new power offer, one well adapted to the industry's new challenges. Gerstner realized that the customer world was evolving again, into one in which IT could provide businesses with strategic solutions and a competitive advantage based on new technologies such as the Internet, networks, servers, databases, and process application software. This was a compelling proposition of direct interest for CEOs, and it led to large-scale projects with tremendous potential in customer equity. It required stronger integration of its product lines, a major investment in new consulting services, and alliances with partners. The new power offer revived IBM, gave it renewed momentum, and propelled it on to a new growth course.[6]

It is good to see that momentum can be regained, but it does not have to be lost in the first place. Gaining and maintaining momentum is all about continuously improving the power behind the offers. And this is done by systematically reconsidering their crafting, their compelling proposition, and their compelling target, at the design stage and in the field.

The Business Value of Momentum

As mentioned in an earlier chapter, the word *power* in the expression *power offers* has a double meaning: power with customers and power to generate growth. Obviously, the two are connected. Power with customers provides the traction for the momentum that powers growth. Efficient growth is the ultimate business impact of momentum—it has the power to propel a firm into a different league.

This is not just a dramatic figure of speech. We have empirical research and computer modeling to substantiate it. We often find that even the most talented and experienced business leaders totally underestimate the astonishing returns that momentum can generate, simply because visualizing dynamics over time requires us to think in too many directions at once. If you ever need to convince a financial analyst why momentum matters, the following section, demonstrating the impact of very small changes in a few key drivers of performance, will help you make the business case.

Imagine this two-firm scenario. Momentum-Powered Inc. is a company with a strong power offer. Momentum-Deficient Inc. is one with a perfectly decent and competitive, albeit unexceptional, offer. We have run these two firms through a computerized simulation that shows how a few momentum-based differences between the two firms will have a massive impact on future growth.

At the start of our comparison, both firms are identical in respects other than the power offer. They both generate the same revenue and make the same profit from their current product. Both have the same number of customers, both acquire the same number of new customers through marketing activity each year, and both spend the same amount on marketing to get them. In addition to this marketing spend, their other costs in delivering their products are the same. Furthermore, each firm is launching a new product. The firms are selling their new products at the same price and are making the same margin and the same marketing investment.

Excellent execution accelerates momentum in a number of ways that we review in the following chapters, but in this simulation let's consider just four: sales growth, cost efficiency, cross-selling, and customer recommendations. We will assume that Momentum-Powered Inc. derives advantages from these four drivers. However, to demonstrate the power of these drivers' ability to deliver momentum, for the sake of this simulation we assume very small improvements and investigate the impact on total growth.

Because Momentum-Powered Inc. has a greater understanding of its customers' needs, its offer is more powerful. As a result, its customers buy more. In most cases, this impact can be significant, but for argument's sake, let's assume that its better offer adds just 1 percent a year to its revenue growth. Consider how many more iPods and Wiis are sold than alternative products, and you'll agree that we are allowing Momentum-Powered Inc. a very modest advantage.

In addition, its deeper understanding of what customers truly value and what they don't enables it to shave something off its costs. In the previous two chapters, we saw how the process of optimizing compelling customer value and compelling customer equity reveals areas in which costs can be eliminated. Remember that lower hardware costs enabled Nintendo to make a profit on the Wii while Sony and Microsoft were selling their games consoles at a loss. More dramatically, recall the way that some of the power offers we examined, such as Dell and First Direct, shaved 40 percent off the traditional cost base for their sector. Again, however, let's assume that this process skims just 1 percent a year from the costs of delivering value to the customer.

With the new product, we see the effect of the third way that momentum can impact results: cross-selling. The fact that Momentum-Powered Inc. enjoys greater customer engagement than Momentum-Deficient Inc. means that the two firms will have differing fortunes when it comes to convincing their existing customers to adopt their new product. Momentum-Powered Inc.'s customers trust it to deliver exceptional value, and its greater customer focus means that it is better at creating powerful offerings that will be enthusiastically adopted. Momentum-Deficient Inc.'s customers, on the other hand, although probably not dissatisfied, are not particularly engaged with it. They do not believe that its new product will be anything exceptional and might even view it with deep suspicion.

As a result, for the sake of this example, we have assumed that each year 5 percent of Momentum-Powered Inc.'s existing customers, just 1 in 20, will adopt its new offering. Because of their lower levels of trust and engagement, just 1 percent of Momentum-Deficient Inc.'s customers will do so with its new product.

Finally, let's consider a fourth accelerator of momentum: customer recommendations. Power offers tend to be so good that existing customers recommend them to friends. As a result, momentum-powered firms acquire a number of new customers every year solely by the free tool of recommendations. For instance, almost all Skype's customers came through recommendation, and many other Internet firms have also based their growth on such a model.

Our research has established that momentum-powered firms in more traditional industries can attract between a third and two-thirds of their new customers through word of mouth. At its peak, First Direct's acquisition from word-of-mouth recommendation every year equated to 15 percent of its existing customers convincing a friend to join. We'll continue to lowball our estimates and say that each year 5 percent of Momentum-Powered Inc.'s customers recommend it strongly enough to talk a friend into buying. Although some of Momentum-Deficient Inc.'s customers might recommend it, they rarely do so with much vigor. Consequently, a statistically insignificant number of people come to Momentum-Deficient Inc. via recommendation.

With these relatively modest differences in momentum drivers, how different will the destiny of these two firms be? Well, within five years, these two formerly comparable businesses have begun to operate in totally different leagues. Momentum-Deficient Inc. is performing well, but as Momentum-Powered Inc.'s performance accelerates, it leaves Momentum-Deficient Inc. in its wake. At the end of just five years, its profits are increasing more than twice as fast as Momentum-Deficient Inc., and it is generating 50 percent more profit than its former equal.[7] Managers usually wildly underestimate the impact of small improvements on key momentum drivers.

As discussed in the following chapters, these are only some of the momentum accelerators that firms can harness to drive performance— and our scenario allowed for only partial, modest improvements. Consider the possibilities if they were all harnessed and delivered their full potential! As the chain reaction of momentum takes hold and power offers help the business build more and more impetus, momentum-powered firms sail along on efficient long-term growth. Their potential for growth appears to be unlimited.

The Chain Reaction of the Power Offer

The ability of momentum-powered firms to deliver higher revenue and simultaneously reduce or redirect costs powers their performance. Think back to the Pushers and Pioneers we looked at in Chapter 1, "The Power of Momentum." Powered by their momentum, the Pioneers achieved almost double the revenue growth of the Pushers over 20 years. By achieving more for less, they deliver greater value to their customers and their stockholders. In the process, these firms become better and more rewarding places to work and more admired and respected by their other stakeholders. The momentum continues. The firm's performance improves further. On it goes. A chain reaction!

The Virtuous Circle of Momentum

The execution of a power offer is the beginning of a chain reaction that builds momentum and drives profitable growth: vibrant execution. At each link in the chain, the results get more powerful—each one provides further acceleration. And, as with the compelling design of a power offer, what sets momentum-powered firms apart is the scale of their ambition. They want their *power offer* to provide a deeply fulfilling customer experience. They are aiming for intense responses—responses at an emotional level, responses that are vibrant and alive.

This vibrancy and ambition runs through the whole second engine of momentum strategy: not just good customer satisfaction, but *vibrant satisfaction;* not just better-than-average customer retention, but *vibrant retention;* not just a level of customer engagement, but *vibrant engagement.* As shown in Figure 8.3, each of these four drivers of momentum accelerates the chain reaction of vibrant execution and increases the intensity of the momentum effect.

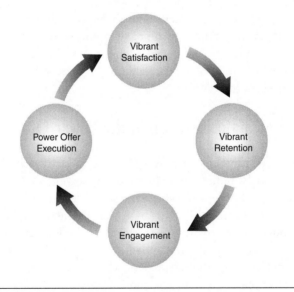

Figure 8.3   How momentum execution accelerates growth

The higher the level of customer satisfaction, the greater the vibrancy about it, and the more emotionally positive customers will become. The more positive the emotions, the more customers will be inclined to develop their relationship with a firm. Customer retention translates that emotional state into the action of continued, repeat business—if the retention is vibrant enough. The more vibrant their retention, the more likely they are to become engaged. The more vibrant their engagement, the more compelling their equity will become and the more compelling value they will reveal to a firm, enabling it to improve its offer further and create yet more vibrant levels of satisfaction.

It is an ambitious virtuous circle in constant motion, attracting customers, retaining them, and building their equity. Remember the example of Skype in Chapter 3, "The Road to Momentum." The vibrant levels of engagement it built up were the direct result of its customers' vibrant satisfaction and the fact that these customers have vibrant reasons for being retained. The level of engagement is evidenced by the way Skype's customers care about the firm—fans regularly contact Skype to offer advice on how the company can improve its offer. It is almost self-perpetuating. Successful power offers lead to vibrant satisfaction, which leads to vibrant retention, which leads to vibrant engagement, which in turn leads to even more powerful offers, which then further enhance customer satisfaction, and so on. This is real momentum.

After a power offer has created traction, the resources required to maintain momentum are minimal. This is because it is largely driven by the acceleration that each stage of the virtuous circle provides, as the Momentum-Powered Inc. and Momentum-Deficient Inc. scenario showed. The resources to create momentum in the first place have been invested *upstream,* in the exploration of customer value and customer equity that lead to the design of a power offer. This is a much more efficient way to generate growth than the dominant business practice of developing an offer with an internal focus and investing resources *downstream* to convince customers of its value. The momentum business model requires that financial and managerial resources be shifted upstream to generate higher growth more efficiently.

After momentum has been created through customer traction, it needs to be maintained and accelerated. This can be achieved in two phases: First, by ironing out any problems in the execution of the offer at each of three stages—customer satisfaction, customer retention, and customer engagement—by discovering sources of friction and mobilizing the entire organization to eradicate them. Second, by constantly learning from customers and feeding the resultant new insights and opportunities back into improvement of the power offer design.

Breaking the Vicious Circles

In contrast, momentum-deficient firms can be trapped in the vicious circle of peddling weak offers. They generate average satisfaction, which leads to customer defection or the passive retention of not-very-happy customers. This will generate either negative customer engagement or, at best, an absence of engagement. Either way, the offer will be weakened even further.

A vicious circle makes the generation of growth an uphill struggle for momentum-deficient firms. Momentum-deficient leaders are often preoccupied with managing internal forces because there's no momentum to power them along. Frequently, staff within large companies are tired and unmotivated. Their work is a struggle.

Generating growth in a company without momentum is a tall order. Employees need to be motivated, so firms invest resources to improve their effectiveness. Customers are dissatisfied, so money and resources go out to solve that problem. Customer retention is difficult, so firms try solutions such as expensive loyalty programs. And a lack of customer involvement requires higher investments in advertising.

These dreary scenarios show the vicious circle at work. Lack of customer focus forces organizations to compensate by plowing more resources into fueling growth. This is what we have called *compensating strategy*, and it is the exact opposite of momentum strategy. Admittedly, as the Pushers in our study demonstrate, it can work, but companies end up with customer churn. The vicious cycle persists, underlying profitability drops, and costs must be cut to compensate.

In such situations, paradoxically, many businesses still appear successful in terms of industry benchmarks. This is because benchmarks compare like with like. They look at "what is" rather than the unlimited potential of "what could be." Benchmarks in this sense are tools for maintaining mediocrity.

These vicious circles are very damaging for a firm, compensating for weak offers with expensive marketing and sales investments. These resources are often subsidized by other products that are weakened as a result. And they limit the investments that should be made upstream in developing improved offers.

In the end, these vicious circles are unsustainable. Business is likely to collapse when customers become more knowledgeable or when competition turns out a better offer. It is essential to identify vicious circles and break them before they break a business. This can be handled by gradually shifting resources upstream, away from inefficient compensating strategies and toward development of better offers. They must originate new value. To escape the vicious circle, one must craft power offers that will create customer traction and build a new momentum for efficient growth.

Building and Sustaining Momentum

After the power offer has been designed and set into action, the focus shifts. What counts now is the way that the chain reaction that produces momentum is built and nurtured. This process is the subject of the next three chapters. Two fundamental themes recur at each of the three stages of customer satisfaction, retention, and engagement: understanding the emotions that drive momentum, and executing a systematic action program to sustain momentum.

Understand the Emotional Drivers of Momentum

Emotions powerfully affect every stage of the momentum chain reaction. Understanding them is as crucial when executing a power offer as it was in designing it. Certainly every customer is different, but a few psychological drivers of emotions are universal. One of the most pertinent is dissatisfaction: Customers never settle for the status quo.

Consider the market for anti-ulcer drugs. That market has gone through multiple momentum cycles despite the fact that the "nearly perfect" drug was launched more than thirty years ago. Before SmithKline introduced Tagamet in 1976, the only treatment available for stomach ulcers had been highly unsatisfactory (painful, risky surgery). Tagamet's six-week remedy was an irresistible power offer. It cured most ulcers with practically no side effects, quickly achieved annual revenues of nearly $1 billion, and created enormous momentum for SmithKline. Then the firm got complacent. Figuring that the anti-ulcer problem was solved, SmithKline stopped its research efforts in this field.

Bad decision. In 1981, Glaxo introduced Zantac, a product that offered only marginal improvements on Tagamet. But, it was new, and it supplanted Tagamet as the power offer for ulcer treatment, reaching more than $3 billion in annual revenues. Glaxo gained tremendous momentum and became a leading global pharmaceutical firm. Could there be a greater success than this? Absolutely. In 1989, AstraZeneca launched Prilosec, which had a new mechanism of action. This drug achieved annual revenues in excess of $6 billion, created exceptional momentum, and led AstraZeneca to global status.[8] Wisely, the company improved on its own offer with a new drug, Nexium. This is currently the top brand on the market.

What is the root of all this? Human nature. Doctors and patients crave better solutions. Dissatisfaction drives the market, and companies will always develop more sophisticated and effective remedies. Tagamet's huge advance disappeared when more powerful offers became available. The same cycle has repeated itself four times in 30 years. It never stops. That's the human story.

And this fundamental human desire for progress cuts through every market. Human nature is the driving force behind momentum. This simple fact allows business enormous and endless growth potential.

Implement a Systematic Action Roadmap to Momentum

Be ambitious! Standard benchmark targets are not enough for surviving and thriving in business today. It is important that all the conditions that give rise to the momentum effect are in place and aligned, but it is even more important that they are intense. You must aim over the horizon for the ultimate goal of momentum: positive, active, *vibrant* involvement of customers with the firm and its offers.

Firms must understand their customer portfolio in terms of the forces that influence momentum and growth. For each stage of the execution process, they must have a feeling for what proportion of their customers loves them, repeatedly buys their products, and promotes them to their friends, but also what proportion has been disappointed, hates the firm, and actively denigrates it.

Building and sustaining momentum requires an approach to systematically nurture the forces that improve it, and to systematically decrease or eliminate the forces that hinder it. We have developed such an approach, and we will frequently refer to it in succeeding chapters with the acronym MDC. As shown in Figure 8.4, it stands for *mobilize* stakeholders, *detect* sources of frictions and insights, and *convert* customers.

Mobilize first, because momentum requires organizations to unify and motivate their stakeholders toward the single-minded pursuit of vibrant levels of customer satisfaction, retention, and engagement. Employees in particular are the interface between a firm and its customers. If they are not motivated to deliver a momentum-building experience for customers, all your other efforts are doomed to failure.

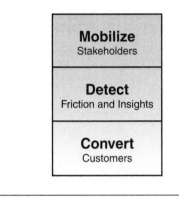

Figure 8.4 The MDC action roadmap to momentum

Detect second, because insights and sources of friction at all levels are the potential boosters and deterrents of momentum. Any factor that can slow down momentum in any way should be identified and removed. Similarly, new insights to increase customer value or customer equity should be spotted and acted on.

Convert third, because momentum ultimately depends on increasing the number of customers with vibrant emotions for the firm and its products. Removing friction and acting on insights will create a strong positive engagement and accelerate momentum. Critical customer feedback is always an opportunity for improvement. Ill-disposed customers and ex-customers can damage momentum, so it is imperative to take action to reverse their negative emotions. Equally important is to continuously search for ways to make existing customers even more satisfied, more loyal, and more engaged. And finally, new insights should always be exploited to help convert noncustomers and bring them into the company's fold.

The MDC roadmap helps firms mount a systematic search for momentum killers and boosters in all three areas: mobilization of people, detection of insights and sources of friction, and conversion of customers. The roadmap, along with the insights that we will develop over the next three chapters, will deepen and sharpen your perspective on momentum. The outcome should guide your actions to foster profitable growth. The momentum execution matrix in Figure 8.5 is a valuable tool to display the key momentum killers and boosters that require your total attention at each of the four stages in the virtuous circle of momentum execution. It is your strategic agenda for momentum execution toward exceptional growth.

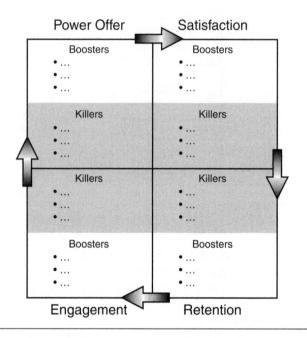

Figure 8.5 The momentum execution matrix

Turn Traction into Momentum

A power offer creates traction. Execution of the offer uses that traction to generate momentum. But execution does not cease once momentum has been established—far from it. The initial momentum must be maintained and enhanced through a process of continuous adjustment and improvement.

We have established five guiding principles for effectively executing power offers:

■ The momentum business model builds and aligns the three pillars of a power offer: a compelling proposition, a compelling target, and power crafting, so that they resonate and create customer traction.

This iterative process extends from design to execution and back again. Design and execution are much more powerful if they are symbiotic.

- Continuous adaptations and improvements must be explored during the execution of a power offer and fed back into its design. Focusing on a power offer's three pillars helps detect tactical opportunities for improvement.

- Relatively small changes in momentum drivers such as retention, cross-selling, and customer recommendations can have a substantial and sustainable impact on a firm's future competitive position.

- The accelerating effects of four related components: power offer, vibrant levels of customer satisfaction, retention, and engagement, lend a potent thrust to momentum. These four components support each other in a virtuous circle.

- Building and maintaining momentum requires a clear understanding of the emotional drivers of behavior and a systematic roadmap for action that we call MDC, for *mobilize, detect,* and *convert.*

One of the telling characteristics of a well-executed power offer is its efficiency. Power offers prove that less is more. Momentum-powered firms achieve more while spending less in the execution phase. They do not have to compensate for a lesser offer with expensive tactics aimed at luring customers. They instead benefit from the tremendous power of customer traction. To follow in their footsteps, we must shift resources from downstream to upstream activities. Engineer an offer with customer traction built-in instead of trying to convince customers of its worth when it has to be sold.

After momentum has been established, a firm must continuously seek to maintain and accelerate it. This is the subject of the next chapters. They show how a systematic approach can help firms develop and maintain the momentum that will make them join the Momentum League—and enjoy exceptional growth.

9

Vibrant Satisfaction

Moments of Truth

The most important moments in the relationship between a company and its customers are the intersections, the points where they encounter each other. This is when value is delivered—the moments of truth,[1] as Jan Carlzon, the former head of Scandinavian Airlines, termed them. It is irrelevant who instigates them or where, when, why, or how these encounters happen. Every single one of these moments matters.

For his company, Carlzon said, they represented fifty million battles that he could win or lose. At the other end of the scale, A.G. Lafley, chief executive of Procter & Gamble, wants his whole organization to focus on two crucial encounters:

There are two moments of truth that we compete for. First, whenever the customer shops, we stand for election, and either we get her vote or somebody else does. The second moment of truth is when she, or a member of her family, uses our products and they are either satisfied or they are not. Being aware of this has proved incredibly focusing.[2]

The accumulation of moments of truth shapes a customer's experiences of a product or service and crafts his or her perceptions of the value received from the firm. If the firm wins, these moments feed customer satisfaction, which in turn fuels customer traction and momentum.

It is up to leaders to frame the concept of moments of truth as they like, whether in Carlzon's millions or by Lafley's focus of merely two. However framed, these moments of truth directly impact customer satisfaction.

If the design and execution of the power offer are successful, the moments of truth will provide superior customer experiences. They will create vibrant customer satisfaction and offer the first evidence of the customer traction inherent in the power offer.

Why Vibrant?

Many companies have a significant number of customers whose relationship with the firm never develops beyond the transactional. There is no emotional connection. To generate the momentum effect requires a much deeper and more committed relationship than that offered by passive customers who just don't complain. Companies should measure their success by the number of *delighted* customers they have—people so thrilled with a product or service that they can't help but tell others about it.[3]

Aiming to satisfy customers is not enough. That is an average, complacent, and mediocre goal. Momentum-powered firms are more ambitious in their customer satisfaction objectives. Their target is truly intense, can't-imagine-any-better satisfaction—vibrant satisfaction.

The basics of customer satisfaction are established early on. It's not based merely on interactions between the customer and the firm. The perception of a product or service hatches during the design and execution of an offer. It is shaped by marketing activities such as pricing, communication, selling, distribution, and other forms of promotion, often before the customer even sees the product.

Targeted customers' perceptions appear in two stages. First, customers make judgments on the initial communications of a product or service that will encourage them to try the offer for the first time. Then, customer satisfaction evolves based on their initial experience.

Vibrant customer satisfaction is essential because it is the first sign that a firm is acquiring customer traction. If a firm has high customer satisfaction, it is likely that customer momentum has already begun. Steps can then be taken to accelerate that momentum. Conversely, if customer satisfaction is low to nonexistent, momentum will never get going unless the causes of low customer satisfaction are addressed.

Adopting the term *vibrant customer satisfaction* indicates that a firm is committed to building intense customer feelings and emotions from its power offers, right through every moment of truth. The use of words such as *intense, feelings,* and *emotions* is deliberate. They evoke the aspects of human nature that have the strongest impact on customer satisfaction.

The Emotions Beneath Satisfaction

Satisfaction is a state of mind. This fundamental fact is totally overlooked when management refers to customer satisfaction in percentages tracked like accounting numbers. The danger in such simple and seemingly objective representations of satisfaction is that they will be mistaken for reality, in place of the subjective but more complete and intense reality—the "real" reality of the customer experience that they are trying to measure.

To ensure that customer satisfaction boosts customer momentum, it is important to keep in mind what it really means. Recall the exploration of how customers perceive the value of an offer. It is often deeply held emotions that drive judgment of the value of a product or service. These same emotions also drive customer satisfaction and lead to the acceleration of customer momentum.

"Dissatisfaction Inside"

Customer satisfaction is transitory. Like other states of mind, it will ebb and flow depending on the latest experience with a firm: the moment of truth. Obviously, consumers' perceptions of a product are based on their experience of it, but increasingly they are also influenced by other, seemingly unrelated experiences. Superior service from an online bookstore or a food retailer will decrease customers' satisfaction with the comparatively poorer service of banks and airlines.

Human beings, as we all know, are difficult to satisfy. On the strength of this observation, Abraham Maslow constructed his theory of the hierarchy of needs, a principle well known to marketers.[4] It describes how humans move up the ladder of different needs. When one need is satisfied, they aim for more sophisticated ones. Maslow portrayed a hierarchy of needs, progressing from basic to more advanced: physiological, safety, love, belonging, self-esteem, and self-actualization. His thesis suggests that human beings are never satisfied, because as one desire is satisfied, another emerges higher up in the hierarchy.

Contemporary research on happiness as a measurement of progress uncovers the same phenomenon. The economist Richard Layard has established that as societies become richer, they do not become happier.[5] He shows that, on average, people have grown no happier over the past 50 years, even though average incomes have more than doubled in real terms.

Internal dissatisfaction is the engine of civilization. Without it, we would still be living in caves and hunting for food rather than aspiring to own two homes and shopping for delicacies in upmarket food shops. This explains why human dissatisfaction is at the heart of value origination, and why it is one of the underlying drivers of profitable growth for momentum-powered firms.

What are the business consequences of dissatisfaction? There are two simple implications: first, that it offers unlimited potential for growth; second, that a company must continuously strive to improve its offers. The relentless rise of customers' expectations is not a result of capitalism, globalization, technology, or any other such fashionable argument. Instead, it is the consequence of the human being's dissatisfaction with the status quo.

The example of the anti-ulcer drug market which we considered in Chapter 8, "Power Offer Execution," is a case in point. When Tagamet was said to have put stomach surgeons out of business, it led to dangerous complacency for its creator. SmithKline presumed that Tagamet was the ultimate treatment for this condition and made the fateful decision to stop its anti-ulcer research program. The company had created momentum but suffered from hubris. It failed to maintain and accelerate that momentum and reap its full benefits.

The great driver of Tagamet's instant success—and of the anti-ulcer drugs that supplanted it—was the intensity of the satisfaction they gave. In customer satisfaction, it is intensity that matters more than anything else.

Why Intensity Matters

There is a very sound reason why firms that provide their customers with vibrant satisfaction do better than those offering normal levels of satisfaction. Like most momentum principles, it is grounded in the emotions of customer psychology.

Customer satisfaction is a state of mind, not an action. Its real value lies in the actions it inspires: purchases, loyalty, or word-of-mouth recommendations. Actions driven by emotions are much more powerful than those motivated by reason. This is why it is important to relate different levels of customer satisfaction to three different states of mind: cognitive, affective, and emotional. Let's now investigate this relationship.

When most customers interact with a product or service—whether they are "just browsing," actively contemplating purchasing it, or already using it—they will think about it. Possibly not in a particularly active manner, true, but at some level their brain will be engaged in reflecting on their experiences as customers. Psychologists call this thinking "cognitive" because it is normally founded on fact and experience and is reasoned and logical.

The depth of these cognitive processes varies widely. As customers, we think deeply about the purchase of high-ticket items, such as a TV, a car, or a house. In the business world, some important purchasing decisions can require task forces working for months and writing detailed reports. On the other hand, we are much less involved when buying low-cost or impulse items.

Sometimes, however, customers go beyond the cognitive stage and enter what is called the "affective" level. This occurs because they either like or dislike something and develop positive or negative feelings. At this point, they become more involved. Many people struggle to recognize their feelings as readily as they acknowledge their thoughts, but they are inescapably present, affecting our decisions. How many customers have agonized while comparing different car models before making a decision based on a feeling, a first impression, a detail, or a color? In most cases, though, a decision based on feelings is a good decision, because ultimately customers live in a world governed by their feelings rather than their logic.

Sometimes these affective processes become so overwhelmingly strong that customers enter what is called the "emotional" stage, in which they become excited or angry. The more intense a customer's state of mind, the stronger the emotions, and the more likely it is that he or she will act.

A customer's state of mind is naturally influenced by satisfaction. A neutral level of satisfaction creates no significant mental reaction. It takes a higher level of satisfaction or dissatisfaction to create feelings and affective responses. If the satisfaction or dissatisfaction becomes more extreme, emotional reactions can be expected.

It is only when customers start to be truly satisfied that they begin to develop positive feelings, and only when they become very satisfied that they get emotional. This is why it is essential for businesses to set ambitious goals and strive toward vibrant customer satisfaction, rather than just tolerating the mediocrity of mere satisfaction.

Champions and Desperados

But affections and emotions are still states of mind, even if stronger than average satisfaction. The link between customer satisfaction and momentum happens when a customer's state of mind is translated into levels of engagement, as shown in Figure 9.1.[6]

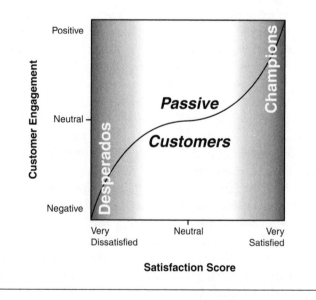

Figure 9.1 Customer satisfaction and behavior

Most of the time, customers are merely satisfied. They are passive, not engaged. But if satisfaction is very high, customers will have positive emotions toward an offer. They will be loyal to the company, quick to adopt its new products and to recommend them to others. They are positively engaged. They are the firm's *Champions*.

Strongly dissatisfied customers lie at the other end of the scale. Customer dissatisfaction creates negative feelings, and extreme levels of dissatisfaction create powerful negative emotions. This can lead to harmful customer actions against the firm that apply a brake to momentum. If dissatisfaction becomes so high that it creates negative emotions, these disgruntled customers will endeavor to discourage other customers, causing damage to a company's reputation. They are negatively engaged. They are the firm's *Desperados*.

Customer momentum will be influenced at the two extremes of the satisfaction scale. It will be impaired by customer dissatisfaction and by Desperados sniping at the firm. Consequently, any source of dissatisfaction needs to be hunted down and eradicated, as shown later in this chapter. Customer momentum requires the positive engagement of Champions, and commitment like that is only earned through vibrant customer satisfaction. This is why it is essential to be ambitious about customer satisfaction and to monitor progress toward these ambitious goals with appropriate metrics.

Satisfaction Metrics

Many firms use no customer satisfaction metrics. As a general rule, these firms lie at either end of the customer satisfaction spectrum. The best firms have an intuitive grasp of it—it is part of their DNA. They are often small businesses led by an inspirational entrepreneur who is deeply focused on customers.

The other firms—the majority—do not measure customer satisfaction because they believe it is not a priority. Disconnected from their customers, they cocoon themselves in a misplaced confidence based on their own selection of anecdotal, positively biased evidence. These firms do not experience customer momentum. They are momentum deficient.

Customer satisfaction metrics should not be a matter of choice for large companies. The gaping distance between big business and its customers means that formal measurement is a necessity. Financial analysts expect to have access to reports covering all the factors that influence the value of a firm's physical assets, right down to office furniture and stationery. Why shouldn't they also expect to know the factors that are affecting the value of an asset as fundamental as customers?

Although there is no universal measure for customer satisfaction, there are a number of accepted standards. Often companies will proudly announce that they have a 66 percent customer satisfaction rating, or 82 percent or whatever—but what precisely does this mean?

The most common method of measuring customer satisfaction is surveys. Companies ask their customers to fill in a questionnaire, typically noting their satisfaction on a five-point scale that moves from very dissatisfied to very satisfied, with satisfied, dissatisfied, and no opinion in between. The standard customer satisfaction ratings are reported as a percentage, combining the customers who say they are "satisfied" and those who respond "very satisfied."[7]

As a result, a customer rating of 70 percent could mean a variety of different responses: from 70 percent satisfied and none very satisfied, to 70 percent very satisfied, or any point in between. This is misleading in a serious way. There is a crucial difference between "satisfied" and "very satisfied" in terms of future customer behavior.

This kind of basic reporting provides overly generous ratings. At best, it can guide companies badly in need of catching up, but it is a totally inadequate measurement of customer satisfaction to help guide vibrant execution. A firm that aspires to join the Momentum League needs to aim much higher and use more demanding metrics.

The difficulty is that satisfaction is a state of mind, an attitude of customers toward the company, something not easy to capture on a questionnaire with just five boxes to choose from. Customer satisfaction surveys use very simple measurement tools that don't take into account customers' deep affective and emotional states. Notwithstanding this limitation, the link we saw between very high levels of satisfaction and emotional engagement can help us go some way to extracting a meaningful benchmark from these metrics.

Top Box Ambition

A high score based on the standard measurements of customer satisfaction creates an inflated and inaccurate view of the real level of customer engagement. An 80 percent "satisfaction" rating sounds very high, but it means that 20 percent of people who paid for a product or service were not satisfied, even at the most basic level. That is an unacceptably high proportion. In addition, that 80 percent could be composed of customers who all responded "satisfied" rather than "very satisfied." Customers who are just satisfied are passive customers and provide little traction for momentum. Momentum doesn't come from, "Yeah, it was okay, I guess."

Customer *delight* should be the only outcome that makes management jump with glee and trumpet the news about their satisfied customers. It's also what customers deserve when they pay for a product. One good way to make certain that a firm has become ambitious about customer satisfaction would be to report, at least internally, only scores for very high levels of satisfaction. Companies need higher expectations. Above average is not good enough—they have to focus on the "top box," because this is essential to drive customer action.

The term *top box* was coined by Andy Taylor, chairman and CEO of Enterprise Rent-A-Car, an American business founded in 1957 by his father, Jack, on the premise that the company would always provide a level of service that would stick in customers' minds. As the family firm grew into an international business with 500,000 rental cars, cracks began to appear in the foundation of its success.[8]

In the mid-1990s, Taylor began getting an uneasy sense that Enterprise's customer service was not as good as it should be. A number of letters, calls, and anecdotes trickling through to him implied that the company was placing too much emphasis on financial metrics and not enough on pleasing its customers. Taylor decided to adopt a simple and meaningful measurement system that would give overall metrics of customer satisfaction and also indicate whether customers would rent from Enterprise again.

Enterprise's new measurement system tracked only completely satisfied customers—the top box. The new ratings were obviously much lower than the previous ones, which had included the "somewhat satisfied" category. To counter any resulting employee demotivation, Taylor insisted that the whole point of measuring satisfaction was not to come up with figures that make the firm look as if it was doing a great job. Instead, it was to guide its efforts to be even better, to make the firm perform more effectively for its customers.

Taylor and his father then made it clear to managers and employees that the highest corporate priority was its customers—more important than growth and more important than profits. Top box customer-satisfaction scores were integrated into monthly operating reports, and no one was promoted without a customer score equal to the corporate average or higher.

Insights from the regular customer satisfaction survey were plowed back into the business, and its top box score has steadily climbed ever since. As a result, Enterprise has been winning more repeat business, benefiting from more referrals and growing much faster than the industry as a whole.

"Top box" shows the importance of being ambitious about customer satisfaction. Determined to recapture its reputation for customer service, Enterprise realized that a robust benchmark was the only way to overhaul its corporate culture. The impact? Enterprise is now a $9.5 billion business and has enjoyed annual compound growth of 20% over the past 25 years.

Top box is just another way of saying *vibrant customer satisfaction.* You choose the expression that's most relevant to your firm. Whereas top box centers on clear measurement, vibrant focuses on the desired impact. Whichever is chosen, what counts is that a firm sets its ambition much higher than average customer satisfaction, because it must engage customers at an emotional level if it is to generate positive, momentum-building action.

The Impact of Vibrant Satisfaction

Vibrant customer satisfaction is not just for the good of customers. It makes business sense because it is a very efficient way to drive momentum growth through customer traction. This is vividly illustrated with the example of First Direct, the world's most recommended bank, as outlined in Chapter 6, "Compelling Equity."

The impact of the vibrant satisfaction experienced by First Direct's customers is easy to see in Figure 9.2.[9] To begin with, at over 85 percent, First Direct's customer satisfaction ratings were 25 to 40 points higher than established U.K. banks.

Second, more than 70 percent of the bank's customers have recommended the service to at least one other person. As First Direct has more than one million customers, this translates to a very impressive sales force of more than 700,000 satisfied customers, the very ones who brought in a third of the bank's new customers by recommendation, at zero acquisition cost.

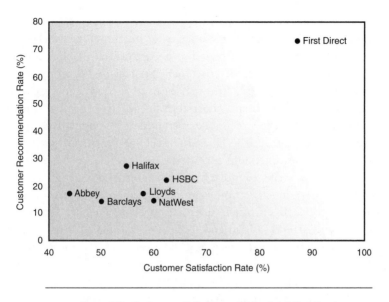

Figure 9.2 Customer satisfaction and behavior at First Direct

Aiming for Vibrant Satisfaction

But how can other firms reach the dizzy heights of First Direct's success? We've already explained how the most effective way to create vibrant satisfaction is through designing and executing a power offer. Second, firms should take a number of actions aiming specifically at customer satisfaction. In our experience, these actions must correspond to adequate objectives that stretch the firm's ambition without discouraging employees. In a firm's journey toward momentum, we have distinguished three different stages for customer satisfaction objectives. But all three—indeed, the central thrust of this entire book—share a single holy grail: progressing toward vibrant customer satisfaction.

It's not easy to get there. In fact, companies that start the trek from a position of weakness such as the "morass" that Lou Gerstner colorfully described upon arriving at IBM might have to manage their way up toward the goal step by step through these stages instead of risking failure and resultant demoralization from trying an overly ambitious great leap forward.

The first stage is about reaching industry benchmarks. Although benchmarks generally betray mediocrity of customer satisfaction, they can also play a vital role for firms that need to catch up. For companies struggling with low levels of customer satisfaction, shining examples such as First Direct and Enterprise might seem unrealistic and unattainable, so a pertinent short-term objective can be simply to increase satisfaction levels to industry standards. We view this approach as "minding the store": It is a useful exercise for firms until a more powerful offer is designed and executed.

Next, firms can strive to move from good to top-box satisfaction. This ensures that they don't become complacent about adequate customer-satisfaction scores. If customer satisfaction objectives are set at higher levels, this will stretch a firm and force it to remain externally focused. Enterprise's top-box initiative is a good example of a more ambitious objective.

Finally, successful firms need to actively nurture the vibrant customer satisfaction they have gained. All the examples of momentum-powered companies discussed so far—First Direct, Enterprise, Dell, Virgin, Skype, Wal-Mart, Microsoft—have at one time created the vibrant customer satisfaction that generated the momentum powering their phenomenal, profitable growth. But it becomes harder when they grow bigger, more complex, and more powerful.

Wal-Mart, for example, is now struggling with pockets of deeply dissatisfied stakeholders, from employees and trade unions to local communities and campaign groups. These are the retailer's Desperados. Wal-Mart needs to manage the situation carefully to maintain the vibrant satisfaction that other stakeholders feel for its services.[10]

Similarly, vibrant satisfaction is no longer as widespread as it used to be for Microsoft. Antagonistic groups, such as Linux fans, antitrust agencies, and industry lobbies, are creating resistance against this global technology group. They are Microsoft's Desperados. Their persistent goal is to halt the firm's customer momentum and erode its dominant position.[11]

Strategies for Vibrant Satisfaction

In chasing the goal of momentum, companies must systematically undertake actions to foster customer satisfaction and eradicate potential sources of friction. Remember MDC, the action roadmap to momentum introduced in Chapter 8. It is the key to accelerating an organization toward momentum at each stage of execution. To foster vibrant satisfaction, MDC will guide us through three steps: *Mobilize* for vibrant satisfaction, *detect* sources of dissatisfaction, *convert* unsatisfied customers.

Mobilize for Vibrant Satisfaction

Vibrant customer satisfaction can be delivered only if a firm is united foursquare behind this ambition. The objective should be clear and present to all levels of employees, from management to the frontline staff. At every moment of truth when the customer meets the firm, all employees must understand the significance of creating a resonant customer experience.

The central task of overhauling a corporate culture to set it on the rails of systematically stalking, enabling, and accelerating customer momentum is so important that we devote Chapter 12, "Internal Momentum," to exploring it in detail. Mobilizing staff to the goal of vibrant customer satisfaction is crucial, but it is not without its caveats. Setting up this mobilization campaign requires care, consideration, and intelligence. First, employees must trust the numbers, so they have to know how they are derived. Second, measuring customer satisfaction should be perceived not as a threatening or controlling mechanism but, rather, as a tool for driving growth. Third, employees will be inspired by details that are relevant to their experience. Many firms communicate nothing more than aggregate results, which are so far removed from employees' daily world that they are meaningless.

To see how very effective mobilization for customer satisfaction can be, consider Harrah's Entertainment. Harrah's invested $10 million in a major customer service initiative that sought to fully understand the key drivers behind its customer's perception of compelling value and then redesigned its entire metrics system accordingly. For example, the general managers' compensation system was changed so that a quarter of their bonus payment was contingent on customer satisfaction results. The casino trained staff specifically for customer service, paying extra wages for the training sessions. Every employee was rewarded if overall customer satisfaction scores improved by 3 percent. In its first year, the scheme paid out $7 million in bonuses. The following year, the impact of the scheme contributed to a 15% increase in revenues, taking them up to $3.5 billion. Within four years, $40 million had been paid out in bonuses, employee turnover had halved, and revenue had more than doubled. Again, the story illustrates the importance of ambition. Although one casino topped the company's satisfaction ratings for four consecutive quarters, its staff did not receive a bonus. Why? Because although it was great, it had not shown any improvement. Momentum-powered firms make sure that the bar always rises.[12]

But it is important to recognize that there is more to mobilizing for vibrant satisfaction than financial rewards for staff. Obviously, stressing the central importance of customer satisfaction to business performance is unlikely to be successful if employees perceive that their contribution to that performance is not rewarded fairly. But there are other "rewards" that arise from vibrant satisfaction and strongly energize employees. Humans' innate sense of fairness, the pride that comes from a job well done, and the more pleasurable working environment that satisfied customers create are all strong momentum-building forces.

Detect Sources of Dissatisfaction

The gap between the design of a power offer and its execution can be enormous. Even the best companies get things wrong. This is why it is essential for firms to be humble enough to systematically hunt down all sources of dissatisfaction.

Tetra Pak offers an illustration of the importance of detecting what has gone wrong and where. This $10 billion company originated a power offer in the form of an aseptic carton for liquid food. This packaging revolutionized the industry, changed the consumption habits of millions of people, and secured 60 percent of the global market for liquid food packaging.

As Tetra Pak grew larger and more successful, its growth and profitability came under threat in a maturing market and intense competition. The company began losing profitability, volume, and customers. The situation was grave.

However, Tetra Pak was wise enough to realize that the key issue was not competition but its own relationship with its business customers. The company's global survey showed that customer satisfaction was just above average. The rating was not so bad that it created a crisis, but it was not good enough to drive continued growth, either. Critically, the dissatisfaction had nothing to do with the product itself. Customers were unhappy with Tetra Pak's failure to help them identify new sources of growth. According to the words used in the report, they were simply asking, "Hear me, know me, grow me."

Tetra Pak's CEO used the survey results as a "burning platform" from which to overhaul the company and bring it closer to customers. Sources of dissatisfaction were pitilessly analyzed in detail. Tetra Pak engineers examined breakdown patterns of customers' filling machines to boost operational cost efficiency, and within a few years machine breakdowns were halved. Tetra Pak regained momentum by creating vibrant satisfaction through opening new growth opportunities for its customers.[13]

It is not always easy for successful companies to spot the source of dissatisfaction, but with humility and effort they can always improve on design and execution of an offer. The impact of customer dissatisfaction is too significant to be left to haphazard discovery. It must be sought out, actively and systematically. The insight discovery matrix presented in Chapter 4, "Compelling Insights," is the right tool. Its four paths are also the appropriate routes for hunting customer dissatisfaction. For this purpose, it might be renamed the friction detection matrix.

The first of the four paths is the knowing-doing. It reflects an inexcusable blind spot for firms. If sources of dissatisfaction are known to both customers and the firm, they must be tackled instantly. The second path—listening to customers—is always the principal one. But some companies are beginning to realize that this path has even more potential than just resolving complaints. Beyond raising problems to be resolved on an individual basis, customer complaints can become a valuable source of insights that lead to innovation. For example, Allianz, a leading global insurer, recognizes that if even a small proportion of its 75 million customers—say 4 percent—complain every year, these complaints represent 3 million opportunities for a double improvement in customer satisfaction: first by resolving the particular complaint and second by applying the lessons learned to improve the experience offered to all customers.[14]

The third path, customer learning, can also be crucial, because sometimes dissatisfaction arises when customers do not understand the nature of offers or how they can be used effectively.

But the most challenging, and rewarding, path for companies tracking down customer dissatisfaction is the white one, the unknown virgin land blanketed in snow. If a source of dissatisfaction is obscure for both the firm and the customers, it will be very tricky to pinpoint. A helpful approach to resolving this problem is to imagine scenarios encompassing different customer experiences. These scenarios can be developed in workshops, in think tanks, or via frameworks such as the customer-activity cycle or the buyer-experience cycle.[15]

Here's a simple example. Amazon, the online book retailer, is frequently praised as an example of great customer satisfaction. It has built customer momentum on the back of a power offer and has incontestably created vibrant customer satisfaction. However, this doesn't mean that it can't be improved. To prove it, we did a little dissatisfaction hunt of our own and discovered one potential source of friction.

We selected a list of ten English-language bestsellers by authors such as Stephen King, Jeffrey Archer, and Dan Brown. We ordered the books, to be delivered to an identical delivery address in France, from both the Amazon U.K. site and the French one. Although the French site offers free delivery, it was 25 percent more expensive for a French customer to order the books from France than to import them from the British site.[16]

Now, there might be myriad reasons to explain why Amazon.fr is more expensive, from exchange rates to internal transfer prices and regulations, but none of these explanations would satisfy a disgruntled customer. It is the customer's relationship with Amazon that is at stake.

A systematic hunt to identify and eradicate customer dissatisfaction should be a planned, proactive program rather than a reaction to crises or complaints—or, worse, a customer discovery such as the one just described. This hunt should be fed with a continuous allocation of resources and become part of a firm's normal operations.

Convert Unsatisfied Customers

At the customer satisfaction stage, momentum is accelerated by converting Desperados and passive customers to Champions. Champions are customers who love the firm so much that they are likely to promote it and its offers. They have taken the first step that enables the firm to move them through the virtuous circle of retention and engagement, as we shall see in following chapters. This is the fulfillment of striving for vibrant satisfaction: converting customers to Champions. This is what builds the foundation for later stages of momentum. Ideally, the firm should aim at having no Desperados at all, and as few passive customers as possible. This ambitious objective is unattainable in full but an indispensable guiding principle nonetheless.

The tool for converting dissatisfied customers is called *customer recovery,* and it takes the hunt for dissatisfaction to the next level. Its first aim is to stop dissatisfied customers turning into Desperados. After it has succeeded, it turns them into positive customers and then, ultimately, converts them to Champions.

Management should begin by encouraging employees to identify dissatisfied customers and empowering them to take corrective action. If they respond to a problem with something as simple as offering customers an alternative or a replacement for an item with which they are unhappy, this could be enough to lead to vibrant customer satisfaction. Customers will tell their story to friends and family, and will return. Some might even be transformed from Desperados into Champions.

A simple example can illustrate this point. Remember our simple calculation of the equity contained in what appears to be a simple $10 pizza-and-drinks transaction if that transaction is repeated once a week over a decade? $5,000! Now imagine a customer in a pizzeria complaining that her pizza is burnt. The price of offering on the spot to make another pizza or giving her a free drink is marginal compared to what's at stake. Let's pretend the pizzeria staff did nothing to satisfy her complaint. What happens next? She leaves disgruntled and, next week, thinks nothing of trying the pizza place one block over.

How to get her back? The conventional method is through advertising. It's a scattergun approach—the company hits people outside its target. Using advertising to bring back dissatisfied customers would cost hundreds of dollars per customer recovered. It might still be worth it given the customer equity at stake, but it's an enormous price compared to the pittance that a free fresh pizza would have cost. One move is made at the source of the problem for a marginal cost of less than $1, with a high probability of success. The other takes place much later and costs hundreds of dollars, with much worse odds. It doesn't take a financial genius to realize which one is the best investment—and yet it rarely happens.

This highlights a paradox stemming from the vertical silos and linear processes that are hallmarks of momentum-deficient firms. On the one hand, there are site managers who put pressure on costs and who deliver margins by counting every cent. On the other, advertising managers are able to negotiate a budget based on the past year plus 10 percent, without counting one dime. Yet it's much more effective to educate all employees to act in a customer-focused manner, to create customer satisfaction and contribute to momentum growth.

The pizzeria example shows how targeted training could help employees identify and recover dissatisfied customers. A systematic approach is crucial. Momentum-powered companies understand the importance of recovering dissatisfied customers via appropriate responses. At Virgin Atlantic, a response to dissatisfied customers can range from a letter of apology or a bottle of champagne to a personal message from Richard Branson and free airline tickets—it all depends on the situation and the customer equity at stake.

At First Direct, agents have standing orders to drop everything else until a customer's complaint is fixed, calling in whatever resources are needed, even the CEO. The employee is highly motivated to get it done, get it done right, and get it done fast. Almost without fail, the customer is happy, and the bank has secured his or her goodwill in a natural and efficient way.

Problems are the test of a company's relationship with its customers, in the same way that crises are a test of friendship in everyday life. Even satisfied customers won't know an organization's heart until they've experienced a problem. Problems encountered by customers make for the most memorable moments of truth. Dissatisfied customers who receive a good and fair response can become more loyal than those who never experienced a problem at all.

A case in point is JetBlue, the low-cost U.S. airline, which delights its customers with an emphasis on inexpensive flying with great service. While other low-cost airlines focused on budget travelers and tourists, JetBlue also cast a spell over upscale business travelers and built incredible levels of customer commitment through exceptional service. Then JetBlue suffered a service meltdown in the winter of 2007. Not only were flights canceled, in some cases passengers were left in unheated planes on the tarmac in freezing conditions, for hours, with no food or drink. It was a customer service disaster.

The effectiveness of the recovery effort that followed is probably due to a number of factors and the fact that JetBlue's customers were more likely to be forgiving, at least once, because of their previous positive experiences. But the way JetBlue CEO David Neeleman handled the problem had a huge impact. He got out in front of as many TV cameras as possible and repeated his unequivocal apology and support for his staff. He repeated his promise that it wouldn't happen again, he made that promise credible by setting out what the firm was doing to fix the problem and prevent a recurrence, and he announced an impressive compensation package, at a cost of more than $20 million. He then took personal responsibility for the problem and, a few months later, resigned as CEO. This appears to have been enough to make sure that the wobble remained just that and didn't become a blowout that wiped out momentum. For the second quarter of 2007, a period that began just a few days after the problem, JetBlue reported revenue growth of 19 percent and profit growth of 50 percent compared to the same quarter the year before. When the influential J.D. Power survey of North American airline customer satisfaction was published in June, four months after the debacle, who was ranked number one in the low-cost sector? JetBlue. Its customers had forgiven it.[17]

The previous examples illustrate the three key steps of customer recovery. First, a firm should be close enough to its customers to detect sources of dissatisfaction as early as possible. It should have some "dissatisfaction nets" in place to catch any problems that customers experience. These nets can take the form of direct observation, quality controls, customer hotlines, easy reporting, or surveys. They should identify disgruntled customers before they consider ending their relationship with the firm or communicate their grief to other customers or prospects.

The second step involves apologizing to the customer for the inconvenience. This should not only express recognition of the initial problem but also acknowledge the grief it has caused. It must be an affective response to an affective situation. Even if it is honest and accurate, a response that justifies the situation by logic at this stage will only aggravate the customer further.

Finally, following prompt analysis, a firm should compensate the customer in a way that will be perceived as better than fair. Not only does the damage have to be repaired, the response must be perceived as taking into account the added aggravations. There are, obviously, costs associated with such effective recoveries and the control systems that need to be established to avoid abuses, but they are small compared to the customer equity at stake, to the costs of acquiring new customers, and to the impact on momentum. In most companies, investment in customer recovery has a higher financial return than any other investment alternative.

Nothing Less Than Vibrant

Customer satisfaction is a crucial phase in the creation of momentum. It is the first test of the customer traction inherent in a power offer. Even if a power offer is properly designed and executed, there are always multiple unforeseen threats and opportunities that can significantly affect its impact. Furthermore, the inherent "dissatisfaction inside" that drives customers' behavior is a permanent source of change and requires attention. However, the rewards are great. The more Champions a firm can enlist, the greater its momentum will be.

To maximize the potential momentum of a power offer at the customer satisfaction stage, this chapter has presented the following guiding principles:

- Customer satisfaction is shaped every time customers encounter a firm, its products, or its services. These moments of truth cumulatively become the customer experience.

- Satisfaction is a state of mind that becomes relevant only when it is so intense that it elicits an emotional response. It is these emotional responses that influence customer behavior.

- Emotions are the reason why simple customer satisfaction does not create momentum, but vibrant customer satisfaction does. As a result, momentum-powered firms set ambitious customer-satisfaction objectives. To reach them, firms must use equally ambitious metrics, such as top-box satisfaction.

- Champions are customers who have positive emotions toward an offer and fuel its momentum. Desperados are customers who have negative emotions toward an offer and hinder its momentum.

- Customer satisfaction is an essential element of momentum. A specific program of action is essential to systematically foster vibrant satisfaction that will further fuel the momentum created by a power offer. Firms must mobilize employees, detect sources of dissatisfaction, and convert dissatisfied customers. Customer recovery is especially crucial to eradicate sources of dissatisfaction and to transform potential Desperados into Champions.

Building customer momentum is a continuous task. Firms must constantly strive to reach higher and higher standards of satisfaction. Only the top box will do. But even vibrant satisfaction is not enough on its own: momentum requires that customers repeatedly buy the power offer. This—vibrant retention—is the next phase in the virtuous circle and the subject of the following chapter.

10

Vibrant Retention

For Want of a Key...

After a hard day at the office, a business executive goes out to his new car, gets in, turns the key. Nothing. Zip. Not even the fateful "errrr" of a dead battery. It turns out that there's nothing wrong with the car. It's the key. It's got a newfangled security device that has malfunctioned. He travels home by train.

The next day, his wife calls the dealership where they bought their car and asks them to replace the dud key. She encounters a guy with an attitude problem. He calls her "Honey." He says she'll have to come in and wait in line while they sort it out. She asks to make an appointment so she won't have to wait. She's busy and probably already annoyed at having to run her husband's errands. The guy says no can do. Oh, and he calls her "Honey" again.

She calls her husband, who gets angry. The car is under warranty, and it's their job to fix it—now. He's also mad at his wife's abusive treatment. He calls the dealership and growls. He uses strong language and an aggressive tone. He speaks to a different guy, who sorts the problem out in just five minutes and promises to have the key ready to collect when he comes by. In theory, this gesture should have ensured satisfaction for this customer, but it's too little and too late.

One bad moment of truth has transformed this man and his wife into Desperados. They'll certainly never use the dealership again. In coming years, they will probably warn many others about the service they received. Even worse, the husband writes an article about their experience for *Fortune*.[1]

Chapter 9, "Vibrant Satisfaction," showed how customers can become seriously dissatisfied because of little things that could have been easily resolved—things like that dud key. Customers make decisions about companies based on their ability and willingness to solve problems. Firms that fail will lose them. When dissatisfaction becomes intense enough, customers will run away. For this dealership, the business executive and his wife are no longer just Desperados, they have become Runaways.

Loyals and Runaways

Keeping hold of targeted, truly valuable customers is one of any firm's most important tasks, because customer retention has a staggeringly strong impact on long-term growth. We have already seen how vibrant satisfaction can accelerate customer momentum once a power offer has been designed and executed. Like customer satisfaction, if customer retention is vibrant enough it can become the next stage in this chain reaction, and it has a much more obvious effect. It has a direct impact on revenues, profits, and growth. It accelerates momentum.

Retaining customers is not enough. As with every stage of the momentum-execution model, it is the vibrancy of retention that counts. Vibrant retention is much richer and more nuanced than it might appear. For one thing, a business shouldn't run after every potential customer. Employees tend to unconsciously focus on the painful ones—customers who shout the loudest for attention—but high-maintenance types who scream louder to get more for less may actually be liabilities. Customers of this sort are so difficult and expensive to serve that they shouldn't always be kept.

In addition, customer retention is influenced by customer satisfaction, certainly, but satisfaction does not guarantee retention. Satisfaction is a state of mind, whereas retention is an *action*. Not every satisfied customer is a retained customer, and not every retained customer is satisfied.

Sometimes, dissatisfaction instantly leads to defection, as in the case of the woman badly treated by her dealership. The *Runaways* are these unhappy customers who decide not to buy from the company anymore. But often, dissatisfied customers may linger. We all know people who badmouth a company whose products they continue to buy. Retention is indeed different from loyalty, despite the fact that these two words are often used interchangeably. Retention is about customers who keep buying the same product over time, whereas loyalty refers to people who have positive emotional feelings about a company. Loyal customers tend to be retained, but retained customers are not necessarily always loyal. The *Loyals* are those who keep buying over time a product for which they have strong positive emotions. It is these emotions that determine the vibrancy of their retention.

The Emotions Beneath Retention

In the same way that vibrant customer satisfaction is a deeper, much richer concept than a series of percentage ratings can show, understanding vibrant customer retention involves much more than analyzing statistics of repeat buying. Two key aspects of human nature have a particular impact on retention: freedom and temptation.

"Freedom Inside"

Just as the human animal was invented with dissatisfaction inside, it was engineered with a lust for freedom. Born free, people resent being forced to think or behave in certain ways. It's even stronger than that: We actively resist it.

Yet on a daily basis, we are prepared to sacrifice some of our freedom in exchange for something else we value more. The difference is that it's our choice. Buying a house, a car, a mobile phone, a drink—all these actions engage us and reduce our freedom for a time, each to its own degree.

Freedom is an essential ingredient in the bartering process between customers and companies. Customers add up the costs and benefits of reducing their freedom. Sometimes when customers surrender that freedom, they don't even perceive it as that, because they have trust. Some customers will repeatedly buy the same product because it simplifies their life, so long as they don't believe they're losing too much of their freedom in exchange.

However, if they perceive that they are forced to buy the same product, either because of a quasi-monopoly or because the switching cost is too high, then they resent it. These undercurrents and nuances of customer behavior would never be spotted by glancing at corporate statistics on retention. But an understanding of "freedom inside" is important for anyone who aspires to create and nurture momentum. Equally, it is vital to understand that it is the perception that matters, not objective reality. Take Apple, for example. Many of its products could be seen as restrictive of their users' freedom, but they are not perceived as such by Apple users.[2] On the contrary, they feel that Apple's products set them free from the frustrations of the poor usability and graceless design of competing products.

"Temptation Outside"

"I can resist anything but temptation," Oscar Wilde quipped one day. Human nature has always been tempted by alternatives. Well, consumers today are bombarded with temptation from every angle.

The dynamism of business, the flexibility of technology, and the forces of globalization mean that customers have more alternatives than ever before. At the same time, information walls have come down, so everyone is aware of the multiplicity of options, through the media, advertising, the Internet, and international travel. Word of mouth now travels, if not literally at the speed of light, then at least at the speed of a pretty good broadband connection.

Temptations, temptations, temptations, as far as the eye can see. Retaining customers is not easy. Gaining their loyalty is even harder. There is an ever-increasing pressure for customer defection. The more customers are bombarded by enticement, the stronger is their perceived need for freedom. They might briefly be lured by a great offer, but they'll soon be on the lookout for the next, even better one.

Temptation and freedom reside inside, side by side. Firms need to understand these human drivers because the evolution of technology and communications is constantly increasing the potential for customer mobility. Whereas this poses a serious threat to mediocre firms, increasing customer mobility offers opportunities to create customer momentum via power offers—and for momentum-powered firms to snatch customers from their competitors.

The captive customer is slowly becoming a thing of the past. Firms that rely on captive customers may still enjoy short-term growth, but they will be unable to sustain it in the long term unless they turn to value origination based on an understanding of and respect for customers. Captive users around the world knew very well that they were being outrageously overcharged for telephone services, especially long-distance calls. Millions of them fled gleefully to new operators and to Skype as soon as they could.

Retention Metrics

Bartenders and small shopkeepers who see their customers every day undoubtedly have an intuitive grasp of customer retention levels. They see the real thing and don't need metrics. Most of us, physically distant from our customers, have to measure it.

Indeed, just as with customer satisfaction, it should be compulsory for large firms to measure customer retention using formal processes.[3] After all, customers are a firm's most valuable asset. It is extraordinary that conventional management practice places enormous emphasis on internal audits, while the measurement of customers is less of a priority—especially as these assets are more able to disappear and more likely to do so than any other.

The problem is that measurement is valuable only if it measures the real thing. There is no standard measurement for customer retention, but the most commonly used method tells a firm how many of last year's customers are still doing business with it.[4] This is the easiest measurement to use for most business relationships and for situations that consist of repeated multiple transactions.

Everyone in an organization should understand precisely the implications of customer retention numbers, and why they are important. What precisely does a retention rate of, say, 50 percent mean? Well, it obviously means that a firm is losing half its customers every year. But what is less appreciated is that if this retention rate continues, and 50 percent of customers keep leaving every year, the average length of time that a customer continues to do business with the firm is just *one year*. This is a very short average customer lifetime.[5] A 50 percent retention rate is mathematically the same as if a firm kept all of its customers for one more year and then lost them all at once. It's shocking but true. Admittedly, the emotional impact on employees, shareholders, and management is not as dramatic if customers leave over time, but the financial impact is the same.

The calculations underlying this observation may not interest everyone in a firm, but the result will, because it's more than just a percentage—it's about the future of the company. It is a figure that will shock management and employees and make them realize how essential customer retention is to a healthy business.

The Business Impact of Retention

The business impact of retention relates directly to its effect on average customer lifetime—and that effect is dramatic. For instance, while a 50 percent retention rate means that, on average, customers stay with the firm for one year, if a firm were able to achieve a retention rate of more than 90 percent, that figure would stretch out to ten years, as shown in Figure 10.1.[6]

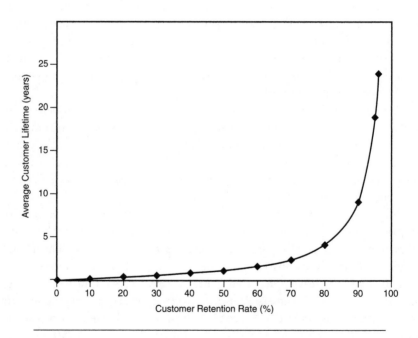

Figure 10.1 The accelerating impact of retention on average customer lifetime

We believe the minimum retention rate to qualify as a momentum-powered firm must be 90 percent. Only momentum-powered firms with a vibrant retention rate as high as this can consider customers as assets. This is because of the acceleration effect that each progressive gain in retention delivers. Anything below a 70 percent retention rate means that the average customer lifetime is insignificant. Even at an 80 percent retention rate, which sounds good on paper, the average relationship with a customer lasts just four years. Retention provides a stunningly progressive acceleration. Just look at the chart and consider the relative impact of a 1 percent gain at different points: An improvement in customer retention from 50 percent to 51 percent adds only two weeks to the average customer lifetime. But the same 1 percent gain from 95 percent to 96 percent adds five years!

Any increase in retention automatically increases average customer lifetime, which in turn increases the value of customers as assets. Of course, it also works in reverse—a drop in retention rate can disproportionately impact the future equity represented by a firm's customers. I recall listening to a pre-float presentation by some very bright young entrepreneurs. Doing some back-of-the-envelope calculations about their figures, it was easy to estimate that their projections assumed a customer retention rate of 90 percent. A bit optimistic and risky for the investors, you might think. Especially as, if they only managed a 50 percent retention rate, their customer equity would have been out by a factor of ten! In other words, if the retention rate they achieved turned out to be just 40 percent lower than their implicit promise, the projected worth of their business would prove to be at least 1,000 percent overvalued! It is fair to say that a misunderstanding of the accelerating impact of customer retention on lifetime value is behind some of the more unfortunate investment mistakes.

It is this acceleration effect that momentum-powered firms are able to exploit to power their exceptional growth. We are unaware of any other aspect of business in which the impact of each progressive improvement in performance increases so dramatically in terms of its ability to boost the value of an asset.

How does average customer lifetime increase the value of customers as assets? First, it improves the efficiency of acquisition spend. To take a simple example, imagine a gym that finds that every year 20 percent of its members don't renew their membership. It must spend money advertising to acquire new members. But before it can increase its total membership, it must replace every member it lost with a new one. If it managed to keep its members longer on average, it would grow at a higher rate with the same amount of money spent on promotional activities. Furthermore, the longer retained members stay, the better it is—a member staying five years means 25 percent more cash to the company than one staying only four, all for the same acquisition cost.

So in terms of revenue growth, an increase in retention has two positive effects: The total customer base increases more rapidly, and customers provide revenues for a longer period of time.

But improving retention also increases profitability. Again, consider the gym. New members are less profitable than established ones. Not only do they cost money to get, but during their first few months they take up more staff time than existing members do. They must be given a safety induction, they need to be shown how to work the machinery, they ask questions about lockers and class timetables, and so on. After the first year, they are pretty much self-sufficient, and so the cost of serving them decreases, and, because the cost of acquiring them has also now been earned back, they generate much more profit per dollar of membership fee than a new member. The higher the proportion of established customers to new ones in a company's overall customer mix, the more profitable a firm will be.

In short, more customers staying longer means both greater revenue growth and improved profitability. This is why customer retention is such a formidable booster of momentum strategy.

The rocket-like takeoff of the customer retention rate curve in Figure 10.1 should be enough to make any employee's eyes pop, and we cannot recommend its use strongly enough in motivational exercises. Suddenly, at 90 percent, the firm goes into orbit! Everyone in the firm should be helped to appreciate the huge impact—not obvious and therefore commonly underestimated—of the retention rate on future sales and a company's health.

Vibrant Retention

Unfortunately, not all 90 percent customer retention ratings are equal. A bald retention statistic is merely a number. The real essence of retention lies not in percentage ratings, but in a qualitative understanding of retention. To gain the full potential of retention, you should always remember the richness of human behavior lying behind the numbers.

Our typical bartender is directly in touch with the real thing. He *knows* his customers directly, eye to eye, but large firms can't get that close to all their customers. A bare retention figure does not tell us anything about the origin, the power, or the sustainability of the retention.

Facebook, the social networking service, has quality retention. Started at U.S. Ivy League universities but subsequently opened up to anyone over the age of 13, Facebook helps its users keep up-to-date with their friends and colleagues. It has become an essential part of daily life for many of its vast number of users. In October 2007, it had 43 million active users—people who keep coming back to the site at least once a month. More important, of those 43 million, half of them visit the site *every* day. The site is perceived as so vital by its users that they spend an average of 20 minutes per day on it.[7] Nobody forces them to. They just find the experience so compelling that they can't imagine spending even a day away.

As Facebook shows, the real essence of retention lies not in the rate alone but in the quality of the retention. The difference can be further illustrated through the example of two retail banks we examined. They had similar retention rates, but the nature of the relationship between the two banks and their customers was totally different. Upon investigation, we discovered that one had a level of customer satisfaction much lower than the other. It was clear that although both retained customers at a similar rate, the quality of their retention was different, and this significantly affected performance. In the first, customers kept doing business with the bank but at a minimum level, as if reluctantly. In the second, they were easy to serve, reacted positively to new products, and recommended the bank to their friends.

The first bank had *passive* retention: a momentum-deficient firm. The second enjoyed *vibrant* retention: a momentum-powered firm. High-quality, vibrant customer retention is needed for maintaining customer momentum.

This example also demonstrates the potential discrepancy that may exist between customer satisfaction and customer retention. As mentioned at the beginning of this chapter, one does not always follow the other. What is needed is a tool to track both the quantity and quality of retention within a firm's population of customers—the customer-retention portfolio shown in Figure 10.2.

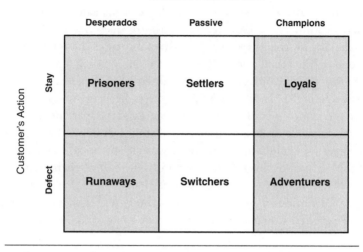

Figure 10.2 The customer retention portfolio

To achieve momentum, one really needs to create not only retention, but the *right* form of retention: vibrant retention. To this end, the next sections analyze the customer retention portfolio further in terms of three different types of retention: passive, forced, and vibrant.[8]

Passive Retention

Passive retention describes customers who buy the same product but have no emotional attachment to it. It is routine. They are apathetic. We start with it because in many companies it is the dominant form of retention. These customers are not usually actually dissatisfied, but neither are they particularly satisfied. If they have no great motivation to change, it might be because they don't believe a better alternative exists.

Our customer retention portfolio distinguishes between two types of passive customers: Settlers and Switchers. *Settlers* are retained, but although they will not actively pillory the firm, they will not actively extol it. They have no real engagement. *Switchers*, while having no strong feelings—good or bad—about the firm, defect easily. They, too, are simply not engaged with the company but, being more mobile than Settlers, will accept an alternative, albeit without any real passion.

The pharmaceutical industry has a huge challenge and opportunity with passive retention—noncompliance, as the industry calls it. It describes patients who have in hand a prescription from their doctor but either don't collect the medication or don't complete the treatment. When they do pick up the medication or start to use the product, these patients fall into the category of Settlers. But their involvement is not really committed. They are one step from quitting the treatment and becoming Switchers. They will not necessarily use another drug—they will just stop taking the prescribed one. The key to this problem is getting the patients more involved and developing an active retention by turning them into Loyals, for their own good and the good of the company.

This issue is costly for both the patients and the healthcare industry. Different studies show that in some categories between 60 percent and 80 percent of chronic patients are noncompliant after 12 months. Patients become unwell, develop complications, or even die. In these cases, the money invested by healthcare providers—in the diagnosis and in the treatment that the patient followed until the point of noncompliance—does not deliver its full potential. Beyond the lives and well-being of patients, billions of dollars are at stake for pharmaceutical companies. And it all hinges on the lack of active retention.

Forced Retention

Forced retention occurs when dissatisfied customers stay with a product or a firm reluctantly. In terms of their satisfaction levels, they are Desperados. In terms of retention, they take on one of two personas: Prisoners or Runaways. We've already encountered Runaways, those customers who leave the company, like the executive and his wife who vowed to never return to the car dealership. Their Desperado status leads them to behave negatively toward the firm and purposefully try to destroy its reputation.

Prisoners are also Desperados, but they have not yet summoned the courage or motivation to defect, and are retained by the firm. This doesn't mean they're any less damaging to it. Unlike Settlers, Prisoners feel trapped. Their dissatisfaction has gone beyond the cognitive state and become emotional. They will actively behave in a negative manner toward the firm, intending to damage its reputation. One day, when they find the right alternative or become even more emotional, they will defect and run away.

There are three common forms of forced customer retention: the quasi-monopoly, switching costs, and "loyalty" programs.

Forced retention through a quasi-monopoly can be a result of restrictions imposed on competition due to a patent or in heavily regulated industries such as many utilities. In the pharmaceutical industry, sales of drugs can plummet by up to 90 percent when a patent expires, demonstrating the extent to which the previous retention was forced.

High switching costs can force retention. Customers may be dissatisfied but are either contractually tied in or lack the time or energy needed to find a better alternative. High switching costs are common in the retail bank sector, as illustrated by the traditional bank we profiled earlier, with a high retention but low customer satisfaction.

So-called loyalty programs are another form of the same thing. Remember the difference between the words *retention* and *loyalty*. Whereas genuine loyalty creates positive affection and emotion toward a product or service, "loyalty" programs rarely engender these emotions. Rather, they entice customers to stay because of economic benefits. "Loyalty" programs are misnamed. They certainly build retention, but few of them create any loyalty.

Consider frequent-flyer programs, which often manage to create both higher customer retention and higher customer dissatisfaction. Of course, these programs create retention, but in the long term, they are a liability if they lead airlines to mistake retention for commitment and hence reduce the urgency for a more customer focused approach that could create a momentum.

Naturally, loyal customers should be rewarded, but that's different from imprisoning them. Virgin Atlantic's loyalty program understands the importance of rewarding customers for their loyalty, rather than forcing them to act in a certain way. Virgin's emphasis is on satisfying customers first and rewarding them second. Its rewards can be reclaimed for other experiences aside from flying Virgin—a trip in a hot-air balloon, for instance, or a stay on Richard Branson's Necker Island in the Caribbean. Virgin's customers actively choose the airline. Their retention is not forced. They have *chosen* to stay. This form of active retention is infinitely more powerful than the passive or forced retention most firms secure: Virgin has vibrant retention.

Vibrant Retention

If active retention refers to customers who are actively interacting with the firm, *vibrant retention* describes those customers who are really committed. In terms of satisfaction, they are your Champions. Apart from repeatedly buying your product, they play a vital role in promoting your company to their friends and family. In terms of retention of customers, Champions fall into two different categories: Loyals, those champions inside the firm; and *Adventurers*, the champions outside.

Loyals are so satisfied that they have actively decided to carry on buying a product or service, despite being offered real alternatives. They've weighed a product's costs and benefits and remain loyal customers. They will actively promote the reputation of a firm, boost the frontline staff's morale, and contribute to the firm's operations. They are your most valuable customers.

Adventurers are also satisfied but will continue to shop around, perhaps because they are curious or simply because they enjoy exercising their freedom. Despite the Adventurers' desire to try alternatives, they are extremely valuable because they will always champion the firm, even when they're not using its products or services—and they may return, stronger Champions than ever, after trying other options and determining that they are no better.

When going on a vacation, most people first choose a destination and then an airline. Many customers of Virgin Atlantic do the opposite. They first look at where the airline is flying, and then choose a destination. This is real loyal retention—it is vibrant retention, so much that it turns the paradigm of vacation decisions upside down and, of course, contributes to the company's momentum.

The quality of this sort of loyalty is of fundamental importance. Momentum-powered firms aim at high customer retention, but they also make sure that their high retention rate is matched with retention quality. The majority of their retained customers choose to stay with them through satisfaction and loyalty, not because they are passive or trapped. Both retention quantity and quality are essential for momentum.

Strategies for Vibrant Retention

As with vibrant satisfaction, firms seeking to actively develop and nurture vibrant retention should follow the MDC framework: mobilize, detect, and convert. It should build on previous actions to create vibrant satisfaction and further accelerate the momentum of a power offer.

Mobilize for Vibrant Retention

Vibrant retention can be achieved only if a firm is united behind this aim. The objective should trickle down to all levels of employees, from management to the frontline staff.

As is the case for vibrant satisfaction, the mobilization of management and employees is the first step to building vibrant retention. A critical mass of the organization must be inspired. Achieving this will require targeted training, coaching, and measurement metrics.

To tap into the momentum potential of vibrant retention, employees need to be educated, inspired, and empowered. This can be achieved, for example, by organizing workshops for selected groups to debate customer retention in terms of specific situations. Remember that simple calculations are inspirational and can be understood by everyone in the organization. Let's return to the story of empowering a pizzeria's employees by demonstrating that the average individual customer is worth $5,000. Now the question could be this: How do our actions have an impact on this figure? The graph in Figure 10.1, showing the relationship between retention and average customer lifetime, can be used to answer this question. It shows that the $5,000 figure can drop by half if the retention rate falls from 90 percent to 80 percent, but can rise to $10,000 if it increases to 95 percent. These observations strike the imagination and are a strong source of motivation for exploring potential actions.

What happens when a company already enjoys a high retention rate? If it is a vibrant retention earned by merit, mobilization is not an issue, because the work force is already committed. The real problem is when in fact the high retention rate includes a high proportion of Prisoners and Settlers in the portfolio. If this is the case, the retention rate's true nature should be exposed and put on display so that employees understand the importance of combining quality with the quantity of customer retention. Prisoners are all too ready to become Runaways, and Settlers could become Switchers at any moment.

One approach to achieve this involves asking groups in a workshop to estimate how many of their "retained" customers show signs of active and positive interaction with the firm. The discussion on how to define active retention will already be enlightening and motivating. The general guideline is that it should represent the proportion of customers who are eager to maintain or increase their relationship with the firm. In the case of the retail bank mentioned earlier, this exercise revealed an estimate of 30 percent as opposed to the official retention rate of more than 90 percent. This lower number demonstrated that there was great room for improvement, and it motivated the team to investigate new solutions for increasing active retention. The point is that a high retention rate is not evidence of vibrant retention—vibrant retention will only come from a high *active* retention rate.

In the short term, passive and forced retention may give the illusion of contributing as much to the economics of an organization as vibrant retention. However, there are costs involved in forced retention, and they include discounts, low staff morale, and negative word of mouth. These costs build inefficiencies and underline the need for an alternative. Only vibrant retention can drive sustainable profitability. Management and employees alike must grasp this essential fact.

Detect Sources of Defection

In many companies, customers leave and go unnoticed. Look out! Once customers are lost, it may be too late to get them back or, at least, much more expensive. You have to be proactive, systematically seeking out and identifying potential sources of defection.

Customers often take a long time to leave. Reasons that could lead to their defection can be investigated and corrected before they make the irrevocable decision. In the financial services sector, alarm bells should ring when customers don't use their credit cards as regularly as before. Car dealerships should notice when customers cease bringing their vehicles back for servicing after the warranty expires. Business-to-business firms should prick up their ears as soon as a client company's management changes or key contacts move on. There are often early signs of trouble ahead, and the proper alarm systems should be set up to detect them.

Another approach is to investigate this issue in depth with customers' active cooperation. Although this might be too expensive and time-consuming to carry out on a large scale, it is easy and rewarding with a selected group of customers. The customer retention portfolio is a useful tool for focusing on customer groups with different retention challenges: Prisoners, Settlers, and Loyals. Within each group, who are those most likely to defect and become Runaways, Switchers, and Adventurers? Taking each of these groups separately helps to see different perspectives and detect a broader range of different problems. The objective here is not to convert them individually—that is the next stage—but to identify potential sources of defection that could affect a larger number of customers.

The hunt for potential sources of defection must be continuous. When there is urgency because of an intense competitive struggle, for example, it should be carried out in stages, focusing first on the customers with the highest equity. Not only are they most important in terms of the firm's future, they are also the most likely to defect because their economic value makes them the preferred target for competitive initiatives.

This approach was adopted by one of our clients where we focused our retention investigation on the top 10 percent of its customer base. The company organized workshops and invited these valuable customers to share reasons that might cause them to do less business with the firm, or to switch to another. It was obvious that in this group of top customers there were Loyals, Settlers, and Prisoners. Some were already contemplating an exit. The discussions were lively, and, interestingly, they centered less on the price of products as on other issues such as flexibility and customer service. The company addressed these observations, which were also relevant for a wider range of customers. And it created a special program for its most valuable customers, whose retention rate increased by 18 percentage points.

Convert Defecting Customers

The next stage after detecting and eradicating sources of defection is to convert customers toward a more active form of retention. The ultimate objective is to have no Prisoners, no Runaways, no Settlers, no Switchers, no Adventurers—only Loyals! Only vibrant retention! Although this is unrealistic as a specific goal, it is a stimulating vision that clearly communicates the real issues underlying retention.

There are two vectors of conversion: changing customers' action from defecting to staying (moving from bottom to top in terms of the retention portfolio in Figure 10.2), and simultaneously altering their state of mind from that of Prisoners and Settlers to that of Loyals (moving from left to right in terms of the retention portfolio).

Companies with a low retention rate should first concentrate on mobilizing employees and detecting sources of friction. The holes in the bucket must be plugged before there is any point in trying to recover the water that has leaked out.[9] They should then prioritize their defector recovery on those customers who represent the highest equity for the firm. This does not necessarily mean only financial. If a highly prestigious and visible client is considering switching to another supplier, for example, it is crucial to concentrate on this particular challenge and do whatever it takes not only to recover the situation but also to secure him or her as a loyal Champion.

With companies enjoying a high retention rate, however, the picture is rather different. These happy firms gain more value in converting those few customers who do defect, and they can engage in a systematic recovery of defectors. It is one of the trademarks of momentum-powered firms. They understand that a high retention rate is no cause for complacency—indeed, it is a motivation to do even better. This is because a small increase in a high retention rate has a proportionally greater impact on the average customer lifetime than the same size increase has on a low retention rate.[10] Think back on the rocket-like curve that kicks in at around 90 percent. This is why, rather paradoxically, defector recovery is even more crucial for well-performing firms.

Whatever a firm's customer retention situation, an effective program to systematically recover potential and confirmed defectors involves the following components: open communication, identification, and actual recovery.

The first step is establishing a two-way communication with existing customers that makes it easy for them to report their concerns. This should be above and beyond normal internal hierarchical reporting, where defensive mechanisms have a tendency to bury problems rather than share them out in the open. Staff must be committed to speed and efficacy of response, to ensure continuous communication beyond the initial phase of enthusiasm for the novelty of the initiative.

The second component is to set up systems to identify potential defectors. Obviously, their unsolicited complaints must be managed, but beyond that proactive surveys should also be undertaken periodically and, just as obviously, any reduction in the activity of specific customers with the firm should be monitored and treated as the early warning sign that it is.

Finally, potential defectors must be approached to gain an understanding of their position and the reason for their change in behavior. An initially soft approach will often go a long way in showing potential defectors that the company cares. Even though such an approach may create a change in attitude by itself, it must be followed by specific actions to resolve the concerns. This must continue until there is evidence that the customer has become a Loyal. In the case of business relationships with major customers, this could involve "SWAT teams" whose mission is to solve customers' concerns to their total satisfaction and the renewal of a contract.[11]

Nothing Less Than Vibrant

Everything up to now has been building to this moment: vibrant customer retention. Here's where the traction starts to really bite and accelerate momentum. But it will do so only if the ambition is high enough. The traction built through the successful execution of a power offer and the positive emotions resulting from vibrant customer satisfaction finally starts to show tangible returns with vibrant customer retention.

To review the steps we have outlined in this chapter, five guiding principles enable the maximization of the potential momentum of a power offer at the customer retention stage:

■ Unlike satisfaction, customer retention is not just a state of mind. It is an action: the result of customers' decision to either continue or abandon their relationship with a supplier. It is influenced by the perceived value contained in an offer, but it also expresses customers' desires to exercise their free choice in a world marked by an increasing number of alternatives.

■ The business impact of retention is generally woefully underestimated. Retention offers an extraordinary acceleration of profitable growth by exponentially increasing average customer lifetime and, as a result, by lowering customer acquisition costs.

- The quality of retention has at least as much impact on the future of a business as the actual rate of retention. Although passive or forced retention does contribute to short-term profitability, it is only vibrant retention that offers sustainable profitable growth. Without the positive and active customer behavior that characterizes vibrant retention there can be no momentum.

- The customer retention portfolio helps by analyzing a firm's customer mix in terms of six groups: Runaways, Prisoners, Switchers, Settlers, Adventurers, and Loyals. Each of these groups has to be handled specifically, with a view to creating and retaining as many Loyals as possible. It is these Loyals who display the vibrant retention that fuels momentum.

- Customer retention is vital for establishing a sustainable momentum. As a result, a specific strategy is required to boost vibrant retention. The three main components of such a strategy are: mobilize for vibrant retention, detect sources of defection, and convert defecting customers.

This chapter has highlighted the importance of retention and provided the tools to increase it to the point where it can fulfill its role as one of the main driving forces of momentum growth: vibrant retention. The aim is to have zero Prisoners, zero Runaways, zero Settlers, zero Switchers, and zero Adventurers. Only Loyals! The next chapter explores the final booster of momentum: vibrant engagement.

11

Vibrant Engagement

Harry Potter and the Exceptionally Engaged Readers

Imagine you launched a new product and it sold 11 million units in its first 24 hours in a market where 1 million units over an entire year is the measure of exceptional success. That is what happened when the last two volumes in the Harry Potter series of children's books were published.[1]

These books' astonishing success is a striking example of the force of what we call *vibrant engagement*. The impact that customer engagement of this sort delivers is not just recommendation from friend to friend or colleague to colleague, but unsolicited *enthusiastic* recommendation—not just repeated purchases of a product, but customers actually *going out of their way* to buy it.

Harry Potter and the Philosopher's Stone[2] by British author J. K. Rowling was published in 1997. The seventh and final novel in her series was published in the summer of 2007. Total sales worldwide had passed 325 million copies, even before the publication of the final volume. They have been translated into more than 60 languages and have made their author a billionaire in a world where most children's authors struggle to make a living. Our point here is not to explain why Rowling's books, rather than any one of a number of other kids books published in 1997, connected with readers in the first place,[3] but to demonstrate the power that this level of vibrant engagement can deliver.

The first book itself was a power offer, as demonstrated by the way that kids enthusiastically recommended it to friends. Next, their parents and teachers began noticing that their children were suddenly much more interested in reading. They spoke about the book to other parents, further increasing its momentum.

The passion with which Harry Potter fans engaged with the novels can be judged from the customer reviews on Amazon.com. Almost 26,000 people have taken the time to write a review of one of the seven volumes in the series, with most of the books achieving more than 80 percent "top box" five-star ratings.[4] As a result of this powerful recommendation, virtually the only advertising that the books' publishers have needed to carry out to secure those 325 million sales has been simply to announce when the next episode would be available for purchase.

The vibrant engagement these books have engendered has also increased customer equity beyond the children who first read them. The intensity of their involvement incited parents to start reading them to see what the fuss was about, thus creating a new adult market. The level of engagement naturally led to cross-selling in movies and other forms of merchandise— toys, computer games, and so on.

The novels' serial nature—they follow the readers' development as they age and become more sophisticated, growing with them, as it were—makes them all the more irresistible and has brought this work of imagination to worldwide cult status.[5] Although some of them are more than 500 pages long, the books enjoy the vibrant engagement of readers and nonreaders alike, accelerating their momentum.

Advocates and Detractors

With this example, we have taken the concept of Champions, and Desperados, Runaways, and Loyals from the preceding chapters, one step further. Within their respective spheres of engagement, Champions now became *Advocates*, and Desperados became *Detractors*.

As Rowling's novels grew more and more successful, journalists picked up and amplified the story. In newspapers, TV, and radio, Advocates passionately debated Detractors. Anything that got a 9-year-old boy with a poor school record interested in reading was a good thing, argued the Advocates. The books were derivative and poorly written in comparison to other works, riposted the Detractors.

In some countries, Detractors vigorously campaigned against the books, which they felt promoted an unchristian belief in magic and the occult. In a few instances, book burnings were held, and public libraries were asked to remove the volumes from their shelves.[6] Despite this, the books charged on to success after success, powered by the advocacy of children who loved them and parents who loved seeing their children read. The Advocates significantly outnumbered the Detractors and fueled an extraordinary momentum.

Why "Vibrant" Engagement?

This chapter demonstrates the importance of vibrant engagement for any firm's future success; whether they are customers or not, Advocates and Detractors pull and push a company's future in different directions. They have a huge impact on momentum—Detractors slow it down, Advocates speed it up—and both affect a firm's efficiency and effectiveness at delivering sustainable, profitable growth. The next section examines the elements of human nature that underlie this phenomenon.

The Human Nature of Engagement

In our consultancy work, we regularly encounter both Advocates and Detractors—persons who promote or denigrate a firm purely on their own initiative, with no apparent prompts or incentives. Advocates and Detractors are like activists or partisans. Through their consumption, communication, and influence, they invest their time, emotions, and energy in a cause they believe to be worth the effort.[7] In this way, they pledge allegiance to or against a firm or a cause. What drives this behavior? Remember how the customer value wedge showed that emotions lie at the heart of human nature and behavior. To become engaged, the key driver is our emotional need for belonging, and this is increasingly facilitated by ever-more-effective connecting technology.

"Belonging Inside"

As mentioned in an earlier chapter, Abraham Maslow described a hierarchy of needs that human beings seek to satisfy. Beyond the lower physiological and safety requirements, Maslow identified higher needs such as love, belonging, self-esteem, and self-actualization.

It is the higher ones, and especially the need for belonging, that drive vibrant engagement. As with any emotional state, this need to belong is manifested in different levels of intensity. For some consumers, buying a product or service is simply a transaction—a fair exchange of value from which they seek nothing more than satisfaction. For others, it is more than just a purchase—it is a way to connect, to become a member of a club or make a statement. In some extreme cases, it is through their vibrant engagement that consumers express something even greater than belonging: Their relationship with a product can become fundamental to their sense of self. Consider how many Ferraris or Rolls-Royces are bought as a means of transportation compared to how many are really purchased for the love of beautifully wrought machinery, and self-esteem.

Fortunately, there are cheaper ways to belong and self-actualize. Facebook, the social networking service, is probably one of the best examples of this. Many other such sites exist, but Facebook is the one that has generated the greatest levels of engagement. As mentioned in Chapter 10, "Vibrant Retention," its users keep coming back—most of them every single day. Why? Because unlike many other networking sites, Facebook has belonging built in to it. This is hardly surprising. After all, it started as an enclosed environment where only students at the same campus could join in. Thus, users already "belonged" before they joined. Facebook, however, has kept that sense of membership as it has grown.

But it is more than belonging to the same school or work group that engages Facebook's users—after all, 45 percent of users who joined while at college continue to visit the site every day long after they graduate—it is the fact that Facebook shows you that other people care about you that is at the heart of its levels of vibrant engagement. Every day, your friends are checking the site to see what you're up to, and sending you updates on what they're doing. It proves that you matter, that you belong.

In the same way, top executives and professional managers demonstrate where they belong, whether they're customers or not, by the decisions they make. Choosing whether to do business with Goldman Sachs or Merrill Lynch, McKinsey or Accenture, Harvard or MIT, Dell or IBM, Microsoft or SAP is obviously based on a professional decision-making process, but it also expresses a statement of belonging to the group of companies that do business with a specific prestigious firm.

"Broadcasting Outside"

Human beings are communicative. We like to communicate all the more as our emotional commitment to something grows: We broadcast our commitment to the outside world. In the process of vibrant engagement, a happy customer can influence decisions by connecting and communicating with others. Where connections were once restricted to local communities, technology means that consumers now connect globally, and at lightning speed. Skype blossomed around the world almost overnight.

The Internet instantly brings together consumers through e-mail, websites, chat rooms, and blogs. Cheap flights, both short hop and long haul, have vastly eased communication. Where only a generation ago, friends and family living a few dozen miles apart would rely on the postal service, saving phone calls for special occasions and visits for births, deaths, and weddings, today we can be in video contact every day, free of charge, or hop on a plane for a weekend visit at a cost of little more than what an extended long-distance call cost a decade ago. It's a cliché, but we really do live in a connected world.

Our natural desire for self-expression and communication has combined with technology to exercise a huge impact on business. It is much easier than ever before for customers to have a voice. One of the most powerful developments of recent years has been the blog.[8] Bloggers are today's equivalent of the man on the street with a megaphone. Facebook takes that further. Its initial growth was no doubt driven by the pleasure young students take in broadcasting their wild and crazy behavior. But older, or more restrained, users still enjoy being able to express their opinions to the world. We live in a world where the reviews of your products that influence many buying decisions are not those of a few trade journalists who you can schmooze at industry events, but those written by thousands of customers prepared to let the world know what they think of your wares on Facebook or similar websites.

Customer engagement is becoming more intense and easier to broadcast. This has two important consequences for business. First, firms that have created power offers and have begun building momentum will find that customer engagement accelerates their efforts. In contrast, this opportunity will turn into a threat for those firms that disappoint their customers. Second, the increased intensity of the need to belong and the accessibility of new communication channels mean that customers' engagement can switch from positive to negative with terrifying speed, shifting their allegiance from one firm to another. The battle is never won for good.

Ambitious Engagement Metrics

The enthusiasm of customers' support of a firm is the real test of engagement. This is where the impact lies. The problem is that vibrant engagement reflects a degree of emotional attachment to a company that is tricky to measure. Once again, as with satisfaction and retention, we need some kind of measuring tool, but relying too heavily on simplistic and reductive numbers does not help firms understand the richness and subtlety of engagement.

Although there is no standardized measurement system, available approaches include: the recommendations score, Bain's Net Promoter Score, Gallup's Customer Engagement (CE) Index, and the recommended new customers score.

The most commonly used customer engagement metric is the recommendations score, which represents the percentage of customers who have made positive recommendations. Second, the Net Promoter Score developed by Fred Reichheld and his team at Bain & Co.[9] analyzes the difference between the percentage of customers who report a high likelihood of recommending the firm to others and the percentage of customers who report a low likelihood of doing so. Third, the Gallup CE Score, one of the most sophisticated measures, combines 11 different customer engagement indicators.[10]

Finally, the recommended new customers score is the percentage of new customers coming to the firm after a positive recommendation from another customer. Of the four measurement techniques listed here, this approach is the only one that directly reflects the real economic impact of customer engagement. As previously noted, First Direct knows that almost a third of its new customers come from recommendations.

Many different measurements exist for companies wanting to gauge customer engagement. Such measurements are necessary, but unfortunately they remain incomplete. Despite this limitation, they at least demonstrate the firm's ambition to make progress on this important dimension. This can by itself help impress upon employees the importance of engagement.

The Business Value of Engagement

Customer engagement can boost a firm's momentum in three main ways. First, engaged customers can be involved in developing a power offer and improving the value it delivers to other customers. Second, engaged customers become more valuable to a firm by buying more and more products and improving the firm's customer equity as a result. Finally, engaged customers persuade new customers to sample their favorite products or services, boosting customer acquisition.

These are the three accelerator effects of engagement: boosted compelling value, boosted compelling equity, and boosted customer acquisition. Let's examine each in more detail.

Accelerator I: Boosted Compelling Value

First, engaged customers like to get involved in businesses they care about. Their influence and involvement can be as little as suggesting minor improvements to specific features—on the other hand they might reveal ways to significantly reduce delivery costs, or help identify new opportunities. Whatever the nature of their involvement, engaged customers can significantly boost the value of an existing offer, or provide innovative ideas that initiate new, more powerful ones.

Some engaged customers are demanding and try to change the way an organization does business, either because they have good ideas to offer or because they are unhappy about something in the company's operation.

These demanding customers are normally satisfied and loyal, but they feel so attached to the company that they want it to do better. They are very valuable because they are supporters.[11] In many companies, employees try to hide from demanding customers, but truly customer-focused companies do the opposite. They have learned to listen, and actually involve their most valuable customers in the development of new products and services. It makes sense. Channeling their needs and desires into innovation allows them to develop exactly what these people want—and what they want is probably what other customers want, too.

Eric von Hippel, head of the technical-innovation and entrepreneurship group at MIT, calls them "lead users": customers who have a high incentive to solve a problem and the ability to innovate.[12]

BMW has developed a program of workshops and seminars to encourage collaboration among lead users, engineers, and executives.

Since 2001, when the program was launched, the car manufacturer has identified a number of improvements by listening to demanding customers who expect the highest level of quality and performance from their cars.

Companies smart enough to adopt this approach before their Desperados become Detractors must provide the right channels for involving customers. Both Nestlé and Procter & Gamble are using their telephone complaint line to harvest ideas for innovation. They have discovered that customers often want to get in touch to communicate advice or share ideas, truly and sincerely. It would be foolish to neglect this potentially valuable input.

Some contributions from engaged customers might seem marginal, but any opportunity to improve a firm's understanding of customer value is worth seizing. It is part of the process of closing the loop and adding to the feedback effect of momentum. Even what appears to be a marginal contribution to a firm's growth rate or cost structure can have substantial impact over time.

Accelerator II: Boosted Compelling Equity

Previous chapters emphasized the importance of viewing customers as assets. The desire of existing customers to adopt additional offerings from a firm is a crucial test of vibrant satisfaction, vibrant retention, and vibrant engagement. It reflects behavior rather than mere attitude, feeling, or thought. It is truly vibrant engagement.

Engaging customers in this way is commonly referred to as *cross-selling,* but the expression is not appropriate for momentum-powered firms. It suggests firms trying to force products on less-than-enthusiastic consumers whereas momentum-powered firms manage something altogether more powerful. Their customers are so engaged with the firm and have such a high level of trust in its products that they quite willingly adopt new offerings. This phenomenon should therefore really be called *self-adoption* rather than cross-selling. It means they actively trust the company. No customer attitude can be more precious than that.

But not all existing customers buy a firm's new offers out of this kind of engagement. It is necessary to distinguish between self-adoption thanks to customer involvement and cross-selling attributable to the push of marketing resources. The difference comes down to the vibrancy of a firm's engagement.

First Direct offers a fine example of self-adoption through vibrant customer engagement based on trust. It broke every rule in the book by successfully offering mortgages to existing customers. Industry observers had serious doubts that mortgages could ever sell online to premium customers. A mortgage is the largest financial commitment that most people will ever make, and yet First Direct's customers snapped them up because they trusted the bank. After launch in July 2002, mortgage sales grew by 53 percent in 2003, and First Direct secured 25 percent of all the new mortgage lending issued by its much larger parent company. That is serious acceleration. Once again, it is evidence of the feedback that momentum strategy engenders from engagement back to equity, from execution back to design.

The self-adoption that firms achieve through vibrant customer engagement is much more profitable than cross-selling secured through marketing push because it costs much less to make the sale. This explains why small improvements in engagement produce ever-increasing returns in profitability.

Accelerator III: Boosted Customer Acquisition

When customers are positively satisfied, they tend to talk to other people about their experiences. But unsatisfied customers also share their experiences and badmouth companies they perceive to have mistreated them.

It is a common element of every piece of customer service training that customers will talk to more people about a negative experience than a positive one. Numbers vary according to situations, but it is estimated that customers making a positive recommendation will speak to 5 to 10 people, compared to 10 to 15 people for a negative recommendation.

But these numbers reflect the fact that the majority of positive customer experiences are still little more than "They did a really good job, and I got what I paid for." This is not really news—it's only what we all have a right to expect. On the other hand, a negative experience is unacceptable for someone who pays for a product or service. Being unexpected, it is news worth broadcasting. So, it makes sense that we will tell more people about frustrating and upsetting negative experiences than we will about acceptable ones, no matter how agreeable.

What happens, though, when a customer has a good experience that is truly exceptional? The astounding quality of the experience becomes a story worth telling. The fact that it reflects well on the customer for having tracked down such a great experience gives further incentive to broadcast it. The force of the story comes not only from the number of people to whom customers recount it, but also from the intensity with which they speak. It ceases to be, "They did a really good job, and I got what I paid for," and becomes, "It is an amazing product. You have to try some."

Word of mouth is the powerful expression of one of the key emotional drivers of vibrant engagement—broadcasting outside—and one of its most vital signs. It is valuable for a number of different reasons. Since its launch in 2000, JetBlue, the low-cost U.S. airline, has built vibrant levels of engagement with its regular customers—an engagement that, as mentioned in a previous chapter, was strong enough to save it from the sort of execution disaster that would sink a lesser firm. It is also an engagement that delivers a bottom-line impact. JetBlue says 60 percent of its new customers come from word of mouth, compared to just 15 percent from its ad campaigns.

Extensive modeling research we have performed on the power of momentum has demonstrated the enormous impact of improved customer value, customer equity, and customer acquisition on sustained profitable growth. The combination of these three acceleration effects of engagement brings a customer momentum that can appear unstoppable.

The Richness of Vibrant Engagement

Customer engagement is the most powerful driver of momentum— and the richest in its intricacies. Our terms *Advocate* and *Detractor* loosely describe two extreme forms of engagement. But, as shown in the Harry Potter example, engagement involves both customers and noncustomers. In other words, whereas satisfaction and retention referred only to existing customers, engagement can also apply to noncustomers.

What do we mean by this? Well, in addition to the customers who buy its products, a firm can have an impact on thousands, or millions, of noncustomers. This impact can be real or perceived, good or bad. And just as there are paying customers who are passive or active, so there are also noncustomers who are passive or active toward the firm.

For example, there are certainly many more Ferrari fans who have never sat in one of these red beauties than there are Ferrari owners. This is the "T-shirt effect." These are the people who proudly display the name of a brand or the picture of a product on their chest. Why do they do it? In great part, because they feel value from being associated with a firm, like being the member of a club. They are unpaid but content to freely advertise their favored firm. But they are much more than that. They are Supporters. They carry the flag.

On the other side of the coin are those noncustomers who derive value from criticizing a firm. For example, in the early 2000s, Jaguar launched the X-Type, an attractive car for the lower end of the brand's range. To save costs, Ford, Jaguar's owner, used the same chassis as the Ford Mondeo.[13] Many people joked about Jaguar owners buying a $15,000 Ford and paying $15,000 extra to get a Jaguar badge stuck on it. This might have been unfair, but whatever their motives, they were Detractors, and they damaged the momentum of the X-Type.

Those noncustomers who wear Ferrari T-shirts or who joke about the X-Type are emotionally involved in a product or service, positively or negatively. They can foster or hinder an offer's momentum just as its customers can. The difference is that their engagement occurs without actually buying a product.

Paid-For Value and Ambient Value

Every offer contains a core bundle of benefits available only to those customers who purchase it. This is the *paid-for value*. But in addition, there is an *ambient value* surrounding the product, and this is not restricted to those who buy the product—customers and noncustomers receive it alike. For instance, passersbys can enjoy the seductive lines of luxurious cars, the look of fashion clothing, the music wafting out of a store, or the smell of a bakery or delicatessen. They also can be annoyed by the pollution of gas guzzlers, the perceived aggressive attitude of SUV drivers, the bad smell of cheap perfumes, the blaring sound of stereo systems, the smoke of cigarettes, or others' offensively bad taste in dress sense.

Like paid-for value, ambient value is a mix of perceived costs and benefits, and the net total can be positive or negative. What is special about ambient value is that noncustomers enjoy it, or are annoyed by it, even if they haven't spent a penny on the related product. This can make their emotional reactions and their engagement potential even stronger than is the case for customers.

With a beautiful, expensive car like a Ferrari, the paid-for value is the car itself and its associated costs and benefits. The ambient value is the package of images and associations that surround the car and which noncustomers can enjoy: the racy looks, the sound of the engine, the projection of imagining driving it oneself, the shared emotions of the Ferrari team winning Grand Prix races. Supporters love these associations and aspire to own the car. Detractors despise the image and deride everything associated with the brand. Of course, owners also enjoy the ambient value, although their perception of it might well be different from what the Supporters or Detractors see.

Noncustomers can be extremely important to a firm, but they are totally free of commitments toward it. Any form of engagement from them, whether positive or negative, is under their own initiative. This means it's harder to obtain their engagement, but that engagement is more powerful once it has been set in motion.

Consider how many people talk about your products even when they've never bought them, as with Ferrari. Imagine the influence of these noncustomers on fostering the momentum of your firm, if you manage to engage them.

The Customer Engagement Portfolio

The customer engagement portfolio set out in Figure 11.1 represents the mix of customers and noncustomers in terms of their engagement, positive or negative. The two extreme forms are the Advocates and Detractors we have already met: positively engaged customers and negatively engaged noncustomers, respectively.

Although very negative customers can do a lot of damage to the reputation of a firm, we call them *Complainers* to distinguish them from noncustomers with negative behavior, the Detractors. These latter ones may well have been customers in the past, but, dissatisfied, they turned into Desperados, then Runaways, and finally the worst category: Detractors.

In a similar fashion, noncustomers will have difficulty in becoming Advocates in the sense of credibly recommending the purchase of a product they have not bought themselves. But they can certainly influence the opinions of others. We call them *Supporters* to distinguish them from positively engaged customers who are the real advocates.

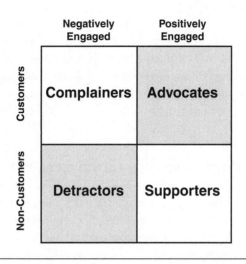

Figure 11.1   The customer engagement portfolio

Ideally, the perfect mix is totally biased to the right side. This might be unattainable, but the reason we mention Ferrari as an example is that the company probably comes the closest to this ideal situation. For most products, even the best power offers, some customers will complain about unavoidable imperfections. Ferrari owners seldom do, despite the fact that the car has definite limitations, because they own their Ferraris knowingly and their enthusiasm transcends these imperfections.

It's the same with noncustomers. A segment of the population is annoyed by the sight of luxury cars that, in their opinion, consume scarce resources, pollute the environment, and are an insult to poor, hungry people. In some countries, owners who leave their luxury car parked in the street overnight might find in the morning they have been purposely scratched by some discontented passerby, or vandalized by Detractors. But this seldom happens to a Ferrari. Even the most destructive hooligans know and harbor respect for the brand. It is more an object of admiration than an insulting symbol of dominance by the rich.

The balance of the mix in these four quadrants determines the power of the momentum that can be expected from the engagement portfolio. To determine the mix for any given firm, managers need a clear sense of the current situation. This can be obtained through specifically designed surveys and initiatives. We have, however, also found it enlightening to start the process with a management workshop and to simply ask informed parties within a firm to estimate the profile of their engagement portfolio. The portfolio offers a structure for reflection and an excellent roadmap for an engagement strategy. Its main purpose is to encourage a search for creative solutions that foster engagement, by focusing on the specific situations of each of the portfolio's four quadrants.

Strategies for Vibrant Engagement

Developing vibrant engagement starts with a power offer and is built on vibrant satisfaction and vibrant retention. However, firms also need to be systematic about ensuring that engagement will be vibrant and will further accelerate momentum. As in the previous two chapters, the strategy for action follows the MDC framework: Mobilize for vibrant engagement, detect sources of engagement, and convert for vibrant engagement.

Mobilize for Vibrant Engagement

An effective strategy for momentum requires a shared ambition, an objective that should trickle down to all levels of employees. Everyone within a firm should understand the importance of vibrant engagement. This requires training, coaching, and the use of appropriate metrics. It might involve workshops investigating how the three different acceleration effects of vibrant engagement apply to specific situations: formulating the firm's engagement portfolio as well as actions to influence its evolution, designing simulations to investigate engagement scenarios' potential impact on growth, or initiating a program to increase the recommendation score.

Beyond understanding, employees must behave in a way that demonstrates their own engagement. Customers will not be engaged if employees aren't. If they are unprepared or unwilling to talk positively about the firm and its products to friends and family and to take initiatives that improve an offering, why would customers? We know of a major insurance company that learned that fewer than half of its employees had purchased their own insurance from their employer! The main reason they gave for offering their trade to a competitor was that their own company was too complex and too expensive to do business with. In contrast, we know of other companies whose employees would not even think about buying a competitor's product because they are passionately convinced that theirs is the best. Which employees are most likely to create a positive impression with customers?

The example for internal engagement should be set by top executives through their own behavior. Inspirational leaders such as Richard Branson at Virgin, Steve Jobs at Apple, and Lou Gerstner when at IBM understood this perfectly.

Detecting Sources of Engagement

The second step in an engagement strategy is to systematically search for any source of engagement that could foster momentum and any source of detraction that could slow it down. When these sources have been detected, it is a regular management task to find ways to exploit or eliminate them.

Let's return to the example of Skype in Chapter 3, "The Road to Momentum." We identified some positive sources of engagement: the desire to appear trendy, to share, or to communicate something newsworthy. Providing stimulating new features to feed this desire would promote further engagement. On the negative side, some sources of detraction have already been eliminated successfully, such as poor sound quality and complexity of operations. But others are still active, such as the fact that certain corporations invoke security reasons to bar their employees from using Skype. If this concern were addressed to the satisfaction of the Detractors, it would unleash additional growth momentum.

Sometimes sources of engagement or detraction are related not to the product itself but to the broader offer that includes the values that it represents. An extreme form of this is illustrated by the Italian clothing company Benetton, with its provocative 1990s "United Colors of Benetton" campaign based on the sensational photographs of Oliviero Toscani.

The campaign began with the idea of photographing diverse ethnic groups dressed in colorful Benetton outfits. These pictures' initial success and emotional impact uncovered the potential for engaging customers and noncustomers alike around several social values, including race relations, poverty, war, love, and compassion.

The award-winning campaign created heated debate, and while applauded in some countries was banned in others. Benetton systematically tracked the emotionally charged reactions. As many as

75 percent of viewers hated the ads, but others loved them. Overall, the campaign succeeded in engaging customers with Benetton's values and created customer momentum despite a limited ad budget.

Converting for Vibrant Engagement

Once Benetton discovered that its customers engaged positively with the values behind its initial campaign, it extended the concept and provided a platform for communicating about those values. This was especially important to its young customer target group, who felt as if the ads had been done in their name—people who shared these values but lacked the opportunity to be heard. Advertising was a tool for engagement, not to sell the products—not directly, in any case. Toscani famously said, "I am not here to sell pullovers but to promote an image." But obviously, the high level of engagement, the visibility, and the image created did boost Benetton's growth. By 2000, the campaign had run its course, and Benetton decided to stop it when the negative power of detraction appeared to be outweighing the positive effects of advocacy.[14]

There is potential for engaging customers throughout their entire relationship with a firm.[15] The general principle is to create tools and platforms that make it easier and more attractive for customers and noncustomers to engage with the firm and its products. The purpose is not to boost sales in the short term but to nurture Advocates and Supporters, to give them a channel for expression so that they can actively promote the firm, its products, and its values. Their enthusiasm and lack of commercial motives make them much more credible than any communication emanating directly from the firm. Investments made to support this approach will be much more effective than traditional promotional tools.

Events to promote vibrant engagement should be planned with a clear target audience in mind: persons who will derive value through their own engagement. One firm that has been notably successful with this approach is Red Bull, the Austrian energy drink. The Red Bull Air Race ties neatly into the brand's promise that "Red Bull gives you wings." It encourages its Advocates to take part in a wacky air race that sees many of them doing crazy stunts that are particularly effective because they reflect intense fun in activities highly valued by its core customer group. It has become a key component in the brand's integrated marketing campaign. The resulting engagement of Red Bull customers is largely responsible for its explosive growth around the world.[16]

Ferrari has an exclusive club with local chapters and many services offered to its owners, including professional driving lessons on the company's private racetrack in Monza, Italy. Of course, it also builds a broader engagement of both Advocates and Supporters through Formula One Grand Prix racing. Observers at these events agree that the engagement of the Ferrari Supporters is unmatched by any of its rivals. The enthusiasm is, obviously, related to the performance of the racing cars and their drivers, but Ferrari also follows a systematic strategy of taking great care not only of its customers but of its vast army of Supporters. Every event is an opportunity for the fans to express themselves and share the glory, wearing Ferrari clothing and waving Ferrari flags. The Y&F community (You and Ferrari) is open to all Supporters, and its members have access to several free services and goodies. In addition, the Ferrari store sells all types of accessories, clothes, and toy models.

But vibrant engagement doesn't thrive only in the world of luxury cars. All that is needed is a power offer that has already created some form of involvement. Any firm that enjoys customer traction, vibrant satisfaction, and vibrant retention will benefit from positively engaging customers and noncustomers further. This is true in all areas, from consumer goods to heavy industrial equipment—and it includes some unexpected fields. One of the most amazing examples in this respect is Shouldice Hospital in Ontario, Canada. Also known as the Shouldice Hernia Centre, it has specialized in hernia surgery for 50 years. Its patients are so engaged that they organize an annual alumni meeting. This would not happen, of course, if the quality of the service were not exceptional, but it is also fostered by the hospital's positive attitude in organizing the events, as well as traveling clinics, a newsletter, and picture sharing.

Promotion of vibrant engagement is based on creating platforms to help Advocates and Supporters express themselves. Creativity is the only limit to their development. They commonly include events, clubs, user groups, communities, sponsoring, charities, research programs, publications, websites, blogs, and even use of virtual worlds such as Second Life[17] or Whyville (as Toyota did to promote the Scion). A fundamental determinant of their effectiveness is whether they have been set up to reinforce an existing engagement or to compensate for the lack of one. If they are just an attempt to buy commitment, they are no longer tools for vibrant engagement. They are in these cases no more effective than regular advertising or promotion, because they are not based on customer traction.

But converting for engagement is about more that just doing things right, it's also about fixing things when they go wrong. JetBlue's actions to put things right after its problems is a case in point as is Steve Job's reaction to criticism about a price cut early in the life of the iPhone. Within two months of release, Apple cut the price by $200—a move that was met by howls of protest from Apple fans who had in some cases lined up overnight to buy the new phone on its launch.

Now, one could argue that early adopters always pay a premium and prices in technology always seem to come down just after you've brought a product, but Apple realized that more was at stake here. Steve Jobs took the extraordinary step of publishing an open letter to all iPhone customers. In it he defended the decision and pointed out that technology prices always come down, but concluded by saying, "Even though we are making the right decision to lower the price of iPhone, and even though the technology road is bumpy, we need to do a better job taking care of our early iPhone customers as we aggressively go after new ones with a lower price. *Our early customers trusted us, and we must live up to that trust with our actions in moments like these.*" Apple offered everyone who had purchased a phone at full price from them a $100 credit for use in an Apple store. He concluded by saying, "We apologize for disappointing some of you, and we are doing our best to live up to your high expectations of Apple."[18] That is the action of a firm that understands the importance of vibrant engagement.

Competing in the Momentum-Powered League

Let's retrace our steps once more: *The purpose of a momentum strategy is to drive exceptional profitable growth based on customer traction. It offers a firm the chance to lift itself free of the morass of mediocrity and build the momentum that propels it ever faster to a new and more efficient growth frontier.*

Each of the stages of the process—vibrant satisfaction, vibrant retention, and vibrant engagement—builds on what has gone before, increasing the momentum. Momentum is cumulative. As a firm moves toward the new efficiency frontier, constantly improving its power offer, its momentum increases, accelerating its progress as it pulls further and further away from its more limited competitors. As revenue builds, a firm is able to invest more in product design or customer acquisition while still increasing its profitability. These investments might be decreasing in terms of the percentage of revenue they consume, but they are increasing in real terms—adding yet more acceleration, yet more momentum. Remember the Pioneers in our study.

Let's return to our two firms, Momentum-Powered Inc. and Momentum-Deficient Inc., from Chapter 8, "Power-Offer Execution," where we considered the impact of four key momentum accelerators. We have added the impact of retention to this simulation, which further increases momentum's acceleration impact. For the purposes of this illustration we have attributed Momentum-Deficient Inc. a retention rate of 60 percent, corresponding to that attained by many reasonably well-managed companies. Momentum-Powered Inc. enjoys the 90 percent rate that we set in Chapter 10, as a bar for momentum-powered firms.[19]

Figure 11.2 shows the differing fortunes of the two companies. At the start of the simulation, the firms are equals, delivering $30 million profit a year. After five years, Momentum-Powered Inc. is generating a profit three and a half times higher than its former equal. The difference in their profit growth is even more impressive. Although Momentum-Deficient Inc. increased its annual profit by $19 million, this is small compared to the $141 million increase of its counterpart. The difference in profit growth is an astounding 642 percent. The impact of their respective performances on each element that gives rise to the momentum effect is all too obvious. They are no longer in the same league. This is the true power of momentum.

Now, obviously, in real life this level of improvement is challenging to achieve in five years. But even if a firm were able to implement just 20 percent of the improvements we have set out, it would comfortably deliver the double-digit annual growth so prized by executives and management alike. And remember, it might be challenging, but it is not impossible. Our simulation allows for 5 percent of new customers joining through recommendation. Skype went from a standing start to nine million registered users in its first year of operation—almost all through word of mouth.

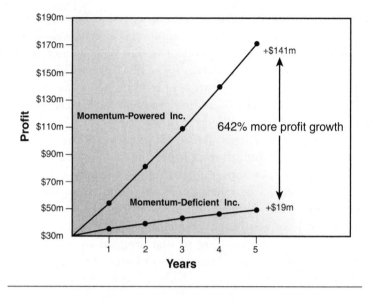

Figure 11.2 The power of momentum

Nothing Less Than Vibrant

Who would have guessed that a book about a 13-year-old orphan could have spawned a multi-billion-dollar business? Obviously not the publishers who turned down the manuscript of the first *Harry Potter* novel! That is the power of engagement, provided it is intense and truly vibrant. Fortunately for us, building vibrant engagement in the commercial world is not the hit-and-miss affair it is in the creative one.

It is the last phase of the virtuous momentum circle that propels firms toward the new efficiency frontier and sustainable, profitable growth. It is much more than customers merely searching for information or trying a product once and then buying it again. It is about getting individuals so positively and emotionally involved that on their own initiative they enthusiastically act in favor of a firm and its products. To best exploit the potential of vibrant engagement and further propel a power offer's momentum, we have presented the following guiding principles:

- Unlike the earlier stages of satisfaction and retention, engagement involves noncustomers as well as customers. Like customers, noncustomers might be involved positively or negatively and influence the future growth of the firm. In the case of highly successful firms, often the number of negatively disposed noncustomers becomes significant to the point of slowing down and even stalling a growth momentum.

- Individuals' desire to engage with others is generally increasing over time, as the need to belong becomes greater and new technologies open up networking opportunities.

- Large, established firms generally underestimate the business impact of engagement. It can significantly promote profitable growth through three acceleration effects: by improving the value delivered to customers, by increasing the equity of customers to the firm, and by making customer acquisition more efficient.

- The customer engagement portfolio can help illustrate the forces that influence a firm's momentum in four groups: Detractors, Complainers, Supporters, and Advocates. Each group must be handled specifically with a view to shifting its position in the portfolio northeastward, developing positive engagement and converting noncustomers into customers.

- An engagement strategy is crucial for fostering the emotional involvement that has already emerged with the impact of a power offer. The three main components of such a strategy are mobilizing employees for vibrant engagement, detecting sources of engagement, and converting customers and noncustomers toward higher levels of engagement.

In Chapter 1, "The Power of Momentum," you saw how some firms deliver exceptional growth and maintain it over a long period of time, thus demonstrating the power of momentum. Through simulations such as the preceding one, we have replicated the momentum effect and tested the impact of different key accelerating factors. Through clinical studies of companies, executive workshops, and our experience in consultancy, we have tested further the implementation of the eight essential components of momentum strategy, from compelling insights to vibrant engagement. We have devoted a chapter to each of these eight components that drive momentum. They allow you to systematically harness this powerful, sustainable energy that can take your firm to the new efficiency frontier, driving the exceptional growth that will propel you into a different league.

We have so far concentrated on the customer as the basis for momentum strategy. However, behind many of these concepts and examples lie implications about the way a firm is managed—specifically, the culture of the firm and its leadership. Both are of paramount importance because they provide the context in which momentum strategy can flourish. In the next two chapters, we describe how the momentum approach can be applied to employees and other stakeholders. The momentum-powered firm is indeed fueled by both external and internal momentum and builds the same levels of satisfaction, retention, and engagement among its customers, its employees, and all its other stakeholders.

PART **IV**

Total Momentum

12

Internal Momentum

Give Me a Squiggly!

As mentioned earlier, Wal-Mart is a firm that enjoyed a phenomenal momentum for years, lost it, and is trying to regain it. Let's first look at slices of Wal-Mart's life that fostered its momentum under the leadership of Sam Walton and then focus on some incidents that presaged its loss of momentum.

Of the many practices that contributed to Wal-Mart's success, there is one that I most enjoy sharing because it creates emotions. It is actually the one that is most frequently disliked and rejected by outsiders. The point is that it would not work in most companies and most environments,[1] but it was beautifully designed to boost Wal-Mart's internal momentum. It is the Wal-Mart cheer. Every day, hundreds of thousands of Wal-Mart employees, bosses, and visitors stand up and perform "the cheer." The energizing exercise takes just 30 seconds, and everyone participates:

Give me a W! ... **W!** Give me an A! ... **A!** Give me an L! ... **L!**
Give me a Squiggly!
(*Everybody moves and twists up, down, and sideways.*)
Give me an M! ... **M!** Give me an A! ... **A!**
Give me an R! ... **R!** Give me a T! ... **T!**
What's that spell? **Wal-Mart!**
Whose Wal-Mart is it? **It's my Wal-Mart!**
Who's number one? **The customer! Always!**[2]

Leading the cheer is an honor that can be bestowed on anyone, from the highest-ranked employee to the newest junior. Everyone stands, and the cheerleader begins, while the rest of the group responds. The most incredible part of the whole exercise is the "squiggly," when everyone, without exception, must wiggle and wriggle around.

Not only are many external observers skeptical about the impact of the Wal-Mart cheer, some are even shocked by it. This reaction demonstrates the need to deeply understand the requirements of a firm and of its environment in order to design specific approaches that will boost its internal momentum.[3] At Wal-Mart, the cheer is an integral part of the company style and its customer-centered culture. Most important is the punch line: "Who's number one? The customer! Always!" It could have easily been written as, "Who's number one? Wal-Mart!" But this could have encouraged a corporate culture of arrogance. Instead, the punch line serves as a constant reminder for employees to keep priorities straight.

The cheer is, of course, only one small aspect of the Wal-Mart success story, but it is a telling one. It contributes to energizing employees, developing a customer-focused culture, and creating an internal momentum. All of these are crucial issues for building sustainable success in any firm.

Mobilizing the Energy Within

The customer is always at the center of momentum strategy. But although customer momentum is the fundamental source of sustainable, profitable growth, a firm will never feel the full power of the momentum effect if its employees are not fully mobilized. Indeed, it is the *M* in our MDC roadmap for the vibrant execution of momentum strategy.

Just as a firm must build external momentum to harness the full potential that customers offer, so it must build an *internal* momentum to mobilize all the energy its employees can offer. Once started with a small group of employees and extended to a critical mass, internal momentum will carry the whole organization forward. It helps the most motivated employees and managers bring out the best in their colleagues. It is behind millions of actions, big and small, that further accelerate customer momentum.

Everyday actions build the future of a firm. Some of these are the result of detailed analyses and well thought through decisions, but most result from spontaneous behavior driven by perception, beliefs, values, and emotions. Every organization has a set of reflexes—those instant, knee-jerk responses that improve our efficiency by allowing us to act without thinking. Written corporate-value statements describe what the organization would like to be, but reflexes betray its true colors.

What is important is to make sure that these corporate reflexes are momentum-building ones. If they are, an organization can grow smoothly through its own energy. If they are not, then, as in the external world of customers, the consequent absence of momentum in the internal world of the organization must be compensated for by the use of resources. It means leaders have to plan continuously, rationalize continuously, remind people continuously, and constantly try to create enthusiasm. It can be exhausting in terms of resources and managerial effort. Indeed, the symptoms caused by the absence of internal momentum are remarkably similar to those induced by a lack of customer momentum. Fortunately, because the problem is similar, so is the solution.

Building Internal Momentum

The momentum framework presented in Part II, "Designing Momentum," and Part III, "Executing Momentum," centered on customers because they are the basis of value origination that lies at the heart of momentum. However, the framework is equally applicable to any of a firm's stakeholders, including employees, suppliers, shareholders, financial analysts, and the media. We now show how a systematic application of the momentum framework can foster an internal momentum that will create superior, sustainable value for employees and the firm.

Compelling Employee Insights

In momentum-deficient firms, employees can often be an enigma. What drives them? What motivates them to work? What current life changes might affect their workplace attitudes? But firms that make an effort to truly understand the concerns and motivations of their employees will be rewarded many times over.

Employees have an unlimited potential for growth. They are not faceless numbers, but human beings, and an exquisitely valuable source of sustainable momentum. Systematically discovering insights into your employees' world is just as important as doing so with customers—and the same tools can be used for both. In particular, the insight-discovery matrix profiled for use with customers in Chapter 4, "Compelling Insights" (refer to Figure 4.1), can also guide a systematic exploration of *employees'* unsatisfied needs.

When applied to employees, all four discovery paths (knowing-doing, listening, learning, and white) can help uncover sources of value and equity that can fuel internal momentum. However, although customers are usually very willing to speak their mind, in many cases employees will not respond freely unless they trust the openness and genuineness of the process. We have sadly witnessed meetings between senior executives and employees that were conducted like elaborate royal visits. The great leader descending, surrounded by his entourage, and condescending to talk at the little people for a while, as nervous supervisors keep watch to ensure that no one creates any embarrassment by suggesting that things are not absolutely perfect, thank you very much. The process of discovering compelling employee insights must be carried out with the same level of humility and openness as is applied to discovering compelling customer insights. Humility and openness can be tough pills to swallow when it comes to one's own employees, but the rewards are substantial.

IKEA swallows the pill effortlessly. Every year, management spends several weeks working in showrooms and warehouses to ensure that they keep in touch with their fellow workers. This is a chance to spend quality time with employees and to truly understand any issues they might have concerning their roles in the firm.

IKEA calls them "anti-bureaucrat" weeks and believes they ensure that managers don't forget the nitty-gritty. This annual exercise leads to key discoveries about employees, new insights, and perceived needs "back on the floor." It is a key source of internal momentum.[4]

Compelling Employee Value

The customer value wedge (refer to Figure 5.2) showed how customers choose to buy a brand for reasons other than its price. So too, most people today are motivated at work by elements other than the simple financial package. The value that employees seek from their employment also involves functional, intangible, and emotional issues such as access to public transportation, availability of daycare centers, personal development, belonging, moral support, meeting interesting people, self-respect, and so on.

For example, ISS, an international cleaning-services firm based in Denmark, stumbled upon a key emotional issue for their employees: their children's feelings about their occupation. Many kids, they discovered, were embarrassed by their parents' profession. In school, when teachers asked pupils what their parents did for a living, most of them were reluctant to admit that Mom or Dad was "just a cleaner." How can you deliver compelling value to your employees if they know their jobs make their kids ashamed of them?

ISS systematically set about increasing the cleaning profession's respectability. This included increasing the technical content of the jobs, offering extensive training, and providing uniforms. But it also appeared that its vehicles played an important role in building the firm's image. ISS decided that they should always be clean and impressive looking. The goal was for cleaners' kids to be able to walk in the street, point to a passing ISS vehicle, and proudly say, "My mom works for that company!"

Value can be created for employees in a multitude of ways. But as with customers, that value lies in their perception of it. For instance, what is the perceived value for a Virgin Atlantic employee of meeting Richard Branson? It can be enormous in many ways. Properly handled, such encounters can foster learning, self-respect, belonging, motivation, and confidence, not to mention the opportunity for bragging rights with colleagues, family, and friends.

To encourage a deeper respect for their staff, some companies have banned the word *employee*. Wal-Mart has associates, IKEA co-workers, Disney parks cast members, and Club Med villages G.O.s—gracious organizers.[5] But here, too, companies that come up with a new name for their employees can create cynicism when it is not coherent with other actions. It is all about perception. Creating value for employees requires a deep sensitivity for the key drivers of this perception.

Compelling Employee Equity

Obviously, different employees deliver different value to the firm, and this has implications for leadership when it comes to allocating attention and resources. But management must realize that every employee should have potential to bring value to the firm, in addition to his or her specific routine tasks.

Employees should be recruited in terms of the values they contribute, and these should be coherent with the company's core values. In some companies, this has led to an "attitudes first, skills second" principle for selecting frontline staff.

At First Direct, for instance, the principal rule of recruitment for call center representatives is that candidates should have no previous banking experience—otherwise, they might have been infected with the virus of poor banking practices. Many of First Direct's finest representatives have previously been employed in teaching, nursing, and other service professions—but not banking.

Recruiting the right people is the first crucial step. Beyond that, management at every level must realize and assume responsibility for an essential fact of business life: All employees do not contribute equally to the firm's prosperity. Those who are delivering great value must be treated as a separate target group and particularly nurtured. With those who are not, the cause of their underperformance must be examined. In many cases, the reason for poor performance is rooted in something the firm itself has done or failed to do. In these cases, the firm must act to remove the block to performance and encourage and assist the employee to reach his or her full potential. However, employees in firms with internal momentum recognize that respect is a two-way street, and that those who do not deliver fair value in return will be challenged to improve or leave.

Employee Power Offers

The two-way street of providing substantial value to employees and, in turn, receiving substantial value from them is the basis of a sustainable win-win relationship. This relationship is strengthened by employment packages that employees perceive as power offers. These offers should be targeted at the type of employees the firm wants to attract, satisfy, and retain. Because there is more than one type of employee, there need to be different power offers, targeted at different parts of the organization, each delivering different compelling value and securing different compelling equity. But they should all deliver a better value proposition than alternative employers' offers for any given employee, while at the same time being cost-effective.

First Direct's understanding of employees' needs saw it discard a range of fringe benefits common to the banking sector. Instead, the bank focused on benefits that aimed to improve the stressful conditions of 24-hour call centers. These included free nursery facilities for working mothers, free vending machines, a 24-hour cafeteria, and nighttime security services. Employees appreciate the firm's generosity in providing services that meet their needs. The value to them is immediately obvious. They are motivated.

Other, established banks offer a more diversified range of benefits accumulated over decades following negotiations between management and unions. The cost of these benefits is much higher than what First Direct spends, yet workers at these competing institutions still perceive their management as stingy because the relevance of the value is less obvious. This is an important competitive advantage for First Direct in terms of both employee mobilization and cost efficiency. It is the same thing as the win-win philosophy of a customer-focused approach: Maximize perceived benefits at the most effective cost.

Vibrant Employee Satisfaction

It often happens that firms realize the importance of employee satisfaction after they have undergone a crisis. This spurs them to try measuring employee satisfaction with surveys. They take some token action, wait for the survey results to demonstrate improvements, and then use it to congratulate themselves that they are good with employees. But this is no way to show the importance of employee mobilization in a competitive environment.

Procter & Gamble did it in a smarter way. The leading global consumer goods company showed it could investigate employee satisfaction in depth and effectively resolve major issues, with benefits accruing to both employees and the firm. In 2000, it was losing market share in half of its top 15 brands, and its stock market price had plummeted. Morale was low. Instead of looking for a quick fix, P&G took the time for a thorough diagnosis. Sources of employee dissatisfaction included a perceived devaluation of the marketing profession, lack of training, and short-termism, leading to cynicism, conflict, and mistrust.

Management had the courage to investigate the problems and make the findings known within the company. Then it drew up a portfolio of initiatives. One of them was to measure how much time marketers spent with consumers—it had dwindled to an average of fewer than six hours a month. This led to a new company mantra: "If you are losing energy, passion, or focus—get out of the building and into the store."[6]

Obstacles to employee satisfaction have to be discovered and eliminated. Inadequate or inappropriate resources, inefficient internal communications, and outdated and bureaucratic processes can all be major sources of friction that frustrate employees trying to do their best.

Employees need to believe in the company if they are to win in today's competitive markets. Companies that excel in employee relations don't make a big deal of it—it's just a part of normal business, a win-win situation.

Vibrant Employee Retention

Employee retention is crucial for a momentum-powered firm, just as much as customer retention. Low employee retention is expensive, ramping up costs in recruitment, training, coherence, culture, and customer interaction.

By *retention,* we mean vibrant retention: The firm's best employees— the ones who have other options—choose to stay with the company. The more valuable the employee, the more alternatives he or she has, and hence the more possibilities for finding work elsewhere.

The smart firm nurtures employees in the same way it approaches customer retention. Loyals should be gratified, Adventurers and Switchers regained, and Settlers and Prisoners motivated and reenergized (or, in the last resort, dismissed) before they damage the organization's reputation. Finally, Runaways must be intercepted so that even if they cannot be turned around (which should be your first goal), lessons can be learned from their reasons for defecting.

William C. Weldon, chairman and CEO of Johnson & Johnson, is known for going out of his way to hold on to his best staffers. When he heard that the head of the pharmaceutical R&D group was considering leaving the company, he called him early the next morning and invited him to his home for breakfast. Weldon himself prepared breakfast for this top executive while discussing his concerns. Within the following week, he had taken steps to address the man's issues, who decided to stay at J&J. Weldon's commitment to showing respect and appreciation for a valuable company asset was the right reflex at the right time.[7]

Vibrant Employee Engagement

Employee engagement is a crucial aspect of sustainability because it motivates outstanding behavior. As we saw earlier in this book, Daniel Vasella's passion to develop the drug Gleevec reverberated throughout the company's oncology division, motivating every employee to a personal involvement in the boss's emergency action. Vasella's inspired leadership brought the drug to cancer sufferers with record-breaking speed and confounded the pessimists who had advised against the development program as a money-loser.

Virgin Atlantic is a completely different kind of company from Novartis, but its boss Richard Branson has instilled the same kind of go-forward culture as Vasella created when bringing Gleevec to market. Every Virgin employee is treated as a potential source of ideas that can affect the future of the entire company.

Employees of momentum-powered firms actively participate in their company's success story by striving for highest standards of value delivery and customer satisfaction—in other words, in executing the customer power offer to the best of their ability. Their motivation derives from a sense of shared intellectual and emotional participation that causes them to act reflexively to power the firm ahead. This is the virtuous circle of internal momentum, as laid out in Figure 12.1.

In the finest moments of the success stories of companies such as Wal-Mart, Microsoft, Southwest Airlines, First Direct, and Starbucks, this circle exists without even being noticed. It's natural. It's just part of the culture.

The model explains the strong internal momentum Wal-Mart had at one point and the way it was lost. Initially, vibrant employee engagement was won through a combination of factors, including the provision of jobs and development opportunities that were lacking in local communities, the physical presence of Sam Walton and his family, stock options for all employees, pride in being part of a successful operation, and team spirit based on being part of a counterculture against "big corporate America." Correspondingly, it was lost through a combination of factors, including the perception of a growing disparity in the sharing of rewards between shareholders and top management on one side and low-wage employees on the other, guilty feelings of contributing to the death of mom-and-pop stores and of the small-community spirit and atmosphere they fostered. The same framework can also be used to systematically identify the actions that Wal-Mart should take to regain its internal momentum.

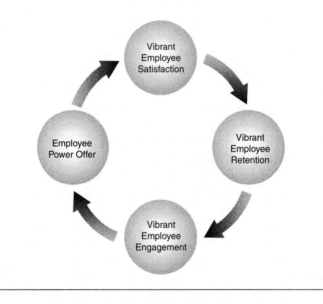

Figure 12.1 The virtuous circle of internal momentum

The Momentum Culture

Momentum cannot be ordered into existence. Employees cannot simply be instructed to act in a way that will generate momentum. To acquire real momentum, the employee behaviors that build it must become instinctive and automatic. They must be reflex actions, not conscious procedures. This is something that manuals, processes, and systems can't force through. Only a strong corporate culture—a momentum culture—can guide the behavior of every single individual, continuously and lastingly.

A momentum culture has many tasks. It has to be respectful to both employees and customers. It has to mobilize staff to search for new growth opportunities. It has to be externally oriented and focused on the needs of customers. It has to prize exploration and discoveries. It has to be sensitive to human nature and emotions. It has to foster ingenuity and promote innovation. It has to be constructive and forward-looking. It has to stimulate spontaneous interfunctional cooperation and break down silos. It has to nurture simplicity, pragmatism, and a sense of urgency. It has to be ambitious and urge to excel. It has to inspire a desire to grow, to succeed, and to win.

That sounds like a tall order, to be sure. But plenty of companies carry it through.

Many firms have tried to encapsulate these dimensions into a set of guiding principles. Hewlett-Packard has enjoyed momentum over a long period of time, largely fueled by a strong corporate culture. In 1939, Bill Hewlett and Dave Packard created the "HP Way." It was never written down, but it was practiced. In times of doubt, employees would ask themselves, "How would Bill and Dave have done it?"

Later on, the company decided to try summing up the HP Way in a few words with a communication tool called "The Rules of the Garage," the garage being the shack in Palo Alto where the founders started their business.[8] It did it in ten rules:

1. Believe you can change the world.
2. Work quickly, keep the tools unlocked, work whenever.
3. Know when to work alone and when to work together.
4. Share—tools, ideas. Trust your colleagues.
5. No politics. No bureaucracy. (These are ridiculous in a garage.)
6. The customer defines a job well done.
7. Radical ideas are not bad ideas.
8. Invent different ways of working.
9. Make a contribution every day. If it doesn't contribute, it doesn't leave the garage.
10. Believe that together we can do anything.

It is amazing how relevant these principles, rooted in the 1930s, remain to today's world of rapid change and intense competition. They are eternal, they drive sustainable growth, and they reflect a momentum culture.

Nothing powers momentum like a strong, collective desire to win. A momentum culture energizes an organization with the will to succeed. It's the same attitude that helps great athletes break world records and then continue improving. The winning ethos appropriate for a momentum culture is based on two components: the customer spirit and the competitive spirit.

The Customer Spirit: "The Real Battlefield Is Outside"

Customer spirit, the first pillar of this winning ethos, goes deeper than merely understanding the customer. It is the recognition that a company's battlefields are the markets it serves. Employees must be mobilized to win on those battlefields.

The problem in large, complex companies is that the battlefields paramount in people's minds are often the internal ones. Managers often fight each other—sometimes with style, sometimes with terrible brutality. The internal battle is with the boss, with subordinates, between departments, between headquarters and subsidiaries.

There is no need to dwell on how much energy is wasted in this internal strife. The resulting inefficiencies are significant and obvious to all witnesses, and it is the customers who lose—that is, until they find better solutions with better companies.

Developing a customer spirit within a company involves raising awareness and a sense of urgency about the external battlefield by continuously emphasizing the importance of the customer. Think of Sam Walton's Wal-Mart cheer, created after Walton visited a supplier in Seoul, South Korea, where he observed factory workers starting the day with gymnastic exercises. This mass participation struck a chord. The cheer he designed after this trip became part of everyday life at Wal-Mart.[9] It is not prescriptive—there are no details on how to deal with customers, as employees face far too many customer situations to make that possible—but it continuously nurtures the "customer spirit."

The only way to keep employees energetically serving customers is through a consistent, unceasing emphasis on putting the customer's needs first. This is the first of the two foundations of a momentum culture.

The Competitive Spirit: "Outsmarting Your Opponent"

Competitive spirit, the other pillar of the winning ethos, is a matter not just of analyzing the behavior of competing firms but of making competition a tangible, human, motivating activity that is actually fun.

True competition is first and foremost a battle of wits. Every employee should see him- or herself not as a faceless soldier in one army fighting another army but, rather, as an individual pitted against corresponding individuals in competing firms. The goal is to outsmart one's counterpart.

For example, product managers have to excel against a maximum of three to five product managers who serve the same markets at other firms. Even if they don't know the names of their counterparts, they should realize that they are not powerful, mythical forces. They are just other people in similar situations. They are probably about the same age. They face the same challenge of balancing their private and professional lives. They all deal with promotions, bonuses, budgets, and other daily issues. These sensitive and vulnerable counterparts are the real competition.

Competing against a giant army can be overwhelming. But doing better than one's peers, that's enjoyable and stimulating. Competition can be a tremendous advantage when used as a source of stimulation. The competitive spirit should be present at all levels of an organization.

In this, the example should come from the top. Sam Walton was very successful in developing competitive spirit. When traveling, he would systematically take the opportunity to visit competing stores. On one trip, when he was already famous as one of the world's richest men, he visited a Price Club in San Diego, talking into a little tape recorder, noting prices and other ideas. He was arrested by security and his tape was confiscated. Sam surrendered the tape gracefully with a note addressed to Price Club CEO Robert Price, congratulating him on the quality of security and asking whether he could get his tape back. A few days later, he received the tape, intact, with a friendly note from his rival.

Internal Momentum in Crises

Internal momentum can be lost for many reasons, internal or external. But the most threatening, even to the best firms, come in the form of unexpected and sudden crises. Such crises can not only stop a firm's momentum, they can even jeopardize its survival—or they can be great opportunities to learn and provide new insights that can reinforce future momentum. Sudden crises are the acid test of an organization's reflexes and of its real culture. Let's have a longer look at how two great firms reacted to such unexpected situations.

Wal-Mart's German Fiasco

Wal-Mart's cheer is only one aspect of its culture and its way of doing business. Whereas the cheer has become a daily staple of its U.S. operations, the retailer has struggled to introduce it in other markets. As Wal-Mart has expanded and grown internationally, it has sometimes faltered in adapting to local culture.

Different people in different cultures can share the same strong values but express them differently. When Wal-Mart expanded into Germany in 1998 and 1999 by buying two existing chains of hypermarkets, it made a number of mistakes. A lack of experience in foreign acquisitions led the American retailer to attempt to transplant its culture—lock, stock, and barrel—to a completely different market.

It moved hundreds of Wal-Mart employees to Germany in an effort to turn the acquired firms into German-speaking Wal-Marts. Trying to impose the Wal-Mart cheer—archetypally American—on disconcerted German employees was a bungle. They viewed the cheer as a ridiculous, demeaning ritual and refused to participate. It should have surprised no one that they hated it. Germans aren't from Arkansas.

By 2006, Wal-Mart had failed to make its German operations profitable. Less than a decade after its entry, the firm decided to sell its 85 stores. Wal-Mart Germany CEO David Wild acknowledged, "We made mistakes. ... Many of our product buyers in Germany were Americans. Some real goof-ups occurred as a result."[10]

Recognizing mistakes is an important aspect of a momentum culture and is essential to better exploit new opportunities. Wal-Mart's German experience should have offered it several valuable learning points for its global expansion. This and other problems it was progressively encountering should have indicated that the company needed to take action to maintain its momentum before it was lost.

Johnson & Johnson and the Tylenol Crisis

Johnson & Johnson is a widely admired firm. Experts in the pharmaceutical industry recognize its corporate culture as a crucial competitive advantage that the company has sustained for decades. This culture is so strong that it's easy to spot J&J alumni years after they've left the company for new pastures.

In the history of crisis management, Johnson & Johnson 's handling of the "Tylenol crisis" is both a remarkable success and a fine example of how a business that has excelled in nurturing a corporate culture can create the right momentum-building reflexes. The internal momentum created by this culture protected the firm during these events and ensured swift, efficient action to contain the situation.

The tragedy struck in America in September 1982. Malicious tampering with the J&J product Tylenol (lacing capsules with potassium cyanide) resulted in seven deaths and a wave of national panic. The Tylenol brand appeared doomed, and Johnson & Johnson lost a billion dollars in market capitalization within a few days.

What happened? J&J reacted quickly and massively, demonstrating that they placed the public health far ahead of cost considerations. J&J halted all Tylenol advertising and alerted consumers across the nation to stop using the product until further notice. Every bottle of Tylenol in the country—31 million of them, with a retail value in excess of $100 million—was recalled. J&J offered to exchange every Tylenol capsule in consumers' homes with tamper-resistant Tylenol tablets. They collaborated positively with law enforcement and offered $100,000, a significant sum in 1982, as a reward for tracking down the killer. They reintroduced Tylenol capsules in November in a tamper-evident package, pioneering a new approach to consumer goods packaging. Throughout the process, J&J chairman James E. Burke kept the public regularly informed of what the company was doing on the case. He obtained the support of both the public and J&J stakeholders. It was clear that from the top down the company's only priority was the safety of the public, and it thus demonstrated that it would not evade its responsibilities. Had the company not developed a strong customer-focused culture, this would not have been feasible.[11]

J&J's actions received much praise. Less than two weeks after the first death, the *Washington Post* published an article headlined "Tylenol's Maker Shows How to Respond to Crisis." Two months after the crisis, Tylenol had recovered 70 percent of its market share—and its market leadership.

J&J had the right reflexes. Its past successes notwithstanding, the company's future was seriously jeopardized. By responding swiftly and without compromise, it recovered and built a new momentum. The high investment of responding to the crisis was recovered many times over. Twenty-five years later, sales of the Tylenol brand exceeded $2 billion and continue to grow. As of mid-2007, Johnson & Johnson was among the world's 20 richest companies in market capitalization and the first among pharmaceutical companies.[12]

This is a remarkable example of momentum at work. From start to finish, J&J focused on safety, fairness, and health above all things. The company was willing to spend unlimited amounts of time and money to correct the situation. Johnson & Johnson today is convinced that it achieved swift and successful resolution of the Tylenol crisis because "company managers and employees made countless decisions that were inspired by the philosophy embodied in The Credo."

Written in 1943 by then-chairman Robert Wood Johnson, the Credo develops earlier ideas that he published in the appropriately entitled pamphlet "Try Reality," emphasizing the corporation's responsibility to customers, employees, the community, and shareholders. An essential feature of the Credo is its flexibility. It is not set in stone and has been carefully updated over time while preserving the original spirit.[13]

So what about this Credo? It's a simple document, less than a page long, expressed in words to which everybody can relate. In four paragraphs, it addresses each one of the firm's four stakeholders: customers, employees, communities, and shareholders. This order is no accident. Robert Wood Johnson believed that putting the customer first would ultimately produce the best returns for all stakeholders.

In the current version, its opening lines read as follows:

> We believe our first responsibility is to the doctors, nurses and patients, to mothers and fathers and all others who use our products and services. In meeting their needs everything we do must be of high quality. We must constantly strive to reduce our costs in order to maintain reasonable prices.

The J&J Credo is not a detailed map—it is a guide to thinking and action. Nor is it a banal public relations tool gathering dust—employees refer to it regularly. When managers get stuck on a difficult issue, somebody often says, "Let's go back to the Credo," or, "How can the Credo help us resolve this dilemma?" At another company, just the mention of an expression like "the Credo" would raise eyebrows and elicit cynical smiles. But not at J&J. That explains why it's easy to spot J&J alumni even when they've gone to work elsewhere. They're believers.

The Best of Human Nature

The interesting thing about J&J's response to the Tylenol crisis is that its employees and managers behaved exactly as we would expect any decent human being to do in such a case. Corporate culture in momentum-deficient firms is often in conflict with instinctive humanity. The final and most fundamental factor in the quest to achieve internal momentum relies on the recognition that behind the employee, the manager, and the CEO, there is a human being with unlimited human potential. In a momentum-deficient company, a cynically opportunistic internal culture is not only inconsistent with its professed external values; it also conflicts with our basic humanity.

Most people are better at "originating value" in their private life than they are at work. Bosses might not even recognize some of their employees if they met them on a weekend. Tame and reined-in during the week, they are charged with energy on weekends, hectically involved in multiple benevolent initiatives. They compete in sports, coach kids' teams, do charity work, organize civic events, play in bands, sing in choirs, and carry on in any number of other such activities.

The ultimate challenge of internal momentum is to have all this energy and these hidden talents contribute to the success of the firm. We have detected two main factors that act as potential-limiting barriers in large established firms: constrained behavior and constrained initiative.

Constrained behavior is the fate of people who have to exercise care to appear and act in a way that is not their "real" self. It happens because many view the workplace as a special universe where a different set of rules applies. They feel continually observed and evaluated. They believe they must project an image.

This artificiality of behavior goes much too far in many companies. Some business environments can seem like battlefields strewn with territories, threats, defenses, attacks, and power struggles. To prepare for it, managers don steel armor every morning, like knights preparing for battle. In other, contrasting cases, prevailing etiquette requires careful decorum and rhetoric, and employees act like members of a royal court. Situations such as this express a real problem. Not only does constrained, artificial behavior represent a major waste of time and resources, it is also a huge barrier to the openness and humility needed for originating value and building momentum.

Constrained initiative is about people feeling they cannot follow through on great ideas that they believe could create value for the firm. This perception is partly fed by the complex processes and multiple interactions that seem to feed on each other and grow inexorably in large corporations. There is a general feeling that it's not even worth trying something that lies outside the set routine, because it is too difficult to get the resources, because it will not be rewarded, or because the penalties in case of failure are too high. Self-imposed constraints of this sort become part of the culture. The morass looms.

Constrained behavior is a waste of time and energy. Constrained initiative is a waste of lost opportunities. Such are the burdens of the momentum-deficient firm.

New firms are increasingly adopting a simple, modern solution: Let employees behave like normal human beings! Do not create conditions that impel employees to be two different persons at work and outside of work. Normal human behavior happens spontaneously in companies such as Virgin, First Direct, Southwest Airlines, and Google. It is not difficult. It is not about creating some special code. It is about not suppressing the rich potential of the human being. It is about recognizing that too much management hinders the potential of the individual and confines us to expensive, growth-limiting rituals.

In Chapters 9, 10, and 11, we mentioned some of the deep elements in human nature that increasingly drive customers' behavior: the "dissatisfaction inside," the need for freedom, and the need for belonging. But what is important for the modern customer is also important for the modern employee. Let the best come out of human nature by helping employees satisfy these higher needs and unleash their frustrated initiatives. In the end, internal momentum boils down to individuals and the choices they have to make every day. Momentum-powered firms achieve sustainability when employees contribute the wealth of their individuality and bring their initiatives to a common direction and culture.

Harness Your People Power

External momentum, centered on customers, is a key to achieving sustainable, profitable growth. To be successfully implemented, this external momentum must be complemented by an internal momentum that harnesses the organization's potential energy. These are the guiding principles that we have identified:

- Most of the daily actions that build—or destroy—a firm's future are the result of spontaneous behavior, or *reflexes,* largely guided by a corporate culture.

- *Internal momentum* can be created by following exactly the same eight-module approach as external momentum. From employee insights to the design of an employment power offer and on to employee engagement, a systematic approach can unveil numerous opportunities to help motivate employees and create an internal momentum.

- A *momentum culture* builds the required momentum reflexes. It is based on a winning ethos marked by two main components. The customer spirit is the realization that a firm's future depends on its ability to win on the external battlefields, rather than the internal ones. The competitive spirit is about outsmarting one's opposing counterparts, performing better than the three to five other people who have similar responsibilities in competing firms.

- *Sudden crises* are the acid test of an organization's reflexes and of its future. They can stop most firms' momentum, but momentum-powered firms take advantage of crises to gain new insights and build a new momentum.

- *Constrained behavior and constrained initiatives* are the deadweights of momentum-deficient firms. Momentum-powered firms know how to get the best out of human nature by helping employees to satisfy their higher needs for self-expression, freedom, and belonging.

This chapter has shown how a strong internal momentum and corporate culture contribute to sustainable, profitable growth by mobilizing employees to seize new opportunities and to have appropriate reflexes in times of crisis. The next chapter tops it all by presenting the requirements that the momentum paradigm places on leadership.

13

Momentum Leadership

Can You Ski the Face?

Val d'Isère, a resort in the French Alps, is widely known as providing some of the world's finest skiing. It has a permanent population of 1,500 and a capacity for 14,000 visitors. The employees in hotels, restaurants, shops, and skiing facilities are multilingual and friendly.

Skiers are always greeted by welcoming smiles and pleasant words as they board the lifts, even at peak times. Although it is in France, it is not a "French" resort. Visitors come from all around the world. In the bars and on the slopes, you will hear more English, German, Dutch, Italian, Spanish, Portuguese, Russian, Swedish, and Norwegian being spoken than you will French.

The town is increasingly known simply as "Val," because this is easier to communicate in a multiplicity of languages. Everything is low-key, but the whole town seems to vibrate with the energy of internal momentum. There's a "feel" to the place that makes it different and somehow exceptional in comparison to most other resorts. But all of this marks a tremendous change.

Until the 1990s, Val was oriented toward "real skiers"—hardly surprising, because it is the hometown of several champions, including the great Jean-Claude Killy, winner of three gold medals in the 1968 Winter Olympics. Most of its ski slopes were extremely challenging, the buildings were not maintained, the accommodation was limited, and the locals tended to be clannish and cold toward visitors. The dominant attitude was this: "This place is for real skiers. If you can't make it down the Face"—the Olympic slope, one of the world's most difficult—"you don't belong here."

It's hard to believe that when you experience the friendly, relaxed, international atmosphere of the place today. How did such a tremendous transformation happen in just a decade? The moving forces were political will and ambition. The mayor recruited a new chief for the town's tourism office, Michel Giraudy, who had headed up tourism at a competing and highly successful upmarket ski resort, Courchevel.

Giraudy understood that change would occur only if he could convince all the resort's different stakeholders to commit to it. He provided leadership that persuaded local hoteliers, restaurateurs, and merchants—as well as ski-slope staff and tour operators—to join in an overarching project of improving the resort's offering to customers. Together over those ten years, they created the enormous momentum and sustainable, profitable growth that today you can almost sniff in the air from one end of the town to the other.[1]

Generating and Directing Momentum

Many excellent books have been written on leadership: Peter Drucker on the skills of managers, John Kotter on leading change, Ram Charan on the CEO's job, Henry Mintzberg on organizations, and Manfred Kets de Vries on the psychology of leadership, to mention just a few.[2] This chapter takes a specific view. It focuses on the leadership required to take a firm on the customer-based pathway to exceptional growth—the sort of leadership that Michel Giraudy provided in Val d'Isère. We call it *momentum leadership*.

By definition, momentum needs direction. Without focus, the human energy in a business dissipates and never reaches the critical point at which its power starts to gather pace. It's not easy, though, to provide direction and focus for today's complex organizations, with their tens of thousands of employees, working in myriad different locations. How do you go about managing the differing, and frequently opposing, demands of multiple stakeholders and bring all their energies together into a common engagement? It requires some very special kinds of leaders: Momentum Leaders.

Of course, a company's culture, reflexes, and momentum are first heavily influenced by the behavior and attributes of its senior managers. But then their momentum leadership has to reverberate in all levels of the organization, from the very top right down through its management and to team leaders.

In light of this imperative, questions need to be asked of managers at every level and in every function of the business, to determine whether they have the competences required to deliver momentum leadership. Do they understand customers? Do they inspire customer discovery? Do they display proper values and lead by example? Do they create customer momentum? Do they create internal momentum?

The challenge facing leaders today is to mobilize both inside and out, to integrate the external with the internal. Everything needs to be coherent, aligned, and focused on momentum strategy—on originating additional value, whether that value be for the customer, the employee, or any other stakeholder. All leaders must constantly seek to build and maintain momentum, both within and without.

The Momentum-Leadership Ladder

Well, just how do we define momentum leadership in brief? It is the ability to realize the unlimited potential that momentum strategy offers. As always in this world, some people perform better than others. Some have it in an innate way, others have to acquire it, but all can improve it.

During our experience in helping leaders implement momentum strategy, we have found it especially useful to create a momentum-leadership ladder, organized into levels from one to five stars, as shown in Figure 13.1. This is certainly not another tool to evaluate executive performance and to bang on the heads of those who under-deliver. Instead, this is a tool for personal development in terms of a specific crucial competency: momentum leadership. We have found it particularly useful as a complement to the momentum-strategy framework. It helps executives focus on their personal progress in leading their organization to explore the various avenues of organic growth. One- and two-star momentum leadership is outlined briefly here. After that, we discuss three-, four-, and five-star leadership, in more detail and with examples.

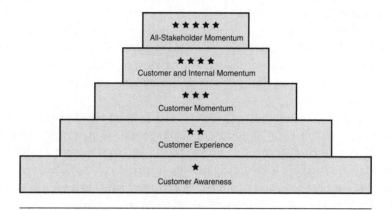

Figure 13.1 The five-level momentum-leadership ladder

A one-star Momentum Leader is already a high performer compared to most. He or she recognizes that customer awareness has an impact on efficient, organic, sustainable growth. We can all think of many leaders who have been successful, at least in the short term, without demonstrating this level of momentum leadership. These zero-star leaders lack an appreciation of the importance of value origination and do not harness the power and sustainability that momentum strategy can provide. Instead, they concentrate on mergers and acquisitions, cost-cutting, or boosting the top line in the short term. These are essential activities, but this is not a sustainable way to lead a firm for the long term. Sooner or later, depending on the competitive environment, their organizations will struggle to grow profitably.

Sometimes it is even worse, and some leaders are so lacking in respect and sensitivity for their customers that their attitude can lead to major value destruction. A notorious example was the British mid-market jewelry chain Ratners. The brand was destroyed overnight when CEO Gerald Ratner gave a speech that was reported in the *Financial Times* and then relayed by the popular press. At a professional conference, he said to his fellow business executives: "We also do cut-glass sherry decanters complete with six glasses on a silver-plated tray that your butler can serve you drinks on, all for £4.95. People say, 'How can you sell this for such a low price?' I say, because it's total crap."[3]

When we approach leaders deserving of stars, their commitment to customer-based growth rises considerably. One-star momentum leadership describes leaders who have developed an awareness of the importance of being customer focused, but without translating this awareness into a set of actions. They have respect for their customers and have made their organization aware of their importance. This is already a great step toward creating growth. This is why such leaders deserve one star and a place on the momentum-leadership ladder.

Going a step further, two-star momentum leadership defines leaders who have launched several successful customer-focused actions that have succeeded in improving the customer experience with the firm and its products. These actions are not yet part of a coherent strategy. It's patchy. It's a work-in-progress. They may be training their frontline staff about the importance of customers, but it isn't tied into a larger project. They may be conducting customer satisfaction surveys, but the measurements do not link with wider business goals or correspond precisely with the high-equity customers they serve. At this stage, a leader succeeds in obtaining some customer traction but has not yet been able to translate this into momentum.

As managers become more advanced and more coherent about momentum strategy, they progress to three- and four-star momentum leadership, and some—a select few—even achieve five stars.

So how can you rise further up the ladder of momentum leadership? By following the roadmap of momentum strategy and exploiting the pathways for exceptional growth that we have explored in earlier chapters. Momentum leadership involves energizing and channeling these efforts and, ultimately, harnessing the active support of all other stakeholders.

Momentum Leadership ☆ ☆ ☆

Leaders who deserve three momentum leadership stars have established customer momentum. They have placed customers at the center of all their activity, so much so that they have created momentum and sustainable growth.

Customer momentum can be achieved by implementing the framework described in Chapters 4 through 11, from compelling insights to vibrant engagement. In small businesses, *customer* momentum is really total momentum. The number of employees is small, and they will be enthusiastically mobilized by customer success. This is why it is easier to single out three-star momentum leadership by looking at small operations.

Take a look again at Skype, an excellent example of three-star momentum leadership. Its founders, Niklas Zennström and Janus Friis, knew and understood their audience and saw the need for a new telecommunications model. They understood the importance of value origination.

They observed the streams of people spending hours on their computers using broadband. This was a generation with new values, notably convinced that all sorts of things ought to be free, because that's what the Internet had taught them. Skype's leaders understood that these customers regarded the value of products and services differently: They were resistant to exploitation by old-fashioned incumbents of quasi-monopolistic situations.

Importantly, Zennström and Friis understood that although these customers were unwilling to pay much (or anything at all) for online services, they were a valuable audience. They were customers with equity, because they spent a lot of time online, they networked, and they were keen and quick to recommend good products by word of mouth.

This is how Niklas Zennström explained the creation of Skype's momentum:

> The model for us is viral growth. We try to get as many people as possible to use Skype for free and then some of them become paying users. We are not pushing it because it is a network effect. If you push too hard to convert free users to paying users, you limit growth. It is like putting too much charcoal on a barbecue.[4]

How does the design of Skype fit its execution? Very nicely. Its customers are satisfied because the service is convenient and low cost. As far as customer retention is concerned, initiates of the targeted customer group stick there forever. Once Skype is installed on their machines, why would they switch? Their friends use it, too. They are engaged customers. Friends tell friends because they want to communicate with them for free, using Skype. The word of mouth passes. The circle enlarges. The virus has taken hold.

Skype has real customer momentum, and its leaders have displayed the competences for three-star momentum leadership. The firm's user growth has been explosive and sustained, which explains why eBay was prepared to pay more than three billion for the company—a price based on a dynamite argument: the compelling equity in that network of 53 million users making free Internet phone calls. Zennström and Friis have definitely been three-star Momentum Leaders.

In large organizations, three-star Momentum Leaders can also be found at many levels, from product managers to CEOs. They have been able to create exceptional growth through compelling design, power offers, and vibrant execution. Behind products that have had a successful launch and sustainable growth is often a customer champion with leadership skills, a three-star Momentum Leader. But in a large organization, real sustainable customer momentum beyond a specific product also requires internal momentum. This takes us to the next level of momentum leadership.

Momentum Leadership ☆ ☆ ☆ ☆

As companies grow, they need to be able to mobilize ever-greater numbers of employees around the same customer-focused goals that drove their early growth. In addition to customer momentum, four-star Momentum Leaders have also achieved internal momentum, as described in the previous chapter. They appreciate how important value origination is for customers and employees alike.[5] Customer momentum and employee momentum[6] fuel each other, creating a feedback effect that generates a result greater than the sum of their individual parts, as represented in Figure 13.2.[7] But the two must be in balance. Imagine these two engines of momentum as a pair of giant rollers. Provided they are running with equal energy, their combined power will be enormous. If they are out of sync, however, the slower one will be a drag on the performance of the faster one.

Compared with small businesses, it is much more challenging for large organizations to emotionally engage employees for growth, but it is a crucial task of leadership. Internal momentum is essential to maintaining customer momentum over time. Many established companies have grappled with this problem. Lacking internal momentum, their growth is directly limited to the success of specific products—and this limited momentum is restricted to the life cycle of its product portfolio. It is a common occurrence in the pharmaceutical industry. Roche, for instance, prospered with the success of Valium and then stalled for a period. SmithKline similarly prospered with Tagamet before struggling and merging with Glaxo. In contrast, the previous chapter illustrated how Johnson & Johnson's exemplary internal momentum enabled it to bounce back after the Tylenol crisis.

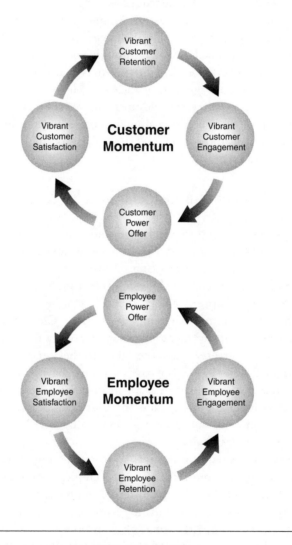

Figure 13.2 Momentum synergy

Creating and maintaining internal momentum is essential for large firms. Indeed, losing it often signals the beginning of a firm's downfall.

Leadership in a modern organization is not the same as it was 50 years ago. There has been a major evolution. In today's world, employees and customers have equal access to information, and both enjoy the freedom to walk away from a company.

Four-star Momentum Leaders recognize that success lies in the ability to convince both customers and employees. They know that they are at the intersection of two different markets: the internal and the external. In both cases, it's not about imposing one's will but, rather, about influencing these different stakeholders in order to keep the momentum going. This requires a capability to understand, design, and execute power offers for both of these markets that they have to lead.

When A. G. Lafley became chief executive of Procter & Gamble in June 2000, he had a lot of persuading to do. Under his predecessor, Durk Jager, the company had issued three profit warnings in just four months. Eventually, Jager was fired for "pushing too hard"—a more persuasive approach was required. From 2000 to 2004, led by Lafley, P&G's profits leaped by almost 70 percent.

Lafley's tenure saw him overhauling and managing both internal and external expectations. There was no single dramatic event responsible for boosting the company's fortunes in this period but, rather, a series of small, interlocking changes.

Lafley recognized that P&G's internal culture had fallen into complacency, and that deep change was needed to transform it. However, he didn't change everything. Beginning with P&G's values, he said, "Here's what's *not* going to change." He cited corporate values such as integrity, trust, and passion for winning. Then he went on to detail what *would* change.

He focused the company mission on its core business and communicated his reasoning to employees, painstakingly and carefully. It was not just slogans. He detailed precisely what this meant, how and where. He made dead sure that everyone understood what P&G's core business was in terms of economics, growth, and return on investment.

Many CEOs fall into the trap of communicating meaningless information to their employees, shot through with management-speak and pitched at a level so far removed from employees' responsibilities that it fails to connect. Not so for Lafley. He spoke in plain language that everyone could understand.

He defined P&G's core aspirations in terms of its markets, categories, brands, technologies, and capabilities—and focused the company's first efforts entirely on that. As he explained:

> If I'd stopped at "We're going to refocus on the company's core businesses," that wouldn't have been good enough. You get questions. Well, I'm in home care. Is that a core business? No. What does it have to do to become a core business? It has to be a global leader in its industry. It has to have the best structural economics in its industry. It has to be able to grow consistently at a certain rate. It has to be able to deliver a certain cash-flow return on investment. So then business leaders understand what it takes to become a core business.[8]

The transformation of P&G's corporate culture created internal momentum. At the same time, Lafley's determination to return the company to a stronger customer orientation fueled a customer momentum as well. Several successful new products have helped to power P&G along. And the successful acquisition and integration of Gillette has probably been helped by and contributed to both the internal and external momentum led by A. G. Lafley.

The longer version of P&G's turnaround is, inevitably, more detailed. But the key elements are simple. Lafley's ability to power both internal and customer momentum is what makes four-star momentum leadership. The ability to sell ideas both inside and outside to obtain momentum is crucial for leaders who want to progress on the journey to sustainable, profitable growth.

Momentum Leadership ☆ ☆ ☆ ☆ ☆

This is the top, the rarest, and the most prized. Five-star Momentum Leaders are aware of their internal and external customers, but they are also able to master even more complexity. They know that everything exposed so far in this book about customers and employees can be applied to every other stakeholder. These lessons are as relevant for shareholders, financial analysts, media, trade unions, distributors, suppliers, government, and communities as they are for employees and customers. In fact, they apply to the whole galaxy of stakeholders, as illustrated in Figure 13.3. Each of these stakeholders is a potential source of momentum, and each requires a specific value-origination approach to get that momentum going.

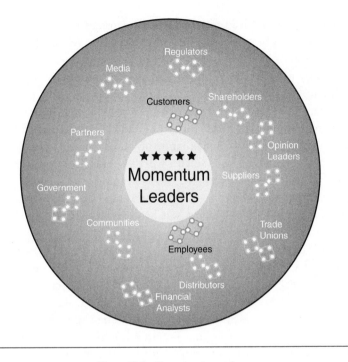

Figure 13.3 The momentum galaxy

Richard Branson of Virgin Atlantic has always been acutely aware of treating his various different stakeholders like customers. One of his greatest fears as a successful entrepreneur is to lose momentum as his company gets bigger and bigger. Virgin's relationship with the press, for example, is enviable, but this is because the company understands what journalists need as customers.

Virgin's understanding of what journalists value is as deep as its understanding of what customers and employees value. Not all journalists are the same, but most of them cherish news above all else. News driven by innovation is best of all, and that's why Virgin has so often dominated the headlines. It's no coincidence that the same innovation that excites journalists also drives customers and makes employees' lives more interesting and fulfilling.

Most leaders fall short of momentum leadership's fifth star. They might be aware of the importance of creating customer and internal momentum, but somehow they don't extend this process to other, less-obvious, stakeholders. This can lead to trouble for them and their companies, and it is most likely to be revealed when least expected. As mentioned earlier, an organization's character comes to light in a crisis. A crisis is when a good reflex by a leader can create and perpetuate momentum, and when a poor or inappropriate one can significantly destroy value.

Not even the world's largest corporations are immune to value destruction through bad reflexes, as Shell chairman Philip Watts discovered to his cost during his handling of a crisis on January 9, 2004. On that day, Shell—ranked as the world's tenth biggest company in terms of market value—announced in a conference call with the financial community that one-fifth of the oil and gas reserves booked on its accounts were not "proved." This was a major disaster for the company. Its share price plummeted by more than 9 percent that very day.[9]

The bad news was compounded by outrage among investors and journalists that such important information had been announced by Shell's chief financial officer rather than by the chairman himself. This was a serious leadership failure, ignoring the needs, feelings, and emotions of these crucial stakeholder groups. The chairman's absence was an extraordinarily poor reflex that inevitably led to this question: If this is how the chairman treats the owners of the company, how do other Shell managers treat customers, employees, and other partners of the firm?

Financial analysts and journalists were so deeply offended by the chairman's cavalier attitude toward such a major announcement that they called for his resignation. One month later, on February 5, Shell organized a meeting with reporters and industry specialists, at which Watts apologized for his absence in the conference call. "I regret it, and I am sorry," he said. "I got it wrong."

At issue in this case was not only the announcement of reduced reserves, but the boss's attitude. It is impossible to calculate exactly how much value was destroyed by the mishandled news conference, but when, less than two months later, Watts was forced to resign, Shell's share price rose 2 percent. How much was this 2 percent worth? More than $3 billion in market capitalization.

Now let's return to Val d'Isère. The rise of this ski resort demonstrates the impetus to be gained from understanding the importance of appreciating the concerns of multiple stakeholders. The station's success is the culmination of five-star momentum leadership.

How did it happen? Michel Giraudy brought some remarkably useful experience with him when he arrived. As a young man, he had been a ski instructor, and then went on to a successful career at Club Med, where he joined, what was then, a first-rate customer-oriented culture. But more important, he understood that he could make change happen only if he could convince all of Val d'Isère's different stakeholders to go along with him. He would have to persuade them that it was in their interest.

He set up extensive consultations while at the same time persuading the town to renovate its own buildings on the main square, most strikingly by facing the old structures with local granite. This elegant design became the model for the rest of the town. Hotel owners and merchants followed suit and upgraded their facades and facilities.

The hardest part was convincing local staff to make the ski runs easier. Here, Giraudy was messing with the heart of Val's elitist skiing culture. He called in professionals to survey the slopes, assess changes to be made, and demonstrate the value of grooming them more for the average skier— not exactly "snow bunnies" but no longer just professional downhillers. The skiing area was expanded and extended, then linked with the neighboring station of Tignes to create the world-renowned "Killy Space," designed by the Olympic champion himself.

At Garaudy's urging, local merchants trekked once a year to tourist stations abroad to observe world-class tourism standards and pick up new ideas. The town got external stakeholders involved by bringing in tour operators and travel agencies for specially organized workshops.

Despite simplifying certain runs, Val d'Isère has maintained its Olympic-level sporting facilities, and the locals are prouder than ever of their town. It has remained the site of many top international competitions, including the 2009 World Ski Championships. Civic values are strong, and evidence of customer momentum is everywhere. Over the past 10 years, capacity in number of beds has not actually increased all that much—the winter season counts about 300,000 visitors staying for an average of one week—but hotels enjoy an occupancy rate of 80 percent and a retention rate of 50 percent, unusually high for this branch of the tourism industry.

Furthermore, as the quality level increased, so have prices. Val is now a very rich village. Five-star momentum leadership has created value for all its stakeholders. The entire town has learned to be sophisticated in its reflexes toward stakeholders, each one slightly different according to its category: individual visitors, tour operators, travel agencies, journalists, or others.

It is much harder to calculate the value of a whole resort than of a single corporation, but a conservative guess suggests that the momentum created through Giraudy's leadership has engineered a change in clientele that has been worth a 20 percent price premium on accommodation and related expenses alone. On the basis of average spending statistics, this suggests an increase in aggregate turnover of $100 million per ski season.

This does not take into account other tourist spending, the increase in property values, or the financial impact of the new jobs that have been created. The future looks shiny, but Val must make sure its success does not lead to arrogance and complacency. All momentum-powered organizations face this same danger.

Like the pursuit of sustainable profitable growth itself, momentum leadership is a journey, not a destination. Leaders can always improve, even if they've reached the dizzy five-star heights. Hubris can strike at any moment. Even the best can fall into it and forget those they are supposed to be serving.

Tips for Aspiring Momentum Leaders

The point of our momentum-leadership ladder is to emphasize that leadership is a journey, and that every leader can and should improve. The best firms and the best leaders never arrive at a destination, because they are perpetually voyaging and seeking. The examples of Shell and Val prove that the best way to get a sense of where leaders are going is by observing their actions rather than their speeches, memos, or other documents. And the most revealing actions are those that are spontaneous and result from reflexes.

One effective way to build proper reflexes and to learn the skills of leadership is to study the lives and actions of great leaders. To provide guidance in this continuous learning experience, we have created a select "Hall of Fame" of five-star Momentum Leaders, displayed in Table 13.1. Although this tribute is presented alphabetically, we would single out Sam Walton, the late founder and chairman of Wal-Mart, and place him at the top, for his multiple competences and the impact and duration of the momentum he created.

Table 13.1 The hall of fame of five-star momentum leaders[10]

Leader	Firm	Years
Richard Branson	Virgin Atlantic	20
Michael Dell	Dell	10
Henry Ford	Ford Motor Co.	20
Bill Gates	Microsoft	20
Lou Gerstner	IBM	10
Steve Jobs	Apple	10
Herb Kelleher	Southwest	10
Jack Taylor	Enterprise Rent-A-Car	20
Sam Walton	Wal-Mart	30
Tom Watson Sr.	IBM	30

In only 30 years, Walton built the world's largest retail operation, becoming the country's richest man, with a personal fortune in excess of $36 billion. When he died in 1992 at age 74, he left a retail legacy that struck fear in the hearts of Wal-Mart's competitors all over the world. Regardless of how the company has evolved since, that is one heck of an achievement.[11]

Leadership has many facets. We are frequently asked to present our views on the most important dimensions of momentum leadership. Building external and internal momentum is the proof of their leadership, of course, but we can offer five tips for managers on their journey toward momentum-leadership stars. We illustrate this final piece of advice with some of the achievements of Sam Walton.

Commit to Value Origination

Momentum starts with value origination, and value origination starts with customers. Momentum Leaders concern themselves with customer focus not because it sounds good, but because it makes business sense. They know that the real sources of value creation are the customers— they are the number-one driver of a successful corporation—and there is no option but to understand and serve them.

Roberto C. Goizueta, former chairman and CEO of Coca-Cola, said that Sam Walton understood customers better than anyone, knew that no business can exist without them, and placed them solidly at the center of everything he did. "In the process of serving Wal-Mart's customers to perfection," Goizueta said, "he also serves Wal-Mart's associates, its share owners, its communities, and the rest of its stakeholders in an extraordinary fashion."[12]

Sam Walton stuck obsessively to a single guiding principle: Give customers what they want. It was a simple, clear stake that he committed to from the beginning. Everything else flowed from that.

Five-star momentum leadership may mean that multiple stakeholders are being served, but value origination is the guiding principle that influences every decision taken with every stakeholder. Walton, for example, built a valuable partnership with Procter & Gamble as a result of his customer-first obsession. A canoeing trip he took with a vice president of P&G brought about a productive new relationship for both companies.

After the canoeing weekend, P&G and Wal-Mart assembled their top 10 executives for a two-day meeting to analyze their relationship. Within three months, a new P&G/Wal-Mart team was formed to collaborate on serving the customer, and thus creating value for both companies.

Sam Walton responded to the soaring U.S. trade deficit by originating value of another Wal-Mart stakeholder: American suppliers. In 1985, he launched the program "Bring It Home to the USA," committing himself to buying from American manufacturers if the price was right. Walton agreed to take a smaller markup and to buy American products rather than imported ones if price and quality varied no more than 5 percent. He estimated that Wal-Mart saved, or created, almost 100,000 American manufacturing jobs through this program. It happened because Walton applied a customer-focused approach to the needs of all of his stakeholders—because he was committed to originating value.

Practice Momentum Concepts Continuously with Your Contacts

Sam Walton understood the importance of treating all his stakeholders like customers. He said that the single most important ingredient of Wal-Mart's success was simple: "If you want the people in the stores to take care of the customers, you have to make sure you're taking care of the people in the stores."

Walton treated shareholders like customers. When he took the company public on the New York Stock Exchange on October 1, 1970,

Walton decided to turn the annual shareholders' meeting into an event rather than a formal ritual, to persuade more of them to make the long trip down to Arkansas.

These Wal-Mart gatherings were popular among investors and often included special activities such as picnics or days fishing or canoeing on the river. One year it featured a camping trip. Walton knew that city-dwelling analysts would need more than a standard annual meeting to lure them to his headquarters in what they regarded as the boondocks. The investors were probably delighted to have an excuse to get out of the big city, especially considering the returns they were getting from their Wal-Mart shares.[13]

Apply the principles of momentum strategy with all your contacts. This is where you have the most impact. If the people with whom you have contact can't feel you creating momentum, how much are they going to pass it on to their teams? This does not mean that you should always do what they want. Momentum Leaders know that customer focus is totally different from customer slavery or customer charity. This is also true for all stakeholders. You will not achieve momentum by being a slave to a boss, a subordinate, a shareholder, or a journalist. Disagreements should be handled with respect and understanding. At the core of momentum leadership is the ability to appreciate what motivates other people so that you can provide value to them while providing value to your undertakings.

Have Respect for People

Respect should be a fundamental belief for all Momentum Leaders. That doesn't mean wanting to be loved but, rather, trying to provide as much value as possible to others. It is not the same as being nice all the time.

Sam Walton placed people at the center of everything he did. However huge his company grew, he continued to treat all its stakeholders with respect. With what could be read today as a sense of foreboding, Walton once wrote, "I worried that we might someday fail to take care of our customers, or that our managers might fail to motivate and take care of our associates. I also worried that we might lose the team concept or fail to keep the family concept viable and realistic and meaningful to our folks as we grow."

Walton was convinced that the key to Wal-Mart's success was the way managers treated those under them (their "associates"), because that behavior would then be mirrored in the way these employees treated customers. This was what would make customers return to the stores again and again. And this, of course, was where the profits lay. It is a lesson that many of Wal-Mart's current detractors would say the company has since forgotten.

The same reasoning explains why Wal-Mart employees are called associates. The idea occurred to Walton during a visit to the United Kingdom, where he saw a sign for retailer John Lewis, which listed its "partners." The idea of a partnership based on mutual respect appealed to Walton very much.

In 1971, he decided to expand his concept of respect for employees from an attitude into something tangible by launching a profit-sharing plan. Anyone who had worked at Wal-Mart a year or more for at least 1,000 annual hours was eligible. Commonplace today, such schemes were quite rare at the time.

There are thousands of authentic stories of loyal Wal-Mart workers who joined in the company success by pocketing hundreds of thousands of dollars in profit sharing. They include a truck driver who accumulated nearly $800,000 in stock after joining the retailer in 1972 and a retired store worker who started out at $1.65 an hour when she joined in 1968 and retired with $200,000 in the bank.

Remember the cautionary tale of Shell's Philip Watts, who neglected to attend an important telephone meeting with press and financial analysts. His lack of respect for these key persons cost him and his company dearly. Walton, on the other hand, understood perfectly that showing respect for all stakeholders—from his boardroom associates to his managers, floor workers, customers, and shareholders—would create momentum and inevitably build financial value.

Spend Quality Time with Customers, Employees, and Stakeholders

Customer time should not be token time. Momentum Leaders understand that what counts is quality time. If managers are told they have to spend 20 percent of their time with customers, it becomes a process or a target. Before long, an assignment such as that ends up destroying value. Key staff members should do it by reflex, as if by instinct.

What's the point of spending time with customers? To *understand* them. Momentum Leaders feel in their gut the importance of observing customers, of keeping in touch with reality, gathering insights, supporting people at the front line, and integrating across different departments of the firm.

There are numerous different ways of spending time with customers. In some instances, we advise putting customers together with managers for several days in a remote location, to discuss specific issues or broad strategies. Spending quality time together develops mutual trust.

At Wal-Mart, Sam Walton insisted from the beginning that every manager, including vice presidents, should spend a minimum of three days a week in stores, enabling them to meet customers and employees at the same time. Gathering information and feedback, they could communicate, educate, and coach—the normal work of any manager. Paperwork went to assistants and secretaries. The role of leaders was to be out in the battlefield three days a week. It was a condition of their employment.

As Wal-Mart prospered, Walton invested in a fleet of aircraft, thus eliminating any excuse for top management not to visit stores. He invested hundreds of millions of dollars in computers and satellite channels to ensure that top management and the archipelago of stores could be in constant contact. Systems for facilitating customer focus became more and more essential as Wal-Mart grew to a hundred thousand employees, then several hundred thousand, and later to more than 1.8 million in over 6,600 stores worldwide.

Be Momentum Consistent

Consistency is what we expect most from leaders. It means repeating the same message and behaving in the same way. This consistency is also essential to build momentum. Of course, everyone has good days and bad, and on bad days it is difficult to behave as well as one would like—difficult but vital. The most effective way to be coherent is to be truthful.

As a Momentum Leader in the discount business, Sam Walton knew that he always needed to act as he wanted his workers and partners to act. He was continuously driving cost efficiencies. This translated into his famous penchant for traveling economy when he took commercial flights. Ditto with managers' expenses. In the early days, when Walton and his partners went on buying trips, they walked rather than taking cabs. They shared hotel rooms to meet Walton's rule that their expenses should never exceed 1 percent of their purchases.

"It's up to me as a leader to set an example," he said. "It's not fair for me to ride one way and ask everyone else to ride another way. The minute you do that you start building resentment and your whole team begins to strain at the seams."

Walton insisted that his managers also set the right example. This was why he founded Saturday morning meetings for managers. At first, many were reluctant to give up weekends with their families—indeed, even Walton's wife, Helen, was famously opposed to the meetings—but Walton was adamant. Wal-Mart couldn't ask its associates to work in the stores on Saturday, he said, while managers were off playing golf. He believed that working Saturdays went hand in hand with choosing a career in retail.

Walton was coherent and consistent as a Momentum Leader, never deviating from his mantra of the customer being at the center of everything he did. As a discount storekeeper, this meant that the savings he negotiated and created had to be passed on to his customers. It was this clear, coherent strategy that powered his business to become the biggest in the world.

It Starts with You

The final step in the process is the only one that's entirely up to you. People who are serving customers and building exceptional internal and external momentum deserve, and need, an exceptional Momentum Leader. That's you. The job isn't easy, but the potential achievements and satisfactions are immense.

This book has presented a new business model and demonstrated a systematic way for firms to operate within it to deliver exceptional growth. This approach creates an external momentum based on customers and an internal momentum based on employees. In this chapter, we have focused on the implications of this momentum model for leadership. These are the guiding principles that we have presented:

- Managers have a dual role: to lead outside and to lead inside, to create an internal and an external momentum. These two forces are synergistic. They are the most efficient way of building sustainable, profitable growth.

- Beyond customers and employees, great leaders obtain momentum from all stakeholders, including suppliers, media, governments, local communities, financial analysts, and shareholders.

- Competences for momentum leadership progress through five levels: customer awareness, customer experience, customer momentum, internal momentum, and all-stakeholders momentum.

- The Hall of Fame of momentum leadership offers valuable lessons to learn from those who have been able to create exceptional growth over extended periods of time.

- Beyond building external and internal momentum, our top five tips for developing momentum leadership are these: commit to building momentum through value origination; practice momentum principles continuously with your contacts; have respect for people; spend quality time with customers, employees, and other stakeholders; be momentum consistent over time and through your actions.

Great leaders must fix upon a vision that is motivating, master the roadmap to reach it, and guide the organization to deliver it. The purpose of this book is to help you achieve just that with the new model of momentum strategy. It has provided you with an ambitious vision for creating exceptional growth based on value origination and momentum strategy. It has described the eight steps through which this vision can be systematically implemented. And it has concluded by focusing on how to mobilize employees and other stakeholders to deliver the ambitious objectives of this vision.

As we emphasize in the Epilogue, the most important point of momentum is the opportunity that is right there before you. You must not miss it.

14

Epilogue

Well, now you know the secrets of the momentum effect—the phenomenon that drives some firms to such exceptional and efficient growth. As mentioned in the Preface, each of its elements is individually simple. It is assembling the pieces of the puzzle that is challenging, but now you have a framework to guide you in this task.

You, too, can deliver exceptional growth by building momentum in exactly the same way that leaders such as Steve Jobs, Michael Dell, Richard Branson, and Sam Walton did.

Yes, they were outstanding leaders, but you can be, too. You might make mistakes along the way, but so did they. There were plenty of moments when Jobs, Dell, Branson, Walton, and others stumbled off course. And so although their stories should serve to inspire and empower all of us, at the same time they caution us.[1] Any one of us can create the conditions to generate exceptional growth, but even great leaders can drop the ball. Never mind: They carried on. Like them, we must all constantly strive for improvement. Momentum is a journey, not a destination.

Seizing the Unlimited Potential

Remember the contrasting stories of Gary Kildall and Bill Gates presented in Chapter 2, "The Source of Momentum." The first lost his momentum and never managed to recover it. The second changed the world of computing and beyond, and in the process became the world's richest man.

The lesson here is simple: There is unlimited potential out there, innumerable opportunities for exceptional growth just waiting to be grabbed, if you have the wit to spot them and the will to seize them. The success of every company that has enjoyed extraordinary growth is founded upon at least one compelling customer insight. It is the strength of these insights that powered Wal-Mart, Microsoft, Dell, Apple, Toyota, Virgin, First Direct, FedEx, Swatch, BMW, Skype, Google, and many others. Building first on some insights, all these firms took the appropriate actions that garnered the conditions required to ignite the momentum effect. All of them harnessed the power of momentum strategies for generating exceptional growth. On the other hand, their success highlights the failings of all the companies that were in place at the time and that could have grabbed these same exceptional growth opportunities, but didn't. When these striving young firms started, their respective fields were dominated by large, established competitors who were convinced that they knew their market inside-out and had a lock on what their customers wanted—but each and every one of them failed to see the enormous potential sitting under their noses.

Business is about continuously discovering and grabbing growth opportunities. Managers talk about catching a wave. But why wait for a wave to appear and hope to grab it? Momentum strategy offers you the chance to build your very own wave and ride it so far your competitors are left floundering in your wake. Don't miss it.

The Momentum Journey

This book offers you the means to exploit this unlimited potential, and we hope it has also given you the desire. The momentum path you will follow to sustainable, profitable growth requires you to supplement the control and logic of managerial analysis with a process of exploration and discovery. This is not how established firms usually operate, so you will probably face challenges as you attempt to convince others of the compelling benefits of momentum strategy. To help you face this challenge, we want to share with you four simple ingredients of successful change toward momentum:

- *Patience* is a precious quality on the momentum journey. It is about diligence, about taking the time to explore more deeply to be more effective. The first handicap managers face in established corporations is the traditional managerial imperative of being overloaded with busywork, rather than taking time to look around and consider whether there are more efficient and rewarding alternatives. By wishing to move too fast along the established paths of tradition, we risk missing great opportunities. Energetic entrepreneurs constantly offer us object lessons in the power of original thinking. They have limited resources, but they have time, and they are not prisoners of established groupthink. Instead of a headlong rush forward in an attempt to improve on the past, momentum strategy requires the patience to take time out and invent a different and better future.

- *Timing* is everything, and it should be chosen carefully to suit both internal and external stakeholders. A momentum strategy should never be launched because of artificial deadlines if chances of success are slim. Often, a good time is just when you begin a new role or assignment, putting you in the best situation to explore novel paths without being hostage to your past decisions. But you still will have to engineer the proper dynamics. Momentum Leaders do not pointlessly push against walls. They wait until they have created the conditions for exceptional growth, and then they surge forward as the walls recede in the rearview mirror.

- *Sense of urgency* is vital. Mobilization is easier when employees sense a strong reason for change. It's not easy. It can be a slog to coax people out of their comfort zones onto the momentum path. Even well-intentioned colleagues can be remarkably blind to the urgency of a situation they don't understand. You must yourself have a clear understanding of the reasons behind the challenges facing your firm's profitable growth and of the changes needed to meet them. Find the "burning platform" that will create a sense of urgency and rally support. Explain why the momentum journey is essential and why it should start without delay. This is the point when transformation toward momentum begins.

- *Powerful images* are essential tools for energizing your people. They can be numbers, graphs, or stories. These powerful images can vary from telling about the pizzeria staff learning that each customer was worth $5,000 to using the top box in a customer satisfaction survey. Tell them Gary Kildall's story so that they don't in their own way "go flying" at crucial times. Tell them about the tailor in the Virgin Atlantic departure lounge. Tell them about the New York students listening to their Walkmans on the sidewalk, and the team at Novartis getting letters and e-mails from cancer patients. Tell them about First Direct, the bank that doesn't like banking. And warn them with the cautionary tales of Gerald Ratner's "crap" and Philip Watts's lackadaisical handling of an important conference call. Use these stories as if they were your own. Take them and mobilize your people with them—they're yours to use on the journey to sustainable, profitable growth.

Some of what we propound may seem contradictory. How can patience be reconciled with the need to create a sense of urgency? Talleyrand, the French revolutionary politician, writer, and rogue, answered it succinctly when he gave an order to the driver of his carriage: "Please go slowly— I'm in a hurry." This is a nicely fitting paradox to keep in mind when embarking on the momentum journey.

Our Momentum Future

We opened this book by presenting our 20-year study showing significant differences in the growth and profitability of three groups of firms: the Plodders, the Pushers, and the Pioneers. These groups represent three standards of growth efficiencies: past, present, and future.

We have revealed the momentum effect, the power of the exceptional organic growth that it delivers, and the conditions under which it arises. We have set out the components of momentum strategy focused on securing those conditions, and described a systematic process for implementing them. Based on a deeper understanding of customers, this process enables the design of power offers loaded with customer traction, ones that create a virtuous circle of vibrant satisfaction, retention, and engagement. With empirical research, company analyses, and computerized simulations, we have demonstrated the significant economic superiority of momentum strategy.

This economic superiority is not good merely for business and customers. It is essential for society and our quality of life. By getting closer to the real needs of customers, by delivering more for less, by providing higher but more efficient growth, we achieve a better use of our resources. One day, the new standards of growth efficiency made feasible by the momentum paradigm will no longer be optional. Firms that fall behind will be unable to survive.

As borderless, globalized competition increases, more and more businesses will be forced to explore new avenues for value origination, and this will build a better world for customers. This new world will be led by colorful individuals, Momentum Leaders determined to create value for their customers, their company, and themselves—and by doing so contribute to building a better world for all.

We will see more Momentum Leaders like Sam Walton, who was convinced there was a way to bring large-scale retailing to rural America; like Luciano Benetton, who saw that the world was starving for colors; like Steve Jobs, who understands that customers can have an affective relationship with gadgets; and like Richard Branson, who believes that air travel need not be boring. New generations will push momentum further with an even deeper understanding of customers, and they will find ways to deliver more value more efficiently. This book aims to help those aspiring Momentum Leaders who embark on their own journey, firm in the conviction that it leads to a brave new world.

Bibliography

Aaker, David A. and Erich Joachimsthaler. *Brand Leadership.* London: Simon & Schuster, 2002.

Alboher Nusbaum. "JetBlue Turning Fliers into Fanatic Loyalists." *Deseret News,* March 24, 2004.

Ambler, Tim. *Marketing and the Bottom Line.* Harlow, UK: Pearson Education Limited, 2003.

Anderson, Chris. *The Long Tail.* New York: Hyperion, 2006.

Angelmar, Reinhard, and Christian Pinson. Zantac (a and b). Fontainebleau, France. INSEAD Case Services, Case No. 09/92, 1993, 236.

Barrett, Amy. "Staying on the Top." *BusinessWeek,* May 5, 2003, 40–45.

Barsky, Jonathan D. *World-Class Customer Satisfaction.* Burr Ridge, IL: Irwin Professional Publishing, 1995.

Barwise, Patrick, and Sean Meehan. *Simply Better: Winning and Keeping Customers by Delivering What Matters Most.* Boston: Harvard Business School Press, 2004.

Bayley, Stephen. "The MT Executive Car of the Year: The Fabulous 5 Series." *Management Today,* March 1, 2004, 72.

Becker, David O. "Gambling on Customers." *McKinsey Quarterly* 2 (2003): 46–59.

Bedbury, Scott. *A New Brand World.* New York: Penguin Books, 2002.

Berner, Robert. "P&G: New and Improved." *BusinessWeek,* July 7, 2003.

Bianco, Anthony and Wendy Zellner. "Is Wal-Mart Too Powerful?" *BusinessWeek,* October 6, 2003.

Bing, Stanley. "It's a !@#$% Man's World." *Fortune,* October 2004, 284.

Blattberg, Robert C., Gary Getz, and Jacquelyn S. Thomas. *Customer Equity: Building and Managing Relationships as Valuable Assets.* Boston: Harvard Business School Publishing Corporation. 2004.

Bossidy, Larry, and Ram Charan. *Execution: The Discipline of Getting Things Done.* New York: Crown Business, 2002.

Braden, Victor et al. *Crisis—A Leadership Opportunity.* Harvard University, John F. Kennedy School of Government, National Security Program, CADRE/PC 2005-003, April 2005.

Bray, Hiawatha. "The Resurrection of Steve Jobs." *Economist.* September 17, 2005, 68.

Bruch, Heike, and Sumantra Ghoshal. *A Bias for Action.* Boston: Harvard Business School Press, 2004.

Burkitt, Hugh, and John Zealley. *Marketing Excellence.* Chichester, West Sussex, England: John Wiley & Sons Ltd, 2006.

Burrows, Peter. "Can the iPod Keep Leading the Band?" *BusinessWeek.* November 8, 2004, 54.

BusinessWeek. "This Volvo Is Not a Guy Thing." March 15, 2004.

CanTech. "Alcoa Sets Sights on Packaging Innovation." November/December, 2005, 9.

Carlzon, Jan. *Moments of Truth*. Collins, 1989.

Charan, Ram, Stephen Drotter, and James Noel. *The Leadership Pipeline: How to Build the Leadership-Powered Company*. San Francisco: Jossey-Bass, 2001.

Charan, Ram. *Profitable Growth Is Everyone's Business*. New York: Crown Business, 2004.

Clancy, Kevin, and Peter Krieg. *Your Gut Is Still Not Smarter Than Your Head: How Disciplined, Fact-Based Marketing Can Drive Extraordinary Growth and Profits*. Hoboken, NJ: John Wiley & Sons, 2007.

Clancy, Kevin J., and Robert S. Shulman. *Marketing Myths That Are Killing Business*. New York: McGraw-Hill, 1994.

Cohen, Marshal. *Why Customers Do What They Do*. New York: McGraw-Hill, 2006.

Cohn, Laura, Carol Matlack, and Dean Foust. "Will Coke's Water Meet Its Waterloo?" *BusinessWeek,* March 29, 2004, 30.

Collins, James C., and Jerry I. Porras. *Built to Last: Successful Habits of Visionary Companies*. New York: HarperCollins, 1994.

Collins, Jim. *Good to Great: Why Some Companies Make the Leap... and Others Don't*. New York: Collins, 2001.

Cook, Victor J. Jr. *Competing for Customers and Capital*. Mason, OH: Thomson, 2006.

Cookson, Clive. "Emotions' Role in Economic Thinking." *Financial Times,* June 13, 2003.

Coughlin, Dan. *Accelerate: 20 Practical Lessons to Boost Business Momentum*. Kaplan Business, 2007.

Cronin, Blaise. "Burned Any Good Books Lately?" *Library Journal,* February 15, 2003, 48.

Csikszentmihalyi, Mihaly. *Good Business*. London: Penguin Books, 2003.

Dalsace, Frederic, Coralie Damay, and David Dubois. "Brand Magic: Harry Potter Marketing." *Harvard Business Review,* February 2007.

De Chernatony, Leslie. *From Brand Vision to Brand Evaluation*. 2nd Ed. Burlington, MA: Butterworth-Heinemann, 2006.

De Martino, Benedetto et al. "Frames, Biases, and Rational Decision-Making in the Human Brain." *Science,* August 4, 2006, 684–687.

Dekimpe, Marnik G., and Dominique M. Hanssens. "The Persistence of Marketing Effects on Sales." *Marketing Science* (Winter 1995): 1–21.

Dekimpe, Marnik G. and Dominique M. Hanssens. "Sustained Spending and Persistent Response: A New Look at Long-Term Marketing Profitability." *Journal of Marketing Research* (November1999): 397–412.

Dell, Michael. *Direct from Dell.* Profile Books, 2000.

Denove, Chris, and James D. Power. *Satisfaction: How Every Great Company Listens to the Voice of the Customer.* New York: Portfolio, 2006.

Drucker, Peter F. *The Effective Executive: The Definitive Guide to Getting the Right Things Done.* Revised Edition. HarperCollins, 2006.

Dutka, Alan. *AMA Handbook for Customer Satisfaction: A Complete Guide to Research, Planning and Implementing.* Chicago: NTC Business Books, 1994.

Economist. "Wal-Mart around the World." December 8, 2001.

Economist. "Virgin Territory." October 2, 2004, 62.

Financial Times. "New Chief Offers a Safe Pair of Hands." March 4, 2004.

Fishman, Charles. *The Wal-Mart Effect.* New York: Penguin Group Inc., 2006.

Focus. "If You Try to Match Complexity with Complexity, It Will Kill the Organization." Vol. IX/1 (2005): 4–10.

Foster, Lawrence G. "The Johnson & Johnson Credo and the Tylenol Crisis." *NJ Bell Journal* 6, no. 1 (1983).

Friedman, Thomas L. *The World Is Flat: A Brief History of the 21st Century.* New York: Farrar, Straus and Giroux, 2005.

Gapper, John. "How to Make a Million Connections." *Financial Times,* July 8, 2005, 12.

Gates, Bill, Nathan Myhrvold, and Peter Rinearson. *The Road Ahead.* Penguin, 1995.

Guardian. "The Miracle of Älmhult." June 17, 2004.

Guardian. "Things Get Worse with Coke: Bottled Tap Water Withdrawn after Cancer Scare." March 20, 2004.

Gerstner, Louis V. Jr. *Who Say's Elephants Can't Dance? Inside IBM's Historic Turnaround.* New York: HarperCollins, 2002.

Gilmore, James H., and Joseph B. Pine II. *Markets of One: Creating Customer-Unique Value Through Mass Customization.* Boston: Harvard Business Review Book, 2000.

Gladwell, Malcolm. *The Tipping Point: How Little Things Can Make a Big Difference.* Boston: Back Bay Books, 2002.

Gladwell, Malcolm. *Blink: The Power of Thinking Without Thinking.* New York: Little, Brown and Company, 2005.

Godin, Seth. *Purple Cow: Transform Your Business by Being Remarkable.* New York: Penguin Books, 2002.

Goldenberg, Jacob, and David Mazursky. *Creativity in Product Innovation.* Cambridge, UK: Cambridge University Press, 2002.

Goldsmith, Russell. *Viral Marketing: Make People Your Willing Advocates.* Upper Saddle River, NJ: Prentice Hall, 2002.

Gratton, Lynda. *Hot Spots.* Harlow, UK: Pearson Education Limited, 2007.

Greene, Jay. "Troubling Exits at Microsoft." *BusinessWeek,* September 26, 2005, 98–108.

Gupta, Rajat, and Wendler, Jim. "Leading Change: An Interview with the CEO of P&G." *McKinsey Quarterly,* July 2005.

Gupta, Sunil and Donald R. Lehmann. *Managing Customers as Investments.* Upper Saddle River, NJ: Wharton School Publishing, 2005.

Hamel, Gary. *Leading the Revolution.* Boston: Harvard Business School Press, 2000.

Hamm, Steve and Jay Greene. "The Man Who Could Have Been Bill Gates." *BusinessWeek,* October 25, 2004, 106–108.

Hanssens Dominique M. and Ming Ouyang. "Hysteresis in Market Response: When is marketing spending an investment?" *Review of Marketing Science.* 419, 2002.

Harari, Oren. *Break from the Pack.* Harlow, UK: Pearson Education Limited, 2007.

Hemp, P. "Managing the Next Best Thing: An Interview with EMC's Michael Ruettgers." *Harvard Business Review,* January 2001, 132–136.

Heskett, James L., Gary W. Loveman, W. Earl Sasser Jr., and Leonard A. Schlesinger. "Putting the Service-Profit Chain to Work." *Harvard Business Review,* March-April 1994.

Heskett, James L., W. Earl Sasser Jr., and Leonard A. Schlesinger. *The Service-Profit Chain.* The Free Press, 1997.

Holzner, Steven. *How Dell Does It.* McGraw-Hill, 2005.

Hoyos, Carola. "Shell Boss Fails to Turn Up for the Bad News." *Financial Times,* January 10, 2004.

Hughes, Arthur Middleton. *The Customer Loyalty Solution.* McGraw-Hill, 2003.

Johansson, Johny K. *In Your Face.* Upper Saddle River, NJ: Pearson Education, 2004.

Kaplan, Steve. *Bag the Elephant: How to Win and Keep Customers.* Austin, TX: Bard Press, 2005.

Kaplan, Tamara. "The Tylenol Crisis: How Effective Public Relations Saved Johnson & Johnson." In Glen Broom, Allen Center, and Scott Cutlip. *Effective Public Relations,* 7th Ed. Prentice Hall, 1994.

Kashani, Kamran. Tetra Pak (A, B, C, D): The Challenge of Intimacy with a Key Customer. IMD Case Study, 2003.

Kashani, Kamran. "Marketing Through Collaboration: How Seller and Buyer Can Benefit." *EBF* 17 (Spring 2004): 37–43.

Keiningham, Timothy L., and Terry G. Vavra. *The Customer Delight Principle.* McGraw-Hill, 2001.

Keiningham, Timothy L., Terry G. Vavra, Lerzan Aksoy, and Henri Wallard. *Loyalty Myths: Hyped Strategies That Will Put You Out of Business—and Proven Tactics That Really Work.* Hoboken, NJ: Wiley, 2005.

Keller, Kevin Lane. *Strategic Brand Management Building Measuring, and Managing Brand Equity.* 2nd Ed. Upper Saddle River, NJ: Pearson Education, 2003.

Vries, Manfred F. R. Kets de. *The Leader on the Couch: A Clinical Approach to Changing People & Organisations.* Wiley, 2006.

Kiley, David. *Driven: Inside BMW, the Most Admired Car Company in the World.* Hoboken, NJ: John Wiley & Sons, 2004.

Kim, Chan W. and Renée Mauborgne. *Blue Ocean Strategy: How to Create Uncontested Market Space and Make the Competition Irrelevant.* Boston: Harvard Business School Publishing, 2005.

Kim, W. Chan and Renée Mauborgne. "Value Innovation: The Strategic Logic of High Growth." *Harvard Business Review* 75, no. 1 (January-February1997): 103–112.

Kim, W. Chan and Renée Mauborgne. "Creating New Market Space." *Harvard Business Review* 77, no. 1 (January-February 1999): 83–93.

Kim, W. Chan and Renée Mauborgne. "Charting Your Company's Future." *Harvard Business Review* 80, no. 6 (June 2002): 76–82.

Kirby, Justin and Paul Marsden. *Connected Marketing: The Viral, Buzz, and Word of Mouth Revolution.* St. Louis: Butterworth-Heinemann Ltd., 2005.

Kirkpatrick, David. "Facebook's Plan to Hook Up to the World." *Fortune,* June 11, 2007.

Koehn, Nancy F. *Brand New: How Entrepreneurs Earned Consumers' Trust, from Wedgwood to Dell.* Boston: Harvard Business School Press, 2001.

Kotler, Philip, and Trias de Bes. *Lateral Marketing: New Techniques for Finding Breakthrough Ideas.* Hoboken, NJ: John Wiley & Sons, 2003.

Kotler, Philip. *Kotler on Marketing: How to Create, Win, and Dominate Markets.* New York: The Free Press, 1999.

Kotter, John P. *Leading Change.* Boston: Harvard Business School Press, 1996.

Kuczmarski, Thomas D. *Managing New Products: Using the MAP System to Accelerate Growth.* 3rd Ed. Chicago: HarperCollins Business, 2002.

Kuipers, Pascal. "Fuelling P&G's P&L." *Elsevier Food International* 8, no. 3 (September 2005).

Kumar, V., Rajkumar Venkatesan, and Werner Reinartz. "Knowing What to Sell, When, and to Whom." *Harvard Business Review* 84, no. 9 (March 2006): 131–137.

Labaton, Stephen and Jeff Gerth. "At Shell, New Accounting and Rosier Oil Outlook." *New York Times,* March 12, 2004.

Landsberg, Max, *The Tools of Leadership: Vision, Inspiration, Momentum.* Profile Business, 2003.

Lanning, Michael J. *Delivering Profitable Value.* Capstone, 1998.

Langreth, Robert, and Matthew Herper. "Pushing Pills: How Big Pharma Got Addicted to Marketing." *Forbes* 177, no. 10 (May 8, 2006): 94–102.

Larreche, J. C., and Anne-Marie Cagna. First Direct 2005: The Most Recommended Bank in the World. Fontainebleau, France: INSEAD Case Study, 2006.

Larreche, J. C. *The Competitive Fitness of Global Firms.* London: Pitman Publishing, 1998.

Larreche, J. C. *The Competitive Fitness of Global Firms 1999.* London: Financial Times Management, 1999.

Larreche, J. C. *The Competitive Fitness of Global Firms 2000.* Harlow, UK: Pearson Education Limited, 2000.

Larreche, J. C. *Measuring the Competitive Fitness of Global Firms 2001.* Harlow, UK: Pearson Education Limited, 2001.

Larreche, J. C. *Measuring the Competitive Fitness of Global Firms 2002.* Harlow, UK: Pearson Education Limited, 2002.

Layard, Richard. *Happiness: Lessons from a New Science.* Penguin, 2005.

Lee, Hau L., and David Hoyt. "Cemex—Transforming a Basic Industry Company." Harvard Business School Case Study, 2005.

Lee, Louise. "Dell's Road to Recovery." *BusinessWeek,* June 1, 2007.

Levitt, Ted. "Marketing Myopia." *Harvard Business Review,* July-August 1960.

Levy, Steven. "Facebook Grows Up: Can It Stay Relevant?" *Newsweek,* August 20, 2007.

Lewis, David, and Darren Bridger. *The Soul of the New Consumer.* Naperville, IL: Nicholas Brealey Publishing, 2000.

Lewis, Elen. *Great IKEA!* London, UK: Cyan Books, 2005.

Liker, Jeffrey. *The Toyota Way.* McGraw-Hill, 2003.

Liker, Jeffrey and David Meyer. *Toyota Talent.* McGraw-Hill, 2007.

Lindholm, Christian, Turkka Keinonen, and Harri Kiljander. *Mobile Usability: How Nokia Changed the Face of the Mobile Phone.* New York: McGraw-Hill, 2003.

Mahajan, Vijay, and Kamini Banga. *The 86 Percent Solution: How to Succeed in the Biggest Market Opportunity of the Next 50 Years.* Upper Saddle River, NJ: Wharton School Publishing, 2006.

Maitland, Alison, and Carola Hoyos. "Shell's Man Who Wasn't There". *Financial Times.* January 14, 2004.

Markides, Constantinos C., and Paul A. Geroski. *Fast Second: How Smart Companies Bypass Radical Innovation to Enter and Dominate New Markets.* San Francisco: John Wiley & Sons, 2005.

Maslow, Abraham. "A Theory of Human Motivation." *Psychological Review* 50 (1943): 370–396.

Maslow, Abraham. *Motivation and Personality.* 3rd Ed. HarperCollins, 1987.

Matlack, Carol. "The Vuitton Money Machine." *BusinessWeek,* March 22, 2004, 50–56.

Matlack, Carol. "Dassault May Be Next in Line for Takeoff." *BusinessWeek,* March 18, 2005.

May, Matthew E. *The Elegant Solution: Toyota's Formula for Mastering Innovation.* The Free Press, 2006.

Mazur, Laura, and Louella Miles. *Conversations with Marketing Masters.* West Sussex, UK: John Wiley, 2007.

McEwen, William J. "Marketing's Missing Link." *Gallup Management Journal* (November 13, 2003): 1–4.

McFadden, Robert D. "Maker of Tylenol Discontinuing All Over-Counter Drug Capsules." *New York Times,* February 18, 2003.

McKay, Betsy. "Thinking Inside the Box Helps Soda Makers Boost Sales." *Wall Street Journal,* 2 August 2002, B1.

McKenna, Regis. *Who's Afraid of Big Blue: How Companies Are Challenging IBM—And Winning.* Addison-Wesley, 1988.

McKenna, Regis. *Total Access: Giving Customers What They Want in an Anytime, Anywhere World.* Boston: Harvard Business Press, 2002.

Middleton Hughes, Arthur. *The Customer Loyalty Solution.* New York: McGraw-Hill, 2003.

Miller, William R. *Change Creators and Momentum Maximizers.* Booksurge, 2002.

Mintzberg, Henry. *Mintzberg on Management.* The Free Press, 1989.

Mooney, Kelly. *The Ten Demandments: Rules to Live By in the Age of the Demanding Customer.* New York: McGraw-Hill, 2002.

Murphy, Victoria. "Microsoft's Midlife Crisis." *Forbes,* no. 6 (October 2005): 88–96.

Nuttall, Chris. "Wii Console Helps Nintendo Raise Its Game." *Financial Times,* July 12, 2007.

O'Brien, Jeffrey M. "Wii Will Rock You." *Fortune,* June 11, 2007: 35–44.

Ortega, Bob. *In Sam We Trust: The Untold Story of Sam Walton and Wal-Mart, the World's Most Powerful Retailer.* Crown Business, 1998.

Parker Woods, Ginny. "Nintendo Targets Nongamers." *Wall Street Journal Europe,* February 23, 2006, 33.

Peppers, Don, and Martha Rogers. *Return on Customer: A Revolutionary Way to Measure and Strengthen Your Business.* New York: Doubleday, 2005.

Pfeffer, Jeffrey, and Robert I. Sutton. *The Knowing-Doing Gap.* Boston: Harvard Business School Press, 2000.

Pinson, Christian, Vikas Tibrewala, and Francesca Gee. The United Colors of Benetton. Fontainebleau, France: INSEAD-CEDEP Case Services No. 01/96-4520, 1996.

Pinson, Christian. Swatch. Fontainebleau, France: INSEAD-CEDEP Case Services, 1987.

Porter, Michael E. *Competitive Strategy.* New York: The Free Press, 1980.

Porter, Michael E. *Competitive Advantage.* New York: The Free Press, 1985.

Powell, Bill, and Martin Kasindorf. "The Tylenol Rescue." *Newsweek,* March 3, 1986, 52.

Power, J.D. & Associates. *2006 Retail Banking Satisfaction Study.*

Prahalad, C. K., and Venkat Ramaswamy. *The Future of Competition: Co-Creating Unique Value with Customers.* Boston: Harvard Business School Press, 2004.

Rajshekar, N., and Kalyani Vemuri. From KaZaA to Skype. Punjagutta, Hyderabad, India: ICFAI Case Services, Case No. TEM0008, 2004.

Rao, Bharat, and Bojan Angelov. Skype: Leading the VOIP Revolution. New York: Polytechnic University Case Services, Case No. 905-003-1, 2005.

Rapaille, Clotaire. *The Culture Code.* New York: Random House, 2006.

Ratner, Gerald. *The Rise and Fall... and Rise Again.* Capstone, 2007.

Reed, Stanley. "Shell's Drama Isn't Over." *BusinessWeek,* February 23, 2004, 24–26.

Reichheld, Frederick F. *Loyalty Rules! How Today's Leaders Build Lasting Relationships.* Boston: Harvard Business School Press, 2001.

Reichheld, Frederick F. "The One Number You Need to Grow." *Harvard Business Review* 81, no. 12 (December 2003) 46–54.

Reichheld, Frederick F. "The Microeconomics of Customer Relationships." *MIT Sloan Management Review* 47, no. 2 (Winter 2006): 73–78.

Reichheld, Frederick F. *The Ultimate Question.* Boston: HBS Publishing, 2006.

Reinartz, Werner, and V. Kumar. "The Mismanagement of Customer Loyalty." *Harvard Business Review* 80, no. 7 (July 2002): 86–94.

Reinartz, Werner, Jacquelyn S. Thomas, and V. Kumar. "Balancing Acquisition and Retention Resources to Maximize Customer Profitability." *Journal of Marketing* 69, no. 1 (January 2005): 63–79.

Ricci, Ron, and John Volkmann. *Momentum: How Companies Become Unstoppable Market Forces.* Boston: HBS Press, 2003.

Rieger, Tom, and Guido M. J. de Koning. "Roadblocks to Customer Engagement (Part 1)." *Gallup Management Journal* (November 13, 2003): 1–5.

Rieger, Tom, and Guido M.J. de Koning. "Roadblocks to Customer Engagement (Part 2)." *Gallup Management Journal* (December 11, 2003): 1–4.

Rocks, David, and Moon Ihlwan. "Samsung Design." *BusinessWeek,* December 6, 2004, 88–96.

Rust, Roland T., Valarie Zeithaml, and Katherine Lemon. *Driving Customer Equity: How Customer Lifetime Value Is Reshaping Corporate Strategy.* New York: The Free Press, 2000.

Sanchanta, Mariko. "Nintendo Wii Success Helps Component Makers Score." *Financial Times,* September 17, 2007.

Schmitt, Bernd H. *Customer Experience Management.* Hoboken, NJ: John Wiley & Sons, 2003.

Sengel, James R., Andrea L. Dixon, and Chris T. Allen. "Listening Begins at Home." *Harvard Business Review* (November 2003): 1–9.

Senge, Peter M., George Roth, and Richard B. Ross. *The Dance of Change: The Challenges to Sustaining Momentum in a Learning Organization.* Currency, 1999.

Serchuk, David. "Harry Potter and the Ministry of Fire." *Forbes,* January 12, 2006.

Shaw, Colin. *Revolutionize Your Customer Experience.* New York: Palgrave Macmillan, 2005.

Shaw, Colin. *The DNA of Customer Experience: How Emotions Drive Value.* New York: Palgrave Macmillan, 2007.

Shill, Walter E., and Robert J. Thomas. "Exploring the Mindset of the High Performer." *Outlook,* October 2005.

Slater, Robert. *Saving Big Blue: Leadership Lessons and Turnaround Tactics of IBM's Lou Gestner.* New York: McGraw-Hill Education, 1999.

Slater, Robert. *Microsoft Rebooted: How Bill Gates and Steve Ballmer Reinvented Their Company.* Portfolio, 2004.

Slywotzky, Adrian J. *Value Migration: Strategies to Preempt the Markets of Tomorrow.* Boston: Harvard Business School Press, 1995.

Slywotzky, Adrian, and Richard Wise. *How to Grow When Markets Don't.* New York: Mercer Management Consulting, 2003.

Smith, Shaun, and Joe Wheeler. *Managing the Customer Experience: Turning Customers into Advocates.* Financial Times Prentice Hall, 2002.

Stern, Chris. *Total Customer Focus.* Philadelphia: Xlibris, 2004.

Stewart, Thomas A., and P. Anand Raman. "Lessons from Toyota's Long Drive" (Interview with Katsuaki Watanabe). *Harvard Business Review* (July-August 2007): 74–83.

Stock, Howard J. "Commerce Bank: Ahead of the Curve." *Bank Investment Consultant* 12, no. 10 (October 2004): 28–34.

Stross, Randall E. *The Microsoft Way.* Basic Books, 1997.

Sull, Donald N., and Alejandro Rueals-Gossi. "The Art of Innovating on a Shoestring." *Financial Times Mastering Series,* September 24, 2004.

Taylor, Andy. "Top Box: Rediscovering Customer Satisfaction." *Business Horizons* 46, no. 5 (Sep/Oct 2003): 3–15.

Teboul, James. *Service Is Front Stage.* Palgrave, 2006.

Tedlow, Richard S. *The Watson Dynasty: The Fiery Reign and Troubled Legacy of IBM's Founding Father and Son.* Collins, 2003.

Thompson, Harvey. *The Customer-Centered Enterprise: How IBM and Other World-Class Companies Achieve Extraordinary Results by Putting Customers First.* McGraw-Hill, 1999.

Treacy, Michael. *Double-Digit Growth: How Great Companies Achieve It—No Matter What.* New York: Penguin Group, 2003.

USA Today. "Women Design Concept Car for Volvo." March 2, 2003.

Vandermerwe, Sandra. *Breaking Through: Implementing Customer Focus in Enterprises.* Palgrave, 2004.

Vandermerwe, Sandra, and Marika Taishoff. SKF Bearings Series: Market Orientation Through Services. IMD Case Study, 1990.

Vasella, Daniel. *Magic Cancer Bullet: How a Tiny Orange Pill Is Rewriting Medical History.* New York: HarperCollins, 2003.

Villanueva, Julian, and Dominique M. Hanssens. "Customer Equity: Measurement, Management and Research Opportunities." *Foundations and Trends in Marketing,* 2007.

Vise, David. *The Google Story.* New York: Macmillan, 2005.

Von Hippel, Eric. *The Sources of Innovation.* New York: OUP, 1988.

Von Hippel, Eric. *Democratizing Innovation.* Cambridge, MA: MIT Press, 2005.

Wall Street Journal. "Tylenol Regains Most of No. 1 Share, Astounding Doomsayers." December 24, 1982.

Walton, Sam, and John Huey. *Sam Walton: Made in America.* New York: Bantam Books, 1993.

Waters, Richard. "Ebay Writes Down Skype Value by $1.4bn." *Financial Times,* October 2, 2007.

Welch, Jack, and John A. Byrne. *Jack: Straight from the Gut.* New York: Warner Business Books, 2001.

White, Ben. "TD Bank in US Push with $8bn Commerce Deal." *Financial Times,* October 2, 2007.

Wierseman, Fred. *The New Market Leaders.* London: Simon & Schuster, 2001.

Wind, Yoram, and Colin Crook. *The Power of Impossible Thinking.* Upper Saddle River, NJ: Pearson Education, 2006.

World Link. "The HP Way Forward." 14, no. 1 (Jan/Feb 2001): 54–59.

Young, Jeffery S. *iCon Steve Jobs: The Greatest Second Act in the History of Business.* Wiley, 2005.

Zaltman, Gerald. *How Customers Think: Essential Insights into the Mind of the Market.* Boston: Harvard Business School Press, 2003.

Zellner, Wendy. "Is JetBlue's Flight Plan Flawed?" *BusinessWeek,* February 16, 2004, 72–75.

Endnotes

Preface

1. We use the word *effect* in the same way that it is used in the phrases "the Doppler effect" or "the greenhouse effect"—to describe a phenomenon. The book is called *The Momentum Effect* rather than simply *Momentum* to emphasize that momentum is first of all a phenomenon, something exceptional that occurs under specific conditions. For a further clarification of the terminology we use, refer to note 1 of Chapter 1.

   Although this book is the first to present a comprehensive investigation of the momentum effect in business strategy, the notion of "momentum" has permeated all spheres of society. It originates in the physics of classical mechanics, where it is defined as the mass of an object multiplied by its velocity, and reflects the property of the object to keep moving. It has been adopted in common language to convey the idea of an intangible force that boosts performance and leads to repeated successes. It has been the subject of many books in a variety of disciplines, including sports, politics, and social sciences.

In finance, *momentum trading* refers to a method to trade stocks that exploits the dynamics in the stock market. In business, the word *momentum* has been associated with innovation, high technology, and leadership. See for instance: Peter M. Senge, George Roth, and Richard B. Ross, *The Dance of Change: The Challenges to Sustaining Momentum in a Learning Organization* (Currency, 1999); William R. Miller, *Change Creators and Momentum Maximizers* (Booksurge, 2002); Ron Ricci and John Volkmann, *Momentum: How Companies Become Unstoppable Market Forces* (HBS Press, 2003); Max Landsberg, *The Tools of Leadership: Vision, Inspiration, Momentum* (Profile Business, 2003); and Dan Coughlin, *Accelerate: 20 Practical Lessons to Boost Business Momentum* (Kaplan Business, 2007).

2. Among the contributions that helped construct the framework for *The Momentum Effect* over time, see the five annual reports on the *Competitive Fitness of Global Firms* published by Financial Times Prentice Hall from 1999 to 2003. Our initial efforts in the field of marketing excellence were built around the *Markstrat* simulation developed in conjunction with Hubert Gatignon, extensively used for developing marketing competences and building customer-focused cultures. *Markstrat* and related simulations are now adopted in three-quarters of all top business schools and by a number of large corporations. They are used, together with other appropriate tools, to help managers create growth through customer focus, innovation, and marketing excellence. To learn more about the author's professional history, see *Conversations with Marketing Masters* by Laura Mazur and Louella Miles and published by John Wiley in 2007.

Chapter 1

1. When the word *momentum* is used on its own, it refers loosely to the momentum effect or momentum growth—that is, the phenomenon or its outcome. As noted in the Preface, we use the word *effect* when we want to emphasize that momentum is a phenomenon, in the same way that the word is used in the phrases "the Doppler effect" or "the greenhouse effect." The momentum effect is a phenomenon by which, under specific conditions, exceptional organic growth is created that feeds on itself. This exceptional growth we will simply call *momentum growth.* Later we also refer to the expressions *momentum strategy* and *momentum process.*

2. See the five annual reports by J. C. Larreche on the *Competitive Fitness of Global Firms* published by Financial Times Management and Financial Times Prentice Hall from 1999 to 2003.

3. We started our investigation with the 1,000 largest companies (on the basis of their 2004 revenues), U.S. or non-U.S., quoted on the New York Stock Exchange. Out of these 1,000 companies, 498 did not exist in 1985, or were the result of mergers and so had to be excluded from the analysis. Out of the remaining 504 companies, some sectors were excluded because of the peculiarities of their competitive situation (oil, utilities, and so on), and full data was not available for all firms. This left a pool of 367 companies for which full data was available. We controlled different sectors of activities. We investigated different definitions of *marketing,* from the narrower and stricter consideration of just advertising to the broadest definition including field forces and all support functions. All analyses showed robust results in the same direction.

4. Of the companies in our sample, 119 belonged to this category. We have chosen this sample because it is the largest sector in the survey and because marketing is an important component of their cost structure. The sample in this example was ranked on the basis of the evolution of their advertising-to-sales ratio over the 20 years, but, as mentioned previously (see note 3), alternative definitions of *marketing* gave remarkably similar results.

5. As with any statistically based study, there are important caveats. Within each group, there are companies that performed outstandingly well, and others that sit at the bottom of the shareholder value-creation table. But what we are interested in here is the broad perspective: How would an investment portfolio made up of Plodders have fared against one of Pioneers or one of Pushers over the long term, and what can the behavior of these firms tell us about which strategy stands the greatest chance of success?

6. When we refer to the Dow Jones Index, or DJI, we always mean the Dow Jones Industrial Average.

7. Among the 119 firms considered in this analysis, 13 are represented in the Dow Jones Index (DJI). Of these 13, 7 are Pushers, 3 are Plodders, and 3 are Pioneers. The overlap between the companies in the DJI and in the Pushers group is thus about 20 percent and not enough to explain the similarity of the evolution of the two groups.

The overlap between the companies in the DJI and in the Pioneers group is about 10 percent, and the two groups have very different evolutions.

8. We looked at changes in the ratios corresponding to the three critical business functions: advertising, operations, and R&D. We know that the gap between the Pushers' and Pioneers' rates of change in advertising ratio was 7 percentage points. But the Pushers more than compensated for this increase in advertising by cutting elsewhere. Compared to the Pioneers, the Pushers cut their cost of goods sold (COGS)-to-sales ratio by 11 percentage points, and their R&D-to-sales ratio by close to 3 percentage points.

Beyond advertising, the Pushers have also increased other aspects of marketing, in the broader sense. Companies record all expenses other than COGS in SGA (sales, general, and administration). We defined OSGA (other sales, general, and administration expenses) as SGA minus advertising and R&D, the two strategic functions we identified. In this way, OSGA includes other marketing expenses, sales-force and sales-support expenses, and the cost of support functions. This is what some authors use as the broader definition of marketing. See for instance Victor J. Cook Jr.'s *Competing for Customers and Capital* (South-Western Educational, 2006). Over the 20-year period, the Pushers increased the OSGA over revenues ratio by 1.3 percentage points more than the Pioneers.

9. Several studies show that most marketing expenditures do not have a long-term impact. The phenomenon whereby marketing does have a durable impact on sales is called *persistence* or *hysteresis* and is more the exception than the rule. See for instance Marnik G. Dekimpe, and Dominique M. Hanssens, "The Persistence of Marketing Effects on Sales," *Marketing Science,* Winter 1995; Dominique M. Hanssens and Ming Ouyang, "Hysteresis in Market Response: When is marketing spending an investment?" *Review of Marketing Science* 419. Persistence is a necessary condition for momentum, although it is not sufficient. As we will discuss in the next chapters, momentum requires a set of specific conditions so that the growth feeds on itself.

10. This estimate is fairly arbitrary because the nature of momentum means that it is artificial to pinpoint the precise moment when it begins and the exact point at which it is lost. However, it is

important to note two things. First, there is no "Game over: You've won" moment with momentum—it must be constantly nurtured to be maintained, or it will be lost. Second, it is possible to maintain momentum for many, many years—even an entire working life.

11. *Made in America: My Story* by Sam Walton with John Huey (Doubleday, 1992). See also Bob Ortega, *In Sam We Trust: The Untold Story of Sam Walton and Wal-Mart, the World's Most Powerful Retailer* (Crown Business, 1998); and for a recent, and excellent, account of the Wal-Mart phenomenon, see Charles Fishman, *The Wal-Mart Effect* (Penguin Group, 2006).

12. A very rich interview of Katsuaki Watanabe is given in Thomas A. Stewart and P. Anand Raman, "Lessons from Toyota's Long Drive," *Harvard Business Review,* July-August 2007, 74–83. This particular quote comes from an interview with the BBC on May 9, 2007, and can be found at http://news.bbc.co.uk/1/hi/business/6637885.stm. Most of the writings on Toyota emphasize its operational excellence. For some recent accounts that offer a broader perspective on the firm's success, see Jeffrey Liker, *The Toyota Way* (McGraw-Hill, 2003); Jeffrey Liker and David Meyer, *Toyota Talent* (McGraw-Hill, 2007); and Matthew E. May, *The Elegant Solution: Toyota's Formula for Mastering Innovation* (The Free Press, 2006).

Chapter 2

1. Note that there is a subtle but profound difference between what most people call exceptional growth and the exceptional growth that is created by the momentum effect. Not all "exceptional growth" is the result of momentum. Remember we said that momentum growth is exceptional in terms of both its quantity and its quality. It is this second aspect that is so often lacking in short-term growth that is so gleefully reported as "exceptional": If it lacks the quality of efficiency that momentum growth has, it has probably been obtained through pushing with resources, is lacking in momentum, and will not be sustainable.

2. There are several accounts of this story. See for instance "The Man Who Could Have Been Bill Gates" by Steve Hamm and Jay Greene, *BusinessWeek,* October 25, 2004. Much has been written about the evolution of Microsoft over the years. See Randall E. Stross, *The*

Microsoft Way (Basic Books, 1997); Bill Gates, Nathan Myhrvold, and Peter Rinearson, *The Road Ahead* (Penguin, 1996); and Robert Slater, *Microsoft Rebooted: How Bill Gates and Steve Ballmer Reinvented Their Company* (Portfolio, 2004).

3. For convenience we generally use the terminology relating to private enterprise (customers, shareholders, profit, competitors, and so on), but the concepts underlying this argument, and the book as a whole, apply to the public and not-for-profit sectors, too.

4. For an early perspective on value creation and distribution, see *Value Migration: Strategies to Preempt the Markets of Tomorrow* by Adrian J. Slywotzky (Harvard Business School Press, 1996).

5. See Michael E. Porter, *Competitive Strategy* (The Free Press, 1980) and *Competitive Advantage* (The Free Press, 1985).

6. See W. Chan Kim and Renée Mauborgne, *Blue Ocean Strategy: How to Create Uncontested Market Space and Make Competition Irrelevant* (Harvard Business School Press, 2005) and a series of excellent articles in the *Harvard Business Review* in the preceding years. Their Strategy Canvass and the ERRC (Eliminate, Reduce, Raise, Create) grid are two of the most powerful diagnostic business tools ever invented.

7. See for instance Jeffrey M. O'Brien, "Wii Will Rock You," *Fortune,* June 11, 2007, 35–44. We return to the Wii in Chapter 5.

8. This example might seem small scale, but it illustrates that momentum-boosting actions can happen at all levels in an organization and that such seemingly small acts can have an enormous cumulative impact.

9. Paul Hemp, "Managing for the Next Big Thing: An interview with EMC's Michael Ruettgers," *Harvard Business Review,* January 2001, 132–136. Again, as with the example cited in note 8, this is a seemingly small scale example. But the point is that, when building momentum, many small steps will collectively have an enormous impact, provided they are consistently taken in the same direction.

10. The key to iTunes' success is the 99-cent price point for individual songs. The site offers users safe and legal access to an extensive collection of music at a price they perceive as fair. Apple has come under pressure from music companies to increase the price but has resisted. Some of these companies don't understand the secret of the iPod/iTunes' success. In May 2007, Apple announced the launch of iTunes Plus offering songs on EMI's catalog at a higher sound quality and with no restrictions on use for $1.29, a premium of 30 cents on the regular iTunes offering. More important, however, the consumer could chose to purchase the "standard" option, still at the 99-cent price.

11. Apple press release, September 10, 2007, http://www.apple.com/hotnews/openiphone/letter. For some insights on the success of the iPod, see Hiawatha Bray, "The Resurrection of Steve Jobs," *The Eonomist,* September 17, 2005, 68; Peter Burrows, "Can the iPod Keep Leading the Band?" *BusinessWeek,* November 8, 2004, 54. For a more complete history of Steve Jobs's road to the iPod, see Jeffery S. Young, *iCon Steve Jobs: The Greatest Second Act in the History of Business* (Wiley, 2005).

12. The expression *inferior product* refers here to a product perceived to be inferior by any relevant customer target. Obviously, a product may be seen as inferior by some customers but as perfectly adequate by others who have different needs. It cannot be called "inferior" from a business point of view as long as it is valuable to a relevant customer target.

13. Building on their work on the persistence of marketing, Dekimpe and Hanssens propose two scenarios for sustained growth: *escalation* (where there is no persistence of marketing effects on sales) and *evolving business practice* (where there is persistence of marketing effects on sales). In a sense, escalation can be considered as a form of compensation strategy, and evolving business practice can be considered as the minimum base for a momentum strategy. See Marnik G. Dekimpe and Dominique M. Hanssens, "Sustained Spending and Persistent Response: A New Look at Long-Term Marketing Profitability," *Journal of Marketing Research,* November 1999, 397–412.

Chapter 3

1. Gleevec is the drug's name in the United States. Throughout the rest of the world, it is marketed as Glivec.

2. This has since been confirmed through the long-term treatment of patients.

3. Throughout Chapters 4–11, we concentrate on the customer in the narrower sense of the word—that is, the person who either pays for, prescribes, or uses the product. This is to simplify matters. However, it is important to remember that the principles exposed in this book reflect the wider sense of the word, and we will examine the crucial importance of employees and external stakeholders in Chapters 12 and 13.

4. The story of Gleevec is well described by Dr. Daniel Vasella himself in *Magic Cancer Bullet: How a Tiny Orange Pill Is Rewriting Medical History* (HarperCollins, 2003).

5. See for instance David Kiley, *Driven: Inside BMW, the Most Admired Car Company in the World* (John Wiley & Sons, 2004).

6. This is not limited to options on new cars. In fall 2004, BMW also sold 12,000 adapters for its car owners to integrate the iPod into their sound system, and there was a long waiting list. See Peter Burrows, "Can the iPod Keep Leading the Band?" *BusinessWeek,* November 8, 2004, 81. For the adoption of the iPod docking stations by car manufacturers, see the June 21, 2004 and August 3, 2006 press releases by Apple at www.apple.com/pr/library/2004/jun/21bmw.html and www.apple.com/pr/library/2006/aug/03ipod.html

7. See various reports and tables prepared by the American Customer Satisfaction Index on its website: www.theacsi.org.

8 . The initial sale price in 2005 was $2.6 billion with an earnout of a further $1.7 billion due in 2009 dependent upon future performance. Performance between 2005 and 2007 was good but not as good as projected, and in October 2007 co-founder Zennström stood down as CEO taking on a role as nonexecutive chairman, in what was described as an amicable arrangement. The final earnout was settled to $530 million, significantly below the anticipated level, bringing the total price to approximately $3.1 billion. See Richard Waters, "Ebay writes down Skype value by $1.4bn," *Financial Times,* October 2, 2007. The

earnout settlement was not as negative as it was portrayed in some quarters at the time. As Friis pointed out on his blog on the day the settlement was announced, "Earnouts are inherently difficult creatures, but we are happy with the result of this one. We are approximately half way into the earnout period and the settlement amounts to one-third of the total possible earnout amount." (Janus Friis, "Not Just Another Monday," www.janusfriis.net/2007/10/01/not-just-another-monday, October 1, 2007).

9. For further details of the Skype story, see *Skype: Leading the VOIP Revolution,* by Bharat Rao and Bojan Angelov, Polytechnic University, New York, case study, 2005; and *From KaZaA to Skype,* by N. Rajshekar and Kalyani Vemuri, ICFAI case study, 2004.

10. When Zennström stood down as CEO in October 2007, Skype had posted four consecutive quarters of profit and was predicted by analysts to be on track to $360 million in revenue for the year, a growth of 85% year on year.

11. Zennström himself pointed this out in his first interview in English after stepping down: "Some people might want to monetize—that is, move users from Skype's free service to paid for ones—faster, but the key is to figure out what is the right speed of monetization. If you act too aggressively, there is a real risk you will lose the huge active user base." Thomas Crampton, "SCOOP: Zennström defends Skype while stepping down," www.thomascrampton.com/2007/10/01/scoop-zennstrom-defends-skype-while-stepping-down, October 1, 2007.

Chapter 4

1. See Louis V. Gernster Jr., *Who Says Elephants Can't Dance? Inside IBM's Historic Turnaround* (HarperCollins, 2002).

2. See Betsy McKay, "Thinking Inside the Box Helps Soda Makers Boost Sales," *Wall Street Journal,* August 2, 2002.

3. See Carol Matlack, "Dassault May Be Next in Line for Takeoff," *BusinessWeek,* March 7, 2005.

4. We are using the word *customer* broadly to include any individual or firm who could potentially become a client. These customers could be existing clients, prospects, or not currently interested in existing offers.

5. One of the most progressive branchless banks in the world is the British-based First Direct, which was named the "most recommended bank in the world" and we will discuss it in Chapter 7.

6. See Howard J. Stock, "Commerce Bank: Ahead of the Curve," *Bank Investment Consultant* 12, no. 10, October 2004, 28–34. Commerce Bank's sale, announced in October 2007, was hastened by the resignation of its CEO and founder, Vernon Hill, in response to regulatory investigations. This doesn't lessen the bank's phenomenal achievement—indeed, according to the *Financial Times,* the sale price of $8.5 billion was lower than would have been expected were it not for the extraordinary circumstances of its sale (Ben White, "TD Bank in US push with $8bn Commerce deal," *Financial Times,* October 2, 2007). In fact, it illustrates that although customers are the most essential part of the momentum mix, getting momentum totally right involves more than just customer focus. Hill was a visionary who revolutionized the retail banking industry and build enormous momentum—but unfortunately his excellent work building momentum with his customers was not matched by comparable care in understanding the needs and values of regulators. We examine the way truly great momentum leaders manage to balance all the competing demands of multiple stakeholders in Chapter 13.

7. For an excellent development of these issues, see Jeffrey Pfeffer and Robert I. Sutton, *The Knowing-Doing Gap* (Harvard Business School Press, 2000).

8. J.D. Power and Associates press release for the 2006 Retail Banking Satisfaction Study, "Commerce Bancorp Ranks Highest in Satisfying Banking Customers in New York," March 26, 2006.

9. J.D. Power and Associates 2006 Retail Banking Satisfaction Study.

10. See Malcolm Gladwell, *Blink: The Power of Thinking Without Thinking* (Little Brown, 2005), 167–76.

11. The first offset mortgage was offered in 1997—perhaps unsurprisingly—by Virgin Direct, a financial services company that was part of Richard Branson's Virgin Group. The product is now sold as the One Account. Another leading provider is First Direct, a momentum-powered firm that we will encounter later in the book.

12. The most comprehensive and strategic approach for discovery of compelling customer insights is provided in the Blue Ocean Strategy work of Chan Kim and Renée Mauborgne, already referred to in the context of value origination. For more specific customer tools, see for instance, Gerald Zaltman's Metaphor Elicitation Technique and Clotaire Raspaille's Cultural Archetypes in Zaltman's *How Customers Think: Essential Insights into the Mind of the Market* (Harvard Business School Press, 2003) and Rapaille's *The Culture Code: An Ingenious Way to Understand Why People Around the World Live and Buy as They Do* (Broadway, 2006).

Chapter 5

1. A "concept car" is one that is not intended to be put into production but is used to test new ideas. Those that work will often find their way into standard production cars.

2. For a detailed account of the design process and of the features of the YCC, see the series of press information documents published by Volvo: "Your Concept Car—a project with women in the driver's seat," "Your Concept Car—by women for modern people," "Your Concept Car—bold but elegant exterior," "Your Concept Car—a personal living room with whatever you want within reach." For some of the press coverage, see "This Volvo Is Not a Guy Thing," *BusinessWeek,* March 15, 2004; "Women design concept car for Volvo," *USA Today,* March 2, 2004. The nine women behind the YCC concept were named Women of the Year by *Automotive News Europe,* a prestigious industry magazine.

3. These comments represented a very small minority considering the adulation heaped upon the car, but the heat in their comments illustrates the strength of their feeling. Amidst all the praise, a dissenting voice posted: "Ok it sounds quite good apart from one little thing—a sealed bonnet!!!....puhlease......and we want men to take us seriously, certainly not with something like that....come on, it's not that difficult to change the oil and water." Feedback: What do you think of the Volvo YCC? November 21, 2005, on Carsguide.com.au, http://carsguide.news.com.au/story/0,20384,17315170-5001400,00.html accessed October 11, 2007.

4. The value story has two sides—value to a customer and value of the customer to the company—and they should not be confused. This chapter focuses on customer value. What a company offers customers and the importance of understanding that value is not the same for everyone. The next chapter investigates the equally important notion of value of the customer to the company, which we have labeled *customer equity.*

5. *Customer myopia* occurs when firms assume that they already know the consumer well, based on past experience. It leads to routine business practices, serving the same type of customers and remaining at a superficial level of understanding of their needs. It is not the same, but is the natural grandchild of *marketing myopia,* an expression coined by Ted Levitt in his famous 1960 *Harvard Business Review* article of the same title, which in some ways marked the beginning of modern marketing. The point of marketing myopia was that businesses should redefine more broadly the markets they serve, not in terms of the products they make but in terms of the customer needs they satisfy. Many companies that escaped marketing myopia and went on to serve customer needs based on superficial knowledge, plunged into customer myopia and made new types of mistakes.

6. See Laura Cohn, Carol Matlack, and Dean Foust, "Will Coke's Water Meet Its Waterloo?" *BusinessWeek,* March 29, 2004, 30. Dasani also initially suffered from some technical problems. Bromide is added to drinking water in the United Kingdom, and Coca-Cola's process had the unfortunate side effect of turning this harmless bromide into small, but illegal, levels of the carcinogen bromate. This was corrected and early batches recalled, but a product that was already holed below the waterline was further damaged by the news: "Things get worse with Coke: Bottled tap water withdrawn after cancer scare," *Guardian,* March 20, 2004.

7. Chris Nuttall, "Wii Console Helps Nintendo Raise Its Game" *Financial Times,* July 12, 2007. See also Jeffrey M. O'Brien, "Wii Will Rock You," *Fortune,* June 11, 2007, 35–44.

8. Marketed in most countries outside North America as Dr. Kawashima's Brain Training.

9. For example, the "Strope" test, where the word *blue* might be written in yellow type and the player must say "yellow" rather than the more instinctive "blue." Next the word *black* might be written in red, and so on. Other tests include simple arithmetic or memory games.

10. See Nintendo Consolidated Financial Highlights, July 25, 2007. *Brain Age* is not the only nontraditional computer game powering the success of the Nintendo DS. The top-selling series is called *Nintendogs,* a dog-owning simulation where players must feed and train their virtual pet. Traditional games such as the Pokemon series continue to be successful, but the key to Nintendo's success is the way they have extended the market by creating new value for new customers. See also Ginny Parker Woods, "Nintendo Targets Nongamers," *Wall Street Journal Europe,* February 23, 2006, 33.

11. When using the customer value wedge, a good visual approach is to systematically write the costs (value destroyers) in red and the benefits (value enhancers) in green, for each of the four elements.

12. See for instance Carol Matlack, "The Vuitton Money Machine," *BusinessWeek,* March 22, 2004, 50–56.

13. See Donald N. Sull and Alejandro Rueals-Gossi, "The Art of Innovating on a Shoestring," *FT Mastering Series,* September 24, 2004. For more details on Cemex's strategy, see also the Harvard Business School case study by Hau L. Lee and David Hoyt, *CEMEX: Transforming a Basic Industry Company,* 2005.

14. See Benedetto De Martino et al., "Frames, Biases, and Rational Decision-Making in the Human Brain," *Science,* August 4, 2006, 684–87. See also Clive Cookson, "Emotions' Role in Economic Thinking," *Financial Times,* June 13, 2003.

15. See for instance Victoria Murphy, "Microsoft's Midlife Crisis," *Forbes,* October 2005, 88–96.

16. For a concise but excellent account of the development of Dell's business model over its first 15 years, see Nancy F. Koehn, *Brand New: How Entrepreneurs Earned Consumers' Trust, from Wedgwood to Dell* (Harvard Business School Press, 2001). See also Michael Dell, *Direct From Dell* (Profile Books, 2000); and Steven Holzner, *How Dell Does It* (McGraw-Hill, 2005).

17. See for instance Louise Lee, "Dell's Road to Recovery," *BusinessWeek*, June 1, 2007. Even before Dell's problems surfaced in the open, Victor Cook had identified some of the issues from a value-creation perspective in his book *Competing for Customers and Capital*. See especially "Why did Dell fall short" on pages 158–60.

Chapter 6

1. To complete this story, one should note that the Rentokil/Initial merger was probably not a proper move for the company's long-term growth. Absorbing a company twice one's size is an obvious challenge and monopolizes management attention. In this operation, Rentokil Initial lost the extraordinary momentum it had created and entered a difficult period of consolidation. Thompson himself was the focus of much public anger in 2006 for his role in what became known as the "Farepack scandal." The details are not relevant here, but this shows again the transitory nature of momentum, both for the firms and their leaders, if it is not carefully nurtured.

2. We use the term *customer equity* to reflect the long-term value to the firm of a single customer or a group of customers. The term is also sometimes used to describe the long-term value of all current and future customers of a firm. The specialized literature on customer equity has progressed substantially in recent years. For an excellent review, see Villanueva, and Hanssens, "Customer Equity: Measurement, Management and Research Opportunities," *Foundations and Trends in Marketing*, 2007.

3. Expertise in one field can often lead us to apprehend readily the essence of situations pertaining to that area of expertise. There are often cases, however, when we are systematically biased because of our experience. *Transaction myopia* is such a situation. For a fascinating account of great successes and failures in the rapid perception of truth, see Malcolm Gladwell, *Blink* (Little Brown, 2005).

4. The pizzeria example finds its genesis in a throwaway line (accompanied by a fetching illustration) in an excellent article by James L. Heskett, Thomas O. Jones, Gary W. Loveman, W. Earl Sasser, Jr., and Leonard A. Schlesinger, "Putting the Service-Profit Chain to Work," *Harvard Business Review*, March-April 1994, 164. It is also referred to in the book by James L. Heskett, W. Earl Sasser,

Jr., and Leonard A. Schlesinger, *The Service-Profit Chain* (The Free Press, 1997), 65. I have found it a particularly effective example to help management teams reflect on the concept of customer equity. It can be built upon in many ways to illustrate different points and it will recur again as we progress through the book.

5. The financial technique used to correct for the time value of money is called *net present value*. It discounts the money amounts to be received in the future to reflect their present equivalent value. For instance, the $5,000 sum calculated in the pizzeria is obtained over a period of ten years and is not the same as $5,000 received today. With a discount rate of 6 percent, the $5,000 would represent about $3,700 in net present value. This is a smaller number by about 25 percent but does not change the implications. For more information on customer lifetime value, see, for instance, Robert C. Blattberg, Gary Getz, and Jacquelyn S. Thomas, *Customer Equity: Building and Managing Relationships as Valuable Assets* (Harvard Business School Press, 2001); Roland T. Rust, Valarie A. Zeithaml, and Katherine Lemon, *Driving Customer Equity: How Customer Lifetime Value Is Reshaping Corporate Strategy* (The Free Press, 2000); Sunil Gupta and Donald R. Lehmann, *Managing Customers as Investment* (Wharton School Publishing, 2005).

6. The *Financial Times* reported analysts' estimates that Nintendo made a profit of around $48 (¥5,600) on each Wii sold in the United States. By comparison, Sony's PS3 units were expected to remain loss making until 2009 (Mariko Sanchanta, "Nintendo Wii success helps component makers score," *Financial Times*, September 17, 2007.)

7. For an overview, see Kamran Kashani's excellent article "Marketing Through Collaboration: How Seller and Buyer Can Benefit," *European Business Forum*, Spring 2004, 37–43. This example is derived from the case studies developed by Sandra Vandermerwe and Marika Taishoff at IMD, *SKF Bearings Series: Market Orientation Through Services*, 1990.

8. Note that we are dealing here with real customers whose prestige should be taken into account when estimating their equity for the firm. This is different from other sources of prestige for which a firm pays. For instance, athletes sponsoring brands are not customers with high equity. They are partners paid by a firm as part of its communication strategy.

9. Malcolm Gladwell, *The Tipping Point: How Little Things Can Make a Big Difference* (Little Brown, 2000).

10. There were, obviously, many other ways in which this situation could have been handled, and each would have had different implications on customer equity. It is worth exploring them as a learning exercise.

11. We are often asked whether these customers that offer compelling equity are the same as those that are called key accounts in many firms. The answer is no. Key accounts are identified in most firms in terms of volume. For instance, "Our 12 key accounts represent 80 percent of our revenues." Customers with compelling equity need not be the largest ones. Their definition is related to the business benefits they bring relative to the business costs they absorb and to their potential for growth. Their equity can be expanded and become a base for momentum growth. Unfortunately, key accounts often have the opposite impact. Because of their volume, they have a tendency to offer limited growth and to place the firm under price pressure.

Chapter 7

1. The bank's commitment to innovation continued after its launch. It was among the pioneers of Internet banking in the United Kingdom in the late 1990s and in 2001 launched one of the first offset mortgages, as outlined in Chapter 4.

2. Personal communication from Alan Hughes, 2007.

3. In their work on persistence, Hanssens and Ouyang have expressed the hypothesis that "the higher the product's perceived value, the stronger the persistence of the advertising effect on sales." See Dominique M. Hanssens and Ming Ouyang, "Hysteresis in Market Response: When is marketing spending an investment?" *Review of Marketing Science*, 419.

4. Effective branding is the result of power offers and not the reverse. Business executives sometimes ask us, "What is the difference between power offers and branding? Isn't *power offer* a different expression for *branding?*" No. The power offer capitalizes on

insights brought by deep exploration of customer value and customer equity that are then integrated into the various components of a company's strategy. This could be interpreted as a broad definition of branding, but the reality of branding is that it is most often limited to increasing the value of a product through communications.

5. Stephen Bayley, "The MT Executive Car of the Year: The Fabulous 5 Series." *Management Today,* March 2004, 72.

6. In our investigations, we have generally considered power offers for which we could claim that status for at least ten years and thus observe a sustained exceptional growth. We have made exceptions to this rule only for recent ventures such as Skype, the iPhone, or the Wii. Several of the power offers we studied lost their momentum because the drivers of this momentum were not understood or not nurtured. All the power offers and all the momentum-powered firms we studied were, however, a source of learning and helped us in building our momentum-strategy framework.

7. See Christian Pinson, *Swatch,* INSEAD Case Study, 1987.

8. An excellent tool to assist when working through the top two boxes of this tool is the ERRC (Eradicate, Reduce, Raise, Create) grid presented by Kim and Mauborgne in their Blue Ocean Strategy framework. Their simple but powerful tool should be used to systematically review the transformation of product dimensions in terms of their value contribution. See *Blue Ocean Strategy,* page 35.

9. This is because the exploration of customer equity will naturally tend to identify a particularly compelling source of equity, whereas with the exploration of customer value the central focus tends to be on a particularly compelling value proposition. Both explorations, however, will provide insights into these two key elements of power offer design. That is why the process of design must be iterative. As the explorations converge, insights from one will feed into the other, constantly changing and improving the end result.

10. The owners of digital cameras have increased their use of inkjet printers, and the toner they consume, to print their snaps. Dell came late into printers, and then did not focus on this segment. The gaming community have ever-increasing demands for ultra-high processing power and graphics performance.

11. As power offers go, the Astra GCT is not yet in the same league as the iPod, but it's doing well. In less than two years, the car had increased its market share by 10 percent. Sales of the new model in 2006 were 30 percent higher than those achieved by the previous model just two years earlier (personal communication from Jonathan Browning, GM Europe's vice president for sales, marketing, and aftersales). The Opel Astra GCT is sold in the United Kingdom as the Vauxhall Astra.

12. "The miracle of Älmhult," *Guardian,* June 17, 2004.

13 See Elen Lewis's excellent book Great IKEA! (Cyan Books, 2005).

14. See J. C. Larreche and Anne-Marie Cagna, *First Direct 2005: The Most Recommended Bank in the World,* INSEAD Case Study, 2006.

15. First Direct marketing material, September 2007.

16. These aspects of power crafting can be considered as the essence of enterprise marketing. See Victor Cook, *Competing for Customers and Capital,* Chapter 1.

Chapter 8

1. To this day, the story of the delicate but skillful introduction of the Walkman is preserved in the Sony history. See "Please Listen to This!" at www.sony.net/Fun/SH/1-18/h3.html.

2. The initial value delivery framework first emerged from the consulting firm McKinsey & Company in the 1980s. For one of the most complete descriptions, see Michael J. Lanning, *Delivering Profitable Value* (Capstone, 1998).

3. See Richard S. Tedlow, *The Watson Dynasty: The Fiery Reign and Troubled Legacy of IBM's Founding Father and Son* (Collins, 2003) for a history of IBM before and at the beginning of the computer era.

4. For simplification, we are using modern vocabulary throughout this example. In the early days of business IT systems, the expressions *information technology* and *chief information officer* had not yet been coined! One referred to "electronic data processing" and "EDP managers."

5. For an early account of IBM's loss of momentum in the late 1980s, see Regis McKenna, *Who's Afraid of Big Blue: How Companies Are Challenging IBM—And Winning* (Addison-Wesley, 1988).

6. See Louis V. Gerstner Jr., *Who Say's Elephants Can't Dance? Inside IBM's Historic Turnaround* (Harper Collins, 2002); Robert Slater, *Saving Big Blue: Leadership Lessons and Turnaround Tactics of IBM's Lou Gestner* (McGraw-Hill, 1999). For the customer-focused approach of IBM after Gertsner's turnaround, see Harvey Thompson, *The Customer-Centered Enterprise: How IBM and Other World-Class Companies Achieve Extraordinary Results by Putting Customers First* (McGraw-Hill, 1999).

7. Full details of this simulation are available on this book's website. Each firm started the simulation making $30 million annual profit. At the end of five years, Momentum-Deficient Inc.'s profit had risen steadily to $56 million annually, while Momentum-Powered Inc.'s had snowballed to $86 million. In other words, over this time, one firm's profits had grown by $26 million, the other's by $56 million. These figures have been rounded to the nearest whole million. Remember that these are just some of the ways that momentum accelerates growth. We examine the equally powerful effects of retention in Chapter 10, and then look at the combined power of all of the stages of momentum in Chapter 11.

8. See the excellent case written by Reinhard Angelmar and Christian Pinson, Zantac (A, B), INSEAD, 1993. Prilosec was originally marketed worldwide as Losec. The name was changed to Prilosec in the United States in 1990. Throughout much of the rest of the world, it is still marketed as Losec.

Chapter 9

1. Jan Carlzon, *Moments of Truth* (Collins, 1989).

2. See "If you try to match complexity with complexity, it will kill the organization," *Focus* IX/1, 2005, 4–10. A. G. Lafley has consistently repeated the "two moments of truth message." See for instance Robert Berner, "P&G: New and Improved," *BusinessWeek,* July 7, 2003; Rajat Gupta and Jim Wendler, "Leading change: An interview with the CEO of P&G," *McKinsey Quarterly,* July 2005; Pascal Kuipers, "Fuelling P&G's P&L," *Elsevier Food International* 8, no. 3, September 2005.

3. For an excellent book on the concept of customer delight, see Timothy Keiningham and Terry Vavra, *The Customer Delight Principle* (McGraw-Hill, 2001).

4. Abraham Maslow, "A Theory of Human Motivation," *Psychological Review* 50, 1943, 370–96; *Motivation and Personality,* 3rd Ed. (HarperCollins, 1987).

5. Richard Layard, *Happiness: Lessons from a New Science* (Penguin, 2005).

6. An early graph linking satisfaction and retention was proposed by the service management interest group at Harvard Business School during the 1990s, as they very skillfully developed an operational model to help service companies to simultaneously increase service quality and profits. See the classic article on the subject by James L. Heskett, Thomas O. Jones, Gary W. Loveman, W. Earl Sasser, Jr., and Leonard A. Schlesinger, "Putting the Service-Profit Chain to Work," *Harvard Business Review,* March-April 1994, 164–74; and the book by James L. Heskett, W. Earl Sasser Jr., and Leonard A. Schlesinger, *The Service Profit Chain: How Leading Companies Link Profit and Growth to Loyalty, Satisfaction and Value* (The Free Press, 1997). They were the first to model the connection between satisfaction and retention as a driver of growth, and the first to make a connection between employee satisfaction and customer satisfaction. Their ideas have since been taken further by others. In this particular instance, we are making three major additional contributions. First, we have linked satisfaction, as a state of mind, to the emotions that drive action, thus demonstrating why extreme levels of satisfaction are so powerful. As a result, the shape of our curve in this figure differs markedly from theirs. Second, and as a direct result of the intense emotions stirred by extreme satisfaction, we show in the following chapters how the process goes beyond mere retention to the much more powerful dynamics of engagement. Third, we are proposing a broader strategic framework that includes design and execution of power offers. On a purely semantic scale, we are using the terminology of *Desperados* and *Champions* rather than *Terrorists* and *Apostles,* respectively, because of political and religious sensitivities.

7. For some comprehensive guides on customer satisfaction measurement, see Chris Denove and James D. Power, *Satisfaction: How Every Great Company Listens to the Voice of the Customer* (Portfolio,

2006); Jonathan D. Barsky, *World-Class Customer Satisfaction* (Irwin, 1995); Alan Dutka, *AMA Handbook for Customer Satisfaction: A Complete Guide to Research, Planning and Implementing* (NTC Business Books, 1994).

8. See Andy Taylor, "Top Box: Rediscovering Customer Satisfaction," *Business Horizons* 46, no. 5, Sep/Oct 2003, 3–15.

9. See Anne-Marie Cagna and J.C. Larreche, "First Direct 2005," INSEAD, 2006. The reported customer satisfaction ratings are based on the percentage of customers who are extremely or very satisfied. The customer recommendation ratings represent the percentage of customers who have recommended in the past 12 months.

10. Anthony Bianco and Wendy Zellner "Is Wal-Mart Too Powerful?" *BusinessWeek,* October 6, 2003.

11. See for instance Jay Greene, "Troubling Exits at Microsoft," *BusinessWeek,* September 26, 2005, and the related online interview of Microsoft's CEO, "Online Extra: Steve Ballmer Shrugs Off the Critics."

12. For the service revolution at Harrah's, see David O. Becker, "Gambling on Customers," *The McKinsey Quarterly,* 2003, no. 2, 46–59; Shaun Smith and Joe Wheeler, *Managing the Customer Experience: Turning Customers into Advocates* (Financial Times Prentice Hall, 2002); and Walter E. Shill and Robert J. Thomas, "Exploring the Mindset of the High Performer," *Outlook,* October 2005.

13. Kamran Kashani, "Marketing Through Collaboration: How seller and buyer can benefit," *EFB,* Issue 17, Spring 2004, 37–43; "Tetra Pak (A, B, C, D): The challenge of intimacy with a key customer," case IMD-5-0604.

14. Personal interview with Jan Carendi, member of the Allianz Management Board in charge of a customer-focus initiative.

15. See for instance Sandra Vandermerwe, *Breaking Through: Implementing Customer Focus in Enterprises* (Palgrave, 2004) and W. Chan Kim and Renée Mauborgne, *Blue Ocean Strategy: How to Create Uncontested Market Space and Make the Competition Irrelevant* (Harvard Business School Publishing, 2005).

16. On Amazon.uk, the total cost of the transaction was €105.58, which included a €20.24 shipping charge. On Amazon.fr, despite "free" shipping, the order cost €131.62. The cost of the books themselves, excluding shipping, was 54 percent higher!

17. See J.D. Power press release: "JetBlue and Continental Continue to Rank Highest in Airline Customer Satisfaction," June 19, 2007, www.jdpower.com/press-releases/pressrelease.aspx?id=2007097. JetBlue press release: "JetBlue Announces Second Quarter Results," June 24, 2007, http://investor.jetblue.com/phoenix.zhtml?c=131045&p=irol-newsArticle&ID=1029705&highlight=. See also Marci Alboher Nusbaum, "JetBlue Turning Fliers into Fanatic Loyalists," *Deseret News,* March 24, 2004; and Wendy Zellner, "Is JetBlue's Flight Plan Flawed?" *BusinessWeek,* February 16, 2004, 72–75.

Chapter 10

1. See Stanley Bing, "It's a !@#$% Man's World," *Fortune,* October 14, 2002.

2. For example, for many years choosing to use an Apple Mac meant forgoing access to hundreds of programs designed for PCs. In addition, the first generation of iPods were not compatible with PCs running Windows. Tunes purchased on iTunes could only be played on iPods, which themselves will not play music files except those in Apple proprietary formats. And when the iPhone was launched, the phones were locked so that they could only be used on Apple's chosen network provider (AT&T in the United States and others in different territories). However, unlike the restrictions and barriers to change we often see other companies employing, Apple's approach doesn't seem to alienate its most dedicated customers. Apple fans simply do not perceive the restrictions as infringing on their freedom. In the case of the iPhone, some users did resent being forced to adopt Apple's choice of network. Initial "hacks" to get around this were negated by Apple with software updates that rendered unlocked iPhones virtually unusable. Despite this, most Apple users continue to feel that the company's products provide benefits that outweigh the imposed restrictions and, from their perspective, offer greater freedom than competitors' offerings. Interestingly, having built a strong, dedicated fan base, Apple then tends to open its products up to drive even greater growth. For example, the iMac now comes with software that will help a user load Microsoft Windows as an alternative operating system if they so choose. Likewise, songs from consenting music companies are now available on iTunes in a format that is compatible with any music player.

3. For some fundamental contributions on customer retention, see Frederick F. Reichheld, *Loyalty Rules! How Today's Leaders Build Lasting Relationships* (Harvard Business School Press, 2001); Arthur Middleton Hughes, *The Customer Loyalty Solution* (McGraw-Hill, 2003).

4. There are many others, most notably measurement on a purchase-occasion basis. This considers the percentage of customers who bought the same product last time and works well for businesses like the personal car market, where customers might buy a new car only every three or so years. More complicated measurements can be used or combined with an annual basis measurement, but these often end up becoming very detailed statistics, which can be difficult to decipher.

5. For the purposes of this illustration, we have assumed that defecting customers go at the end of the year. The figure therefore represents the average number of years that existing clients will keep doing business with the firm after the end of the current year. One could have an estimate including the current year in which case one should add one year to all the reported numbers. Or, one could reflect the fact that customers might defect regularly throughout the year, and add half a year to all reported numbers.

6. This graph shows the average customer lifetime value corresponding to a retention rate, as per the remark in the previous note. The formula used to produce this graph is CLTV = R / (1 − R), where CLTV is the customer lifetime value in years and R is the retention rate expressed as a fraction. For instance, for a customer retention rate of 50 percent, this gives 0.5/(1−0.5), which is equal to one year, as reported earlier. More quantitative developments are available on the book's website (www.themomentumeffect.com) for the mathematically inclined reader. These calculations do not make any adjustment for the time value of money.

7. See David Kirkpatrick, "Facebook's plan to hook up the world," *Fortune,* June 11, 2007; Steven Levy, "Facebook Grows Up: Can It Stay Relevant?," *Newsweek,* August 20, 2007, and www.facebook.com/press/info.php?statistics (retrieved October 2, 2007).

8. There are a number of traps in the management of customer retention. They are in great part related to a simplistic treatment of retention statistics that do not differentiate between passive and

active retention. For a better understanding of the pitfalls of retention, see Werner Reinartz, and V. Kumar "The Mismanagement of Customer Loyalty," *Harvard Business Review,* July 2002, 86–94; Timothy L. Keiningham, Terry G. Vavra, Lerzan Aksoy, and Henri Wallard, *Loyalty Myths: Hyped Strategies that Will Put You Out of Business—and Proven Tactics That Really Work* (Wiley, 2005).

9. The powerful image of the "leaking bucket" was offered by James Teboul, *Service Is Front Stage* (Palgrave, 2006), 89.

10. As we saw earlier, a seemingly small increase in retention from 95 percent to 96 percent will increase the average customer lifetime from 19 to 24 years, a 25 percent impact. A firm that moves from 50 percent to 51 percent manages just a 4 percent improvement in average customer lifetime.

11. Defector recovery covers a wide range of situations depending on the firm and the industry. At one end, it includes cases such as magazine readers who will not renew their subscription because they are furious that the rate they have to pay as loyal customers is above the one offered to new subscribers. At the other end, it concerns contracts in millions of dollars that might not be renewed because of real or perceived issues. The defector-recovery strategy we expose is valid in all these cases, although the resources used and the specific approach will be totally different to fit the situation. *SWAT* is a military term that stands for "Special Weapons And Tactics." The use of this military term can help to stress the importance of the situation when it involves a major customer relationship with a lot at stake.

Chapter 11

1. These last two volumes are the sixth and seventh in the Harry Potter series: J. K. Rowling, *Harry Potter and the Deathly Hallows* (Bloomsbury, 2007) and *Harry Potter and the Half-Blood Prince* (Bloomsbury, 2006). For the impressive statistics on their launch, see http://news.bbc.co.uk/1/hi/entertainment/6912529.stm, July 23, 2007.

2. Published in the United States in 1998 as *Harry Potter and the Sorcerer's Stone.*

3. One of the great advantages that all the other power offers in this book had over *Harry Potter* was that they didn't have to be perfect the first time. Building power offers, and the momentum they generate, is an iterative process, unlike publishing a book!

4. By July 31, 2007, a total of 5,331 customers had left reviews on Amazon.com for *Harry Potter and the Sorcerer's Stone.* Of those, 4,518 (85 percent) gave it the maximum five-star rating; only 65 (just over 1 percent) had given it the minimum one star. Subsequent books in the series achieved top-box ratings of 83 percent, 88 percent, 85 percent, 66 percent, 61 percent, and 73 percent. By way of comparison, on the same day Dan Brown's *The Da Vinci Code,* another recent publishing phenomenon, had 2,000 fewer reviews and a top-box rating of just 39 percent.

5. The idea of the heroes in *Harry Potter* aging at the same rate as their readers has led some to suggest designing brands that would follow a certain customer cohort as they age. This would definitely be a more effective strategy to build loyalty than segment markets in terms of age groups. See Frédéric Dalsace, Coralie Damay, and David Dubois, "Brand Magic: Harry Potter Marketing," *Harvard Business Review,* February 2007, 6. This would capitalize on a phenomenon that exists without being an explicit marketing strategy: Often people divulge their age because of what they buy. Indeed we tend to keep consuming some brands that were most fashionable when we were young, especially for hygiene and cosmetic products.

6. See Blaise Cronin, "Burned Any Good Books Lately?" *Library Journal,* February 15, 2003, 48; David Serchuk, "Harry Potter and the Ministry of Fire," *Forbes,* January 12, 2006.

7. The strength of this sense of belonging can be seen when customers perceive a threat to it. The Body Shop, the U.K.-based ethical cosmetics company, built up an intense level of dynamic customer engagement with a specific group of consumers over the years through its public opposition to animal testing and advertising that they perceived as damaging to women's self-image. As soon as the sale of the business to L'Oréal was announced in early 2006, online bulletin boards filled with despairing postings from customers

appalled at what they perceived as a "sell-out" to a firm that in their opinion represented the antithesis of the Body Shop's values. They felt they could no longer support an organization that had become fundamental to their sense of who they were.

8. Blogs, short for "web logs," are easily published online diaries that have become influential tools for customers to demonstrate their opinions and belonging.

9. For details on its measurement and correlation with growth rates, see Frederick Reichheld, "The One Number You Need to Grow," *Harvard Business Review,* December 2003, 1–9; "The Microeconomics of Customer Relationships," *MIT Sloan Management Review,* Winter 2006, 73–78; *The Ultimate Question* (Harvard Business School Press, 2006). The term *Net Promoter Score* is a registered trademark.

10. See Tom Rieger and Guido M.J. de Koning, "Roadblocks to Customer Engagement (Part 1)," *Gallup Management Journal,* November 13, 2003, 1–5, and "Roadblocks to Customer Engagement (Part 2)," *Gallup Management Journal,* December 11, 2003, 1–4.

11. Of course, there are also unprofitable, unsatisfied customers who are simply demanding. A customer-focused organization should be able to distinguish between painful customers and profitable customers and understand which ones are worth listening to.

12. Von Hippel defines lead users as "users of a novel or enhanced product, process, or service ... who display two characteristics with respect to it: 1. Lead users face needs that will be general in a marketplace, but they face them months or years before the bulk of that marketplace encounters them, and 2. Lead users are positioned to benefit significantly by obtaining a solution to those needs." In *The Sources of Innovation* (Oxford University Press, 1988), 109. For the active involvement of lead users in the creation of value, see C. K. Prahalad and Venkat Ramaswamy, *The Future of Competition: Co-Creating Unique Value with Customers* (Harvard Business School Press, 2004).

13. The Ford Mondeo was sold in the United States as the Contour. The chassis for the X-Type Jaguar was a modified version of the European Mondeo chassis. To this day, many Jaguar salespeople fail to comprehend customers' emotional reactions to the Jaguar's chassis. Instead, they attribute the car's failure to more rational reasons, such as its size. This demonstrates the importance of investigating the deep emotions of customers, as explained in Chapter 5, on compelling value.

14. See Christian Pinson, Vikas Tibrewala, and Francesca Gee, *United Colors of Benetton*, INSEAD, 1996, Case No. 01/96-4520.

15. Because of lack of space, we are focusing here on promoting engagement as opposed to recovering Detractors. The subject of recovery has already been addressed in the satisfaction and retention chapters and would naturally extend itself to engagement. An extreme example of Detractor recovery is the reaction of Coca-Cola when its customers revolted following its change in formula. The firm soon brought the old formula back as Classic Coke and offered the first case of the revived production to the leaders of the movement as a token of peacemaking. The new drink was referred to as New Coke, then rebranded Coke II, and slowly phased out of the company's portfolio.

16 See www.redbullairrace.com, which demonstrates the excitement Red Bull creates for its customers. The firm has also created the Red Bull Music Academy, which has a similar positive impact on customers. See www.redbullmusicacademy.com.

17. Second Life is a virtual world developed by Linden Lab and progressively built by its users. You can enter the Second Life world in the form of an avatar that you have designed to represent your virtual personality. You can visit it, participate in events, buy real estate, build properties, and sell services. See www.secondlife.com. Second Life is developing rapidly, and already contains the virtual sites of major corporations, political parties, pressure groups, and universities. For instance, INSEAD has developed a virtual business school campus under the direction of Professor Miklos Sarvary.

18. Emphasis added. See Steve Jobs, "To All iPhone Customers," www.apple.com/hotnews/openiphoneletter/, retrieved October 4, 2007. The existence of websites such as www.anythingbutipod.com, a website that reviews alternative products to the iPod with an almost evangelical zeal, demonstrates that even Apple has its detractors. The site states that it "is here to present the other options, not to bash and hate the iPod," but the emotional tone in the rest of its "About" statement demonstrates the strength of feeling of Apple's detractors: "With the iPod there are no decisions to make; you give up your right to choose. You are just another face in the crowd…This website is dedicated to individuals who can think for themselves." Of course, despite this, for much of its life

the iPod has enjoyed over 70 percent market share, and in April 2007, Apple announced that they had sold the 100 millionth iPod: "100 Million iPods Sold," Apple Press Release, April 9, 2007, www.apple.com/pr/library/2007/04/09ipod.html. Detractors like this are unlikely to be recovered, and in many instances their impact will be minimal. But, it is vital that the causes of their perceived grievance be investigated because they might reveal insights into the sort of momentum killers that might be negatively affecting other less-engaged customers.

19. Because Momentum-Powered Inc. is experiencing greater profit growth, it has the capacity to increase its actual spend on customer acquisition more than Momentum-Deficient Inc. In the displayed example, the increases in marketing spend are 7 percent and 5 percent, respectively. Despite this absolute increase, the percentage of its revenue that Momentum-Powered Inc. devotes to acquisition will drop by more than half from 20 percent to 8.5 percent over the course of the five years, adding further acceleration to its profitable growth.

Chapter 12

1. Later in the chapter, we mention the cultural problems that the cheer encountered and that slowed down Wal-Mart's momentum as it expanded across the world. For example, its lack of sensitivity to cultural differences of employees in different countries led to some German employees hiding in the bathrooms when it was time to chant the morning corporate cheer. See "Wal-Mart Around the World," *Economist,* December 8, 2001.

2. Sam Walton, *Made in America, My Story*, 199–200. Also Bob Ortega, *In Sam We Trust: The Untold Story of Sam Walton and Wal-Mart, the World's Most Powerful Retailer* (Crown Business, 1998); Charles Fishman, *The Wal-Mart Effect* (Penguin, 2006).

3. The Wal-Mart cheer was an appropriate solution to develop a unifying customer culture at a time of fast expansion. Its initial acceptance by the organization owes much to the retailer's southern rural culture and Sam Walton's particular form of leadership.

4. See Elen Lewis, *Great IKEA!* (Cyan Books, 2005).

5. Club Med was created by a group of friends who wanted to enjoy a certain concept of vacationing between people who shared common values of nature, fun, and freedom. From the outset, they rejected the use of the words *employee* and *client* and coined the expressions G.O. (*gentil organisateur* in French, translated as "gracious organizers"), and G.M. (*gentil membre,* translated as "gracious members").

6. See James R. Sengel, Andrea L. Dixon, and Chris T. Allen, "Listening Begins at Home," *Harvard Business Review,* November 2003, 1–9.

7. In Amy Barrett, "Staying on the Top," *BusinessWeek,* May 5, 2003, 40–45.

8. The "Rules of the Garage" were included in the 1999 Annual Report to the HP shareholders. They were introduced with these words: "We are—at the end of the day—a **people business,** and therefore, a business for which **customer experience** is the only true measure of success. And so, we are reinventing the way we do business. Getting back to our roots. Back to the **rules of the garage.**" (Emphasis in the original text.)

9. Wal-Mart's culture and values sprang from the organization's environment. This is why the organization was receptive to Sam's proposed cheer after his trip to South Korea. But values can never be artificially imposed from the top down, as the later example of Wal-Mart's experience in Germany demonstrates.

10. See Anthony Bianco and Wend Zellner, "Is Wal-Mart Too Powerful," *BusinessWeek,* October 6, 2003, 46–55. Also "Wal-Mart around the World," *Economist,* December 8, 2001; and *Deutsche Welle,* July 28, 2006.

11. For a complete description of the crisis, see Tamara Kaplan, "The Tylenol Crisis: How Effective Public Relations Saved Johnson & Johnson," in Glen Broom, Allen Center, and Scott Cutlip, *Effective Public Relations,* 7th Ed. (Prentice Hall, 1994). See also, "Tylenol Regains Most of No. 1 Share, Astounding Doomsayers," *Wall Street Journal,* December 24, 1982. A short strategic analyses of the management of the Tylenol crisis is in Victor Braden et al., *Crisis— A Leadership Opportunity,* Harvard University, John F. Kennedy School of Government, National Security Program, CADRE/PC 2005-003, April 2005.

12. A second and similar tampering of Tylenol capsules happened three years later on February 8, 1986, causing the death of a young woman in Westchester County, New York. The company reacted as swiftly as in the first case. With the cooperation of the authorities, another tampered bottle was found before it could do any harm. The company took then the dramatic step to stop producing capsules. See Bill Powell and Martin Kasindorf, "The Tylenol Rescue," *Newsweek,* March 3, 1986, 52; Robert D. McFadden, "Maker of Tylenol Discontinuing All Over-Counter Drug Capsules," *New York Times,* February 18, 1986.

13. Robert Wood Johnson recognized that the Credo would have to evolve to reflect changes in language and in the environment. The Credo has indeed changed several times, and the 1979 and 1989 versions are displayed on the company website with the details of specific additions and deletions. The spirit of the Credo has, however, never changed. It has always stressed the responsibility of the company toward all its stakeholders: customers, employees, communities, and stockholders. See www.jnj.com/our_company/our_credo_history/revisions/index.htm. An excellent article showing how the Credo and the culture it created were essential in resolving the Tylenol crisis is provided by Lawrence G. Foster, "The Johnson & Johnson Credo and the Tylenol Crisis," *New Jersey Bell Journal* 6, no. 1, 1983.

Chapter 13

1. The description of the transformation of Val d'Isère is based on an unpublished work by the author and personal communications with Michel Giraudy.

2. See for instance Peter F. Drucker, *The Effective Executive: The Definitive Guide to Getting the Right Things Done* (Harper Collins, revised edition, 2006); John P. Kotter, *Leading Change* (Harvard Business School Press, 1996); Ram Charan, Stephen Drotter, and James Noel, *The Leadership Pipeline: How to Build the Leadership-Powered Company* (Jossey-Bass, 2001); Henry Mintzberg, *Mintzberg on Management* (The Free Press, 1989); Manfred F. R. Kets de Vries, *The Leader on the Couch: A Clinical Approach to Changing People and Organisations* (Wiley, 2006).

3. For the account of this story by Gerald Ratner himself, see his recent book, *Gerald Ratner: The Rise and Fall and Rise Again* (Wiley, 2007). Ratner was ousted from his own company, which was renamed Signet Group. The event occurred in April 1991, and had such an impact that the expression "doing a Ratner" is now a British expression referring to a business executive who criticizes the company's products or disparages the customers, with disastrous results.

4. John Gapper, "How to make a million connections," *Financial Times,* July 8, 2005.

5. Alan Hughes, CEO of First Direct from 1999 to 2004, is a case in point. Many of the examples we've looked at from First Direct, including the offset mortgage, come from his period in office.

6. Throughout this book, although we have been centering on customer momentum, we have used the terms vibrant satisfaction, retention, and engagement without specifying who is being satisfied, retained, or engaged. This is because the concept is valid for all stakeholders, and we didn't want to imply that the concept is restricted to customers. However, now that we are looking at the synergy between momentum derived from the internal and external market, we must differentiate between these two groups—hence, vibrant customer retention is mirrored by vibrant employee retention and so on.

7. Note that on a first glance the internal-momentum virtuous circle appears to be different from the version presented in Figure 12.1, but it is not. Although the direction of the arrows has been altered from clockwise to counter-clockwise, the components have also been transposed so that they are still in the same positions, relative to each other. It is as if you are looking at Figure 12.1 from the other side. This is simply to demonstrate the synergy between the two engines of vibrant *customer* momentum execution and vibrant *internal* momentum execution when they are brought together.

8. Rajat Gupta and Jim Wendler, "Leading Change: An Interview with the CEO of P&G," *McKinsey Quarterly,* July 2005.

9. See Carola Hoyos, "Shell boss fails to turn up for the bad news," *Financial Times,* January 10, 2004; Alison Maitland and Carola Hoyos, "Shell's man who wasn't there," *Financial Times,* January 14,

2004; Stanley Reed, "Shell's Drama Isn't Over," *BusinessWeek,* 23 February 2004, 24–26; "New Chief offers a safe pair of hands," *Financial Times,* 4 March 2004; Stephen Labaton and Jeff Gerth, "At Shell, New Accounting and Rosier Oil Outlook," *New York Times,* 12 March 2004.

10. We have restricted this Hall of Fame to leaders who, in our judgment, have achieved a five-star momentum leadership status for at least ten years and whose success is sufficiently documented to serve as a guide. Some of these leaders ended their careers while their firms were still enjoying momentum growth, others are still leading momentum-powered organizations, and others are trying to recover a momentum they once created and then lost.

11. There is a general recognition, inside the company, and among outsiders, including competitors, that Sam Walton was an exceptional leader and his multiple qualities have been detailed many times, including in several books. The emphasis here is that these qualities focused on delivering value to multiple stakehoders with the net result of creating momentum and exceptional growth for a long period of time. See Bob Ortega, *In Sam We Trust: The Untold Story of Sam Walton and Wal-Mart, the World's Most Powerful Retailer* (Crown Business, 1998); Charles Fishman, *The Wal-Mart Effect* (Penguin, 2006).

12. The statements attributed to Sam Walton in the rest of this chapter are taken from his book *Made in America: My Story.*

13. From 1977 to 1987, Wal-Mart's average annual return to investors was 46 percent.

Chapter 14

1. In 1985, Steve Jobs was ousted from Apple, the firm he founded. He was called back ten years later. In the meantime, he had created NeXT Computer, which contributed a number of significant innovations, including some that helped Apple develop its new operating system. In 1986, he bought The Graphics Group from Lucasfilms. This company, renamed Pixar, has made some of history's most successful animated movies, and was sold in 2006 to Disney for more than $7 billion, making Steve Jobs Disney's largest shareholder. Quite an impressive momentum record!

Index

D

N

O–P

Q–R

S

W–Z

⊮ Wharton School Publishing

In the face of accelerating turbulence and change, business leaders and policy makers need new ways of thinking to sustain performance and growth.

Wharton School Publishing offers a trusted source for stimulating ideas from thought leaders who provide new mental models to address changes in strategy, management, and finance. We seek out authors from diverse disciplines with a profound understanding of change and its implications. We offer books and tools that help executives respond to the challenge of change.

Every book and management tool we publish meets quality standards set by The Wharton School of the University of Pennsylvania. Each title is reviewed by the Wharton School Publishing Editorial Board before being given Wharton's seal of approval. This ensures that Wharton publications are timely, relevant, important, conceptually sound or empirically based, and implementable.

To fit our readers' learning preferences, Wharton publications are available in multiple formats, including books, audio, and electronic.

To find out more about our books and management tools, visit us at whartonsp.com and Wharton's executive education site, exceed.wharton.upenn.edu.